The Batterer as Parent

Sage Series on Violence Against Women

Series Editors

Claire M. Renzetti
St. Joseph's University

Jeffrey L. Edleson
University of Minnesota

Lundy Bancroft
Jay G. Silverman

The Batterer as Parent

Addressing the Impact of Domestic Violence on Family Dynamics

S∕∕AW
Sage Series on Violence Against Women

SAGE Publications
International Educational and Professional Publisher
Thousand Oaks ■ London ■ New Delhi

Quotations in Chapter 6 from Johnston, J., & Campbell, L. (1993). A clinical typology of interparental violence in disputed-custody divorces. *American Journal of Orthopsychiatry*, 63(2), 190–199. Reprinted with permission from the *American Journal of Orthopsychiatry*. © 1993 by the American Orthopsychiatric Association, Inc.

For information:

 Sage Publications, Inc.
2455 Teller Road
Thousand Oaks, California 91320
E-mail: order@sagepub.com

Sage Publications Ltd.
6 Bonhill Street
London EC2A 4PU
United Kingdom

Sage Publications India Pvt. Ltd.
M-32 Market
Greater Kailash I
New Delhi 110 048 India

Printed in the United States of America

Library of Congress Cataloging-in-Publication Data

Bancroft, Lundy.
    The batterer as parent: Addressing the impact of domestic violence on family dynamics / by Lundy Bancroft and Jay G. Silverman.
        p.   cm. — (Sage series on violence against women)
    Includes bibliographical references and index.
    ISBN 0-7619-2276-8 (c)
    ISBN 0-7619-2277-6 (p)
    1. Abusive men—United States.   2. Wife abuse—United States.   3. Family violence—United States.   4. Victims of family violence—United States.   I. Silverman, Jay G.   II. Title.   III. Series.
    HV6626.2 .B25   2002
    362.82′92—dc21   2001005105

02 03 04 05 06 10 9 8 7 6 5 4 3 2 1

Acquiring Editor:	Nancy Hale
Editorial Assistant:	Alicia Carter
Production Editor:	Denise Santoyo
Copy Editor:	Steven Holmes
Indexer:	Molly Hall

Contents

Foreword

Twenty years ago, my colleague David Wolfe and I began extensive clinical and research explorations to better understand and counsel children growing up in violent homes. We were troubled to discover through our work that community professionals in various helping and legal systems were largely overlooking the plight of children exposed to the battering of their mothers. Although the potential traumatic effects of child physical and sexual abuse were widely recognized at that time, the similar psychological impact on children of domestic violence was rarely understood. The community appeared to accept the misconception that children without visible injuries could not be suffering great harm.

A further obstacle to expanding professional understanding in this area has been the tendency of batterers to make themselves unavailable for participation in services or research studies, so that they have often remained invisible and poorly understood. Our early studies, for example, often centered on abused women in shelters because of their accessibility to us. Unfortunately, this focus led us to link children's emotional and behavioral problems primarily to their mother's physical and psychological well-being, without adequate attention to how the conduct of batterers was fomenting the dynamics we were observing. While we were correct in observing that children often recovered more successfully when their mothers healed well, we did not always recognize the complexity of the psychological injury to children and the disruption to family dynamics that batterers can cause.

Fortunately, progress in this area has been substantial in recent years. Since we wrote *Children of Battered Women* in 1990, there have been many important scholarly publications on the special needs of children in violent homes, which in turn have contributed to steps forward in policy, research, intervention, and prevention. Many communities in the U.S. and Canada now offer specialized programs for these children, and service providers are sometimes connected to the broader domestic violence network through local coordinating committees or councils.

Lundy Bancroft and Jay Silverman have now further deepened our understanding of the trauma done to children of battered women with this very thoughtful and practical volume that turns the spotlight onto the attitudes and behaviors of batterers as parents, examining in concrete and illuminating detail the home conditions that domestic violence creates. The authors simultaneously clarify many misconceptions that still exist about the short- and long-term impact batterers can have on children.

Bancroft and Silverman move beyond the narrow clinical perspective that is sometimes applied to viewing the emotional and developmental risks to these children, offering in its place a view that takes into account the complex ways in which a batterer's abusive and controlling behaviors are woven into the fabric of daily life. The shift in perspective that the authors bring is perhaps captured most succinctly by their appropriate recommendation that the current term "children exposed to domestic violence" be replaced with "children exposed to batterers." This change serves to underline batterers' accountability and responsibility for the effects of domestic violence in a way that impersonal terms such as "violent homes" or "conjugal abuse" do not. Perhaps more important, the new term draws attention to the fact that the parenting of batterers can bring multiple sources of trauma to children's lives in addition to the terror of violence toward their mothers. For example, Bancroft and Silverman document the evidence that batterers are at a greatly increased risk to physically or sexually abuse children, often use the children as weapons against the mother, can sow important divisions between children and their mothers and among siblings, and may be psychologically abusive to children. They outline the complex and insidious processes through which batterers hamper children's social and emotional development.

Bancroft and Silverman also shed light on the common misconception that the trauma to children of domestic violence ends when the parents separate, devoting much of their text to exploring how the abuse of power and control in violent relationships may continue through disputes over child custody, visitation, and child support. They successfully challenge existing theories about "high-conflict divorce" and "parental alienation" that minimize and misinterpret the batterer's pattern of manipulative and coercive behaviors, and that tend to shift blame for the children's emotional difficulties—including their fear of their fathers—onto battered mothers.

I have observed that family law lawyers and judges often fall prey to becoming the agents of batterers to continue the harassment of abused partners through prolonged court proceedings and conflicts about post-separation parenting. Since batterers are more likely to fight for custody of children and as likely as nonbatterers to be successful in this action, more intensive reading and training in this area is essential for forensic professionals. I happened to be interrupted in the midst of reading *The Batterer as Parent* by an emergency call by a lawyer for an abused mother who had just received a court judgment ordering her to share joint custody with the batterer, on the basis that the batterer had never abused the children directly, only the mother. These words came from a well-regarded judge with over two decades of child custody litigation experience.

To assist in addressing problems of this kind, Bancroft and Silverman offer systematic and useful guidelines for assessing the risk to children from batterers. This assessment tool should become a standard part of the practice of custody evaluators and courts in making decisions that promote the safety and security of children. In addition, the authors offer complementary guidelines on evaluating genuine change in batterers as parents, which are essential given that custody and visitation disputes may continue before the court for many years. Although constructive interventions sometimes take place with the batterer during this period, perhaps including the imposition of supervised visitation, the court may be placed under constant pressure to reduce such safeguards and counseling requirements based on promises rather than on actual changes in the batterer.

This book will challenge communities to extend their services and training on behalf of children exposed to batterers. A clear focus on the impact of batterers as parents will enhance the quality and comprehensive nature of intervention and prevention services. Bancroft and Silverman should also inspire researchers to test the many implied hypotheses about batterers' impact on children as well as warning and hopeful signs for change in perpetrators of domestic violence.

As someone with 30 years of experience working with the police and the courts in a more collaborative response to domestic violence,

I found that *The Batterer as Parent* left me with a fresh perspective and new ideas for clinical practice and research in this area. I am confident that other readers will be stimulated in a similar fashion. I hope that this book comes to be seen as required reading for all judges, lawyers, custody evaluators, child protection workers, therapists, and advocates involved in domestic violence cases.

Peter Jaffe, Ph.D., Director, Center for Children
and Families in the Justice System

Preface

As we have viewed the ballooning collection of published research on the effects on children of exposure to domestic violence, the two of us increasingly have come to feel the need for an in-depth analysis of the *mechanisms* by which psychological injury—and emotional recovery—take place in homes affected by domestic violence. What exactly are the sources and characteristics of the suffering that the children of battered women endure? Is their distress primarily tied to the trauma of witnessing frightening violence toward their mothers? Or is this violence perhaps just the beginning of the challenges that these children face? As we have examined these questions, we have concluded that the behavior of men who batter sends a set of destructive ripples through the lives of families, ripples that are far more complex than has commonly been recognized. The first level radiates from a batterer's day-to-day behaviors toward his partner, each of which has implications for children in the home. The second grows from the batterer's approach to interacting with children, which varies tremendously from case to case. And the third level reverberates in every direction, for it has to do with the family interaction patterns that a batterer engenders, affecting all relationships in the home. A grasp of these dynamics is critical to the task of any provider—and to a battered mother herself—who wishes to promote recovery and healing in a family affected by the actions of a battering man.

Our goal is to prepare the reader to identify and to respond to the range of individual and family dynamics that can be created by battering behavior. It is our belief that men who batter are distinguished both by the fear that they inculcate and by their abusive mental processes. These two elements, which we explore in detail, can play a powerful role in shaping the daily experience of children who live with battering men. Furthermore, the dynamics that arise do not disappear when a battered mother leaves her abusive partner; they live on in the patterns of interaction that have been established and, often more directly, in the batterer's use of litigation for custody or visitation. Therefore, professionals, battered mothers, and others who wish to assist children need to understand a host of pre- and postseparation sources of emotional injury to a mother and her children, as well as appropriate strategies for fostering recovery. In fact, we propose in this book some substantial shifts in the thinking that currently prevails regarding the causes of and solutions to the trauma and other difficulties exhibited by so many children who are exposed to domestic violence.

We direct this book to domestic violence professionals, therapists, child protective and court personnel, battered mothers, and to anyone else who is in a personal or professional position to touch the lives of children of battered women. We believe, for example, that school personnel, parent trainers, custody evaluators, and providers of supervised visitation can all draw from what we have written. It is our hope that the insights that we have shared here, combined with our detailed practice recommendations, can increase the effectiveness of interventions on behalf of the children of battered women.

Although we have referred extensively to published research, this book is grounded largely in our extensive experience working directly with men who batter and (to a lesser extent) with their families. As group leaders in programs for abusers, the two of us have counseled over a thousand battering men and have been involved in approximately an additional thousand cases through supervising other batterer counselors. Our clients have covered a range of socioeconomic backgrounds and racial groups, including men from over twenty different countries of origin. Our clients have included a few hundred voluntary participants, with the remainder court mandated; voluntary clients have tended to be middle to upper-middle class, whereas court-mandated clients have come from across the class spectrum, depending on the community in which a particular court is located. We have also offered a large number of case consultations to child protective workers and attorneys. In addition, Bancroft has performed approximately fifty custody evaluations for various Massachusetts courts, with most of those cases involving allegations of domestic violence. We also have some legal case experience from other states and provinces as a result of our consulting work. Finally, both of us are currently part of a project that is performing in-depth (4- to 5-hour) interviews with battered mothers regarding their experience of domestic violence, its effect on their children, and the responses of courts and custody evaluators to the batterer's use of custody and visitation litigation.

We acknowledge that the clinical experience upon which we have based many of our conclusions, although extensive, has been restricted to a few geographical sites. Our work in batterer intervention programs also involves a preponderance of court-mandated clients; at the same time, our custody evaluations and research interviews largely have involved cases without such criminal proceedings. We wish to emphasize the need for further research to test and deepen the analyses and recommendations that we have put forth in this book, and to expand their applicability to diverse racial, cultural, and socioeconomic groups. We also look forward to refinement by other professionals of the tools we are proposing for distinguishing the level of risk that a particular batterer presents to children's well-being. Finally, we wish to underline the fact that the parenting behavior of batterers appears to fall on a continuum, as we strive to make clear in the pages ahead, and that batterers do not all manifest the full range of parenting problems that we describe here.

We wish to make two notes regarding terminology. First, throughout this book, we have chosen to use the term *batterers* rather than the phrase "men who batter." We understand that the former term runs the risk of creating the impression that battering behavior is unchangeable or inherent, which is not our belief; rather, we employ the term for a different reason, one having to do with gender inclusivity. We believe that the research and clinical evidence available to date on lesbian batterers suggest that the preponderance of our descriptions of battering men may also be substantially accurate for women who abuse their female partners. We therefore have chosen to use the more inclusive phrase.

Second, we have tried to adopt the most widely used legal terms possible, but some definitions are necessary here since terminology and court structure vary from state to state. We have used *family court* to mean any court handling custody, visitation, and child support. We find that in many states these courts are distinct from those having jurisdiction over child protective matters, which are commonly called "juvenile" or "dependency" courts. The terms *custody evaluator* and *Guardian ad Litem* refer to anyone appointed by a court to make recommendations regarding custody or visitation; we find that in most states this role tends to be filled by a lawyer or mental health professional.

Finally, we wish to thank a number of people for their contributions, intended or otherwise, to this book. Both of us are grateful to our editors at Sage, Jeff Edleson and Claire Renzetti; Gillian Andrews, who first suggested a book on the parenting of men who batter; David Adams, Susan Cayouette, Chuck Turner, and Ted German, all currently or formerly of Emerge, the original batterer intervention program in the United States; Lonna Davis and Pam Whitney; Kim Slote and Carrie Cuthbert; Michelle Lambert and Doug Gaudette; Joan Zorza; Anita Raj; Gail Dines; Carlene Pavlos; and Steve Holmes, for his painstaking and caring copyediting. We wish also to thank the Ford Foundation for its funding of research on custody and visitation litigation in the context of domestic violence, research upon which we have drawn in this book. Lundy Bancroft wishes to thank Carole Sousa, who was the pioneer in educating him on the effects of domestic violence on children. He is also grateful to Judge Arline Rotman, whose invitation to present at a conference on custody evaluation led him to write four articles that eventually formed the bases for Chapters 4 through 7 of this book, and to Peter Jaffe, for encouraging him to get those pieces published and for generously agreeing to contribute a Foreword to this book.

For Cathy and John Hosmer

1

The Battering Problem

Over the past 10 years, the traumatic effects on children of exposure to batterers have increasingly entered the public and professional eye. In the United States, more than 10% of women in relationships experience violence each year (Straus & Gelles, 1990), and a high percentage of these assaults are witnessed by one or more children, leading to an estimated 3 million or more children being exposed to acts of domestic violence per year (review in Fantuzzo & Mohr, 1999; Carlson, 1984). Children of battered women have been found to be at increased risk for a broad range of emotional and behavioral difficulties, including suicidality, substance abuse, depression, developmental delays, educational and attention problems, and involvement in violence (review in Kolbo, Blakely, & Engleman, 1996; Gleason, 1995; review in Jaffe, Wolfe, & Wilson, 1990). Furthermore, children exposed to batterers are themselves at high risk to become direct targets of physical abuse (Straus, 1990; Suh & Abel, 1990; Bowker, Arbitell, & McFerron, 1988) and of sexual abuse (McCloskey, Figueredo, & Koss, 1995; Sirles & Franke, 1989; Paveza, 1988). The danger even extends to homicide: One multiyear study found that in approximately one fifth of domestic violence homicides and attempted homicides, a child of the battered woman is also killed in the process (Langford, Isaac, & Kabat, 1999; see also Websdale, 1999). Children exposed to domestic violence are also at risk for other kinds of child fatality (Monemi, Peña, & Ellsberg, cited in Heise, Ellsberg, & Gottemoeller, 1999; Pecora, Whittaker, Maluccio, Barth, & Plotnick, cited in Edleson, 1998), and this risk has tended to be underestimated

(Websdale, Town, & Johnson, 1999). Finally, the violence is a known to be a recurring cycle: Studies consistently have found that boys who grow up exposed to domestic violence have an increased likelihood to batter their own partners as adults (e.g., Silverman & Williamson, 1997; review in Hotaling & Sugarman, 1986).

The sources of emotional and behavioral difficulty for children of battered women are many, with the actual seeing or hearing of acts of violence being only the beginning. The presence in the home of a batterer, usually in the role of parent or stepparent, has a wide range of implications for family functioning. Batterers tend to be authoritarian yet neglectful parents, with far higher rates than nonbatterers of physically and sexually abusing children (see Chapter 2). Battering changes the nature of children's crucial relationships with their mother, through mechanisms that include undermining her authority and interfering with her ability to provide care. Batterers often engage in efforts to create divisions within the family and can be highly manipulative (Jacobson & Gottman, 1998; Adams, 1989). They are more likely than are nonbattering men to seek custody of their children in cases of divorce or separation (American Psychological Association [APA] Presidential Task Force on Violence and the Family, 1996; McMahon & Pence, 1995; Liss & Stahly, 1993) and can have several advantages over battered women in custody litigation (see Chapter 5). We believe therefore that the psychological distress observed in children exposed to domestic violence results not only from their witnessing of periodic acts of violence but also from exposure to a batterer, and to his parenting style, in everyday life; in fact, we believe that the phrase "children exposed to batterers" is often more accurate than the current phrase "children exposed to domestic violence," for reasons that will become clear in the pages ahead. For closely related reasons, we find that a batterer's parenting cannot be assessed separately from his entire pattern of abusive behaviors, all of which have implications for his children.

The mounting awareness that large numbers of children run the risk of being traumatized along with their mothers by domestic violence has led to a recognition of the need for improved interventions in the families of battered women and to specialized services for children. Skilled and sensitive responses are sought from child protective services, battered women's programs, family courts, therapists, and the range of other institutions that serve families affected by domestic violence. In this book, we hope to contribute to the further development of these interventions by offering an extended analysis of the batterer in the family setting. Clinical experience and research on domestic violence over the past 20 year provide a coherent and consistent profile of the attitudes and behaviors that define batterers and that in turn shape the experiences and functioning of their family members. This deepening grasp among domestic violence professionals of the psychology and tactics of batterers creates an opportunity to develop systemic responses to families that take into account the full breadth and complexity of the injuries and challenges caused by batterers.

DEFINING BATTERERS

Given the many interpretations that exist of the term *batterer*, we begin by providing and elucidating our working definition:

> *A batterer is a person who exercises a pattern of coercive control in a partner relationship, punctuated by one or more acts of intimidating physical violence, sexual assault, or credible threat of physical violence. This pattern of control and intimidation may be predominantly psychological, economic, or sexual in nature or may rely primarily on the use of physical violence.*

Two points need to be made about this definition. First, the definition we are using takes into account the presence of considerable variation in abusive style among batterers. This flexibility is important because, as we will see, the impact on children of living with a batterer varies depending on his level of violence, the extent of his cruelty and manipulativeness, his level of respect for sexual boundaries, his treatment of the children's mother, and various other aspects of his behavior.

Second, our definition does not require the presence of beatings, but it does require that there at least be actions clearly intended as threats, such as raising fists, cutting phone lines, or deliberately dangerous driving. Although psychological abuse by itself can cause emotional harm to children (Berlin & Vondra, 1999; Kashani & Allan, 1998), the presence of fear may dramatically intensify those effects; a pattern of name-calling, for example, can have more debilitating emotional sequelae if it is punctuated by, and therefore emotionally interwoven with, periodic physical assault (see, e.g., Adamson & Thompson, 1998). By contrast, violence that is primarily annoying (as opposed to intimidating) and that is not accompanied by a pattern of coercion will not be considered here. Of course, we are not condoning violence of any kind; however, to carry out a meaningful examination of the parenting implications of domestic violence perpetration, we find it necessary to make distinctions, such as between a batterer's aggressive violence and a battered woman's acts of self-defense. Also, definitions similar to ours are currently used and endorsed by many professional organizations, thereby creating a common terminology that facilitates the practical application of our discussion of battering.

The reader already will have noticed that although it is not part of our definition, throughout this book we refer to the batterer as "he" and to the battered partner as "she." We find this gender ascription to be accurate for most cases in which a professional is required to evaluate a batterer's parenting, and it is reflected both in our clinical experience and in most published research. Sexual assault by intimate partners occurs 25 times as often to women as to men, stalking by intimate partners occurs 8 times as often to women as to men, and injuries from physical or sexual assaults by intimates requiring medical attention occur more than 7 times as often to women as to men (Tjaden & Thoennes, 2000). Female homicides of male partners are far less common than the reverse (see Bureau of Justice Statistics, 1996), and those that do occur tend to be carried out by victims of domestic violence rather than by perpetrators (Langford et al., 1999; Websdale, 1999). The disparity between male and female homicides of intimate partners grows even larger postseparation (Langford, Isaac, & Kabat, 1998; Daly & Wilson, 1988). The incidence of parents killing children or other nonpartners during a domestic violence assault is similarly rare with a female perpetrator (Langford et al., 1999; Websdale, 1999; Daly & Wilson, 1988). Finally, we have not encountered persuasive evidence in our cases of mutual abuse, and researchers have concluded similarly that mutual abuse is rare (Berk, Fernstermaker Berk, Loseke, & Rauma, 1983).

Of course, our gendered language does not apply to lesbian and gay male relationships, but recent literature addressing the prevalence, causes, and dynamics of same-sex domestic violence suggests considerable parallel to heterosexual battering (Turrell, 2000; Leventhal & Lundy, 1999; Renzetti, 1997; Waldner-Haugrud, Gratch, & Magruder, 1997). Despite popular stereotypes, same-sex violence may have a significant impact upon children. Lesbians are increasingly choosing to have children and to raise them together. Although joint parenting by gay male couples is less common in our experience, it does exist, and gay men also may have weekend care or primary custodial care of children from earlier heterosexual relationships. The behavioral profile of lesbian and gay male batterers appears to correspond closely to that of heterosexual abusers (Leventhal & Lundy, 1999; Renzetti, 1997), including, for example, the batterer's common mistreatment of children and/or pets and the rarity of mutual abuse (Renzetti, 1997). Clinical experience in this area leads to similar conclusions (Cayouette, 1999). Our book therefore may be useful in addressing the parenting of lesbian or gay male batterers, but professionals should be aware of their need for further education about the particular dynamics of domestic violence in these communities, including the particular tactics used by same-sex batterers and the additional obstacles faced by same-sex victims (Leventhal & Lundy, 1999).

CHARACTERISTICS OF BATTERERS

We believe that the parenting style that batterers exhibit is grounded both in their attitudes and perceptual systems and in their patterns of behavior. In this section, after introducing the overarching concepts of control and entitlement, we go on to discuss other attitudinal and perceptual characteristics, and then other behavioral patterns, that are typical of batterers. (We recognize, at the same time, that attitudinal and behavioral qualities are not entirely separable, as our descriptions will make clear.) Although our descriptions of these characteristics are intended as an aid in assessment, it is important to keep in mind that a batterer may be careful not to exhibit any of these traits to professionals, and so assessment should not be based exclusively on psychological testing of, or interviews with, the alleged batterer but should incorporate collateral sources of information as well.

Control

The overarching *behavioral* characteristic of the batterer is the imposition of a pattern of control over his partner (Lloyd & Emery, 2000; Pence & Paymar, 1993; Adams, 1989). The batterer's control is carried out through a mixture of criticism, verbal abuse, economic control, isolation, cruelty, and an array of other tactics (Herman, 1992). Indeed, a majority of battered women report that the psychological abuse that they suffer has a *more* severe impact on them than the physical violence (Follingstad, Rutledge, Berg, Hause, & Polek, 1990), a finding supported by studies from other countries (review in Heise et al., 1999). Psychological abuse is a strong predictor of continued difficulties for a battered woman even if the violence is suspended (Edleson & Tolman, 1992).

We observe that the batterer's imposition of control typically emerges gradually and intensifies during the early years of the relationship. In some cases, there is a distinct period of a few months (or even days) when the coercive pattern presents itself. Common points for the onset of this pattern include when the couple first begins living together, when the couple gets married, when the first pregnancy begins, and when the first child is born. Subsequently, the woman's efforts to resist these forms of control generally meet with an escalation by the abuser, and thus the pattern of control becomes increasingly coercive over time. A batterer usually perceives his controlling behavior as justified (Pence & Paymar, 1993) and therefore sees his partner's reluctance to be controlled as evidence of her mental instability, volatility, or desire to control *him*. The batterer's control often takes the form of undermining his partner's efforts at independence (Adams, 1989), thus increasing his power and control in the relationship (Dutton, 1995).

Although the relationship aspects that batterers may attempt to dominate are too numerous to list, we can identify the predominant spheres: arguments and decision making, household responsibilities, emotional caretaking and attention, sexual relations, finances, child rearing, and outside social contacts (see also Lloyd & Emery, 2000). The typical batterer will focus more on some areas than others, with his cultural training being an important influence over which aspects of the relationship he feels most entitled to determine.

The controlling nature of batterers has important implications for child rearing. Initially, the batterer may coerce decisions about when and whether to have children. After children are born, a range of decisions about how they are to be treated, fed, trained, and educated may fall increasingly under the batterer's control, even though he is typically contributing only a small portion of the labor of child rearing. Harsh and frequent criticism of the mother's parenting, often audible to the children, can undermine her authority and incite children's disrespect of her. Institutions such as child protective services often hold the mother primarily responsible for the children's well-being, unaware of the extent to which conditions may be beyond her control (Magen, 1999; Whitney & Davis, 1999; Edleson, 1998). A study of restraining order affidavits found that one of the most common reasons that mothers gave for why they needed the order was the batterer's "punishment, coercion, and retaliation against the women's actions concerning children" (Ptacek, 1997, p. 112), including specific references to the batterer's anger at the woman's questioning of his authority over the children.

Finally, batterers tend to be controlling and coercive in their direct interactions with children, often replicating much of the interactional style that they use with the mother (see also Ayoub, Grace, Paradise, & Newberger, 1991). Their coercive parenting has multiple consequences for families, which we will examine in more detail below. In particular, the batterer's tendency to be retaliatory has important implications for children who disclose abuse to outsiders or who call for police assistance during an assault. Professionals intervening in families affected by domestic violence need to remain aware at all times of the high potential for punishment or intimidation of the children by the batterer for discussing events in the home.

Entitlement

The overarching *attitudinal* characteristic of batterers is entitlement. Entitlement may be the single most critical concept in understanding the battering mentality, and so we will discuss it in some detail here (see also Silverman & Williamson, 1997; Edleson & Tolman, 1992; Adams, 1991). Entitlement is the belief that one has special rights and privileges without accompanying reciprocal responsibilities. Batterers tend to have this orientation in specific relationship to their partners and children and do not necessarily carry it over into other contexts. The batterer's entitlement leads him to feel justified in taking steps to protect his special status, including the use of physical intimidation when he considers it necessary (Ayoub et al., 1991). The belief that violence toward a partner can be justified is a strong predictor of which men will batter (Margolin, John, & Foo, 1998; Silverman & Williamson, 1997) and helps to distinguish which boys exposed to domestic violence will grow up to abuse their own partners (O'Keefe, 1998).

A primary manifestation of entitlement is that batterers expect family life to center on the meeting of their needs, often to the point of treating their partners like servants (Pence & Paymar, 1993). If a batterer's partner attempts to assert her own needs, the batterer often characterizes her as selfish or uncaring. Batterers thus are distinguished partly by their high and unreasonable expectations, including forceful and urgent demands for catering (Dobash & Dobash, 1983). They may believe that they are owed services and deference without regard to their own level of contribution or sacrifice.

Batterers' expectations of service may include physical, emotional, or sexual caretaking. The demands for physical labor can involve expecting meals prepared for them in the precise way that they like, shopping and housecleaning done, the children looked after and kept quiet, school meetings attended, the social calendar arranged, and a continuing list of family and household responsibilities. Batterers may retaliate if this work is not done to their satisfaction.

Equally central are a batterer's typical demands for emotional caretaking. The batterers we have seen as clients in batterer intervention programs tend to expect to be the center of their partners' attention. They consider it their partners' responsibility to soothe them when they are upset, to praise and compliment them, and to defer to them in conflicts. Partners are expected to lay their own needs aside and to cater to the batterer even in times of family crisis; for example, one of our clients complained angrily to his wife that she was ignoring him during a 2-day period when her teenage son was missing. In our experience, batterers' demands for emotional caretaking are as likely to lead to verbal abuse or to physical violence as are their demands for physical labor.

Finally, our clients often define themselves as being wronged by their partners if the latter do not cater fully to their sexual needs. Even if his partner does engage in sexual relations, a batterer may feel mistreated if she fails to exhibit adequate pleasure or, contradictorily, if she initiates sexual contact with him at a time when he does not desire it. He may particularly pressure his partner for sex following an incident in which he has been verbally or physically abusive. Sex following soon after a physical assault should probably be defined as rape (Bergen, 1996).

We have observed that the higher a batterer's level of entitlement, the greater his apparent perceptual tendency to reverse abuse and self-defense. The typical batterer defines his abusive behaviors as efforts to protect his own rights and defines his partner's attempts to protect herself as abuse of him (Jacobson & Gottman, 1998). For example, he tends to interpret occasions when his partner refuses to have sex with him as her efforts to control or manipulate him (Mahoney & Williams, 1998). Batterers therefore often claim to be the victim of the woman's abuse or violence (Pence & Paymar, 1993; Adams, 1991). Entitlement can lead a batterer to have double standards, such as the belief that he can have outside sexual relationships but that it is not acceptable for his partner to do so (Ptacek, 1997; Dobash & Dobash, 1983).

A batterer's level of controlling behavior and his level of demand for service can be independent factors. Some of our clients are extremely vigilant regarding their partners' movements or social contacts but contribute substantially to domestic responsibility. Others permit their partners considerable freedom but demand high levels of catering (see also Jacobson & Gottman, 1998). A third category includes batterers who are both highly controlling and severely demanding of service.

Batterers' sense of entitlement influences their parenting, beginning commonly with the expectation that their partners should handle the most unpleasant or demanding tasks of child rearing, such as changing diapers, rising in the middle of the night, or helping children resolve their conflicts. At the same time, they often consider themselves to be authorities on child care, and for this reason they may feel entitled to custody after separation. In some cases, batterers attend only to those aspects of parenting that they find enjoyable or that gain notice from friends, school personnel, or other community members, thus allowing them to develop reputations as excellent fathers.

High entitlement can also lead to role reversal, where batterers expect their children to be responsible for attending to their needs. We commonly observe that our clients maintain poor emotional boundaries as parents, expressing to their children their distresses, insecurities, and worries (including how wounded they feel by the children's mother). Batterers are more likely than other men to use their children to meet their own needs for physical affection or sexual contact, leading to an elevated rate of incest perpetration (see review in Chapter 4).

Selfishness and Self-Centeredness

Largely as a result of their sense of entitlement, our clients perceive their needs as being of paramount importance in the family. They provide less emotional support and listen less well to their partners than do nonbattering men (Adams, 1991). They expect to be the center of attention, to have their needs be anticipated even when not expressed, and to have the needs of other family members postponed or abandoned (see also Ayoub et al., 1991). At the same time, they often expect family members to respond to them as the generous, kind, responsible people that they believe themselves to be, and they may react with a sense of woundedness or injustice when they see themselves perceived as selfish. If a batterer's partner pulls back when he makes a sudden movement, for example, he may become angrily indignant, perhaps saying, "How can you be afraid of me? You know I would never hurt you!"

Batterers are often preoccupied with their own needs and thus not available to their children (Johnston & Campbell, 1993b) yet may expect their children to be always available to *them* in ways that can interfere with a child's freedom and development (Roy, 1988). Some batterers show tremendous emotion when speaking to others about their children, yet quickly lose interest or become enraged when their children's needs or independent personalities inconvenience them or fail to give them the ego gratification that they seek. Children of a batterer are sometimes swayed by his grandiose belief in his own generosity and importance, enhancing their blame of themselves and of their mothers for the violence.

The self-referential tendency of batterers, characterized by grandiosity and an unrealistic self-image, can be mistaken for narcissistic personality disorder. However, we observe that the batterer's self-centeredness is primarily the product of his entitlement, whereas the narcissistic personality appears to result from a severe assault on the self during childhood (see Lowen, 1985). There are two crucial points of differentiation: (a) The batterer's self-centeredness occurs in specific relation to his partner or his children; in other contexts, he shows less grandiosity in his presentation of self, less need to receive awed deference, and a normal ability to take another person's perspective. (b) Apart from his denial of the battering, the batterer tends to have a reasonably realistic view of himself. Moreover, the narcissist does not have a particular tendency to violence by virtue of the disorder alone. At the same time, a battering problem is quite compatible with a narcissistic personality disorder, and the two conditions can coexist; in our clinical experience, roughly one batterer in eight shows significant signs of a clinical level of self-centeredness, and these clients are highly resistant to change.

Superiority

Batterers believe themselves to be superior to their victims (Russell & Frohberg, 1995; Adams, 1991). Our clients tend to see their partners as inferior to them in intelligence, competence, logical reasoning, and even sensitivity and therefore treat their partners' opinions with disrespect and impatience. In conflicts and at other times, a batterer may talk to his partner as if she were a willful and ignorant child whom he needs to educate and to improve. Tones of disgust, condescension, or infantilization are commonplace when a batter addresses his partner, as are harsh criticism, humiliation, and parentlike imposition of punishments.

A recurring element in the tone of most batterers' discussions of their partners is contempt. Our clients have difficulty describing serious conflicts with their partners without expressing ridicule of the women's opinions or behaviors, using such approaches as mimicking their partners' voices or making sarcastic exaggerations of arguments that the latter have made. It is valuable for professionals to note that level of *contempt* and level of *anger* are distinct issues: Both batterers and battered women may exhibit high degrees of anger when describing the histories of their relationships, but the extent of disrespect and ridicule that we hear from our clients does not usually appear in our conversations with their partners, even in cases of severe abuse.

Superiority can sometimes include elements of depersonalization or objectification (Pence & Paymar, 1993). According to Bandura (1978), "Maltreatment of individuals who are regarded as subhuman or debased is less apt to arouse self-reproof than if they are seen as human beings with dignifying qualities" (p. 25). Our clients sometimes are uncomfortable referring to their partners by name rather than as "my girl," "the wife," or similar terms, and they often have limited knowledge about their partners as people, being largely unable to answer questions about the women's interests, personal strengths, or family relationships. A batterer in this category may view his partner as a depersonalized vehicle for sexual gratification and thus be prone to sexually assaulting her (see also Campbell, 1995b). In many batterers, these attitudes of superiority generalize into hostility toward women in general (Pence & Paymar, 1993), although this outlook may take time to detect (Edleson & Tolman, 1992).

The superiority, contempt, or depersonalization that children may observe in a batterer's day-to-day treatment of their mother can shape their views of both parents. Children tend to absorb the batterer's view of their mother over time; we observe in custody evaluations, for example, that children of battered women sometimes describe her in terms similar to ones that the batterer would use, saying that she "nags," that she "doesn't know what she's doing," or that "what she needs is a slap in the face." For similar reasons, children can come to see the batterer as the parent who is most knowledgeable, competent, and in charge.

Possessiveness

One useful way to encapsulate the nature of the batterer's problem is that he perceives his partner as an owned object (Lloyd & Emery, 2000; Adams, 1991). A number of studies have shown, for example, that men who use violence against partners are more likely than other men to believe that a female partner should not resist the man's sexual advances (e.g., Silverman & Williamson, 1997) and to become angry if she does so (Adams, 1991). In discussing an arrest, a batterer may express confusion, saying, "I told the police that she was my wife, but they arrested me anyhow." Referring to times when their partners refused to have sex with them, many clients of ours have made reference to the woman's signing of the marriage certificate as conferring an obligation upon her to consent. In dealing with infidelity, the batterer may assault the other man rather than his own partner because "nobody touches my girl." Sexual jealousy can be an important indicator of possessiveness (Adams, 1989; Dobash & Dobash, 1983) and is present at elevated rates in batterers (Raj, Silverman, Wingood, & DiClemente, 1999), but possessiveness can also take other forms and thus should not be assessed on the basis of sexual jealousy alone.

A batterer's possessiveness sometimes exhibits itself starkly when a relationship terminates, commonly leading to violence against the woman for her attempts to leave (Dobash & Dobash, 1983). Nearly 90% of intimate partner homicides by men have been shown to involve a documented history of domestic violence, and a majority of these killings take place during or following separation (Websdale, 1999). Batterers cite various reasons why their partners "owe" them another chance, including the marriage vows, the good of their children, and their own efforts to change. One illustration of this value system is a client of ours who admitted that he had committed a near-lethal beating of his partner (which led to her hospitalization) yet continued to insist that she had a responsibility to reunite with him because he had stopped drinking and could "help her get her life together," pointing to the other people with whom she was spending time as "bad influences."

In attempting to understand the propensity of batterers to kill or to seriously assault partners who attempt to leave them, some theorists have concluded that batterers have an inordinate "fear of abandonment" or are unusually "despondent" after separation. However, we find no evidence that females are less prone than males to fears of abandonment or to postseparation depression, yet their rates of postseparation homicide are far lower (Websdale, 1999). Nonbattering men rarely commit postseparation homicides (Websdale, 1999), despite sometimes suffering serious emotional crises when relationships end. Our clinical experience reveals no connection between a batterer's level of dependence and his level of violence; rather, our clients who have become the most terrorizing of their partners after separation stand out primarily for their high levels of possessiveness. Those batterers who go beyond the terrorizing behavior to actually commit a homicide do appear to have elevated rates of mental illness *combined with* high possessiveness, although mental illness is much less consistently present than possessiveness (Websdale, 1999).

The extent to which a batterer carries his possessive orientation over to his children has important implications for his parenting. Large numbers of our clients over the years have made comments regarding physical abuse of their children such as "No one is going to tell me how I can discipline *my* children" and "Whether I hit my children or not is nobody's business." At the same time, they commonly express disapproval or outrage at adults who hit children who are not their own (such as stepchildren or grandchildren). For these batterers, the connection between possession and the license to abuse children is stated explicitly. We find our clients especially vulnerable to the existing social tendency to view children as owned objects (see also Liss & Stahly, 1993), with its unfortunate tendency to create a context for child abuse (Ayoub et al., 1991).

Possessiveness plays an important though less-recognized role in fostering child sexual abuse and boundary violations. Sexual abusers are notorious for the attitudes of ownership that they exhibit toward children (e.g., Salter, 1995), and incest perpetrators sometimes perceive sexual access as a parental privilege (Leberg, 1997; Groth, 1982). We have found that an incest perpetrator is sometimes sexually possessive toward a teenage daughter, for example, accusing her of having sex with boys or even assaulting boys who attempt to date her. This style of abuser treats his daughter more like a partner than like a child and can behave like a rejected lover when she begins a serious dating relationship for the first time.

The batterer's mentality of ownership also can shape his post-separation parenting. For example, some batterers are nonthreatening for a period after a relationship ends but revert rapidly to the use of intimidation when their former partners develop a serious new relationship. In session, these batterers make statements such as "No other man is going to be around my kids" and "If she lets them call another man Daddy, she'll be sorry." In some cases, these statements mark the beginning of a pattern of threats to the mother, psychological pressure on the children, and litigation in pursuit of custody.

Confusion of Love and Abuse

Batterers often explain their relationship violence by describing it as a product of the depth or intensity of loving feelings that they have for their partners. Many of our clients see their abusiveness as actually proving their love, stating, for example, "I wouldn't get like that if I didn't care for her so much." We have found that friends and relatives of batterers can adopt similar analyses, as do many mental health providers, court personnel, custody evaluators, and other professionals. The batterer thus may experience strong social reinforcement for this construction.

It is true that a link can exist between love and *anger,* in that intimacy creates vulnerability to hurt feelings and therefore can lead to anger as a response. The error, however, is to connect anger to *abuse.* Anger, including rage, occurs both in abusive and in nonabusive people and thus is not in itself a cause of abuse or aggression; indeed, it need not even necessarily be present (Bandura, 1978) or may appear only after the intimidating acts fail to have their desired effect (Hart, 1986). In any case, anger tends to be overestimated as a cause of battering behavior (Healey, Smith, & O'Sullivan, 1998).

The confounding of love and abuse can contribute to the confusion of children of battered women. For example, they may hear the batterer, with anger mounting in his voice, listing off the generous or loving things that he has done for his partner as he escalates toward finally assaulting her. An hour after a beating, they may hear him crying and saying that he loves her. He may tell the children directly how much he cares for their mother, perhaps in the same conversation in which he also says that she is an incompetent parent or a drunk. Through receiving these contradictory messages, children can form convoluted understandings of how kindness and cruelty interrelate, which may contribute to difficulties in their present or future relationships. One example of this dynamic, commented on frequently by clinicians specializing in working with children exposed to domestic violence, is that some young children struggle with the belief that a person who doesn't abuse them must not really love them.

Moving from emotional to physical impacts on children, our professional experience indicates that adults who believe that abuse is evidence of love are at increased risk to abuse children. Batterers appear to be particularly prone to using culturally supported arguments of this kind in defending their abusive parenting, making comments in session such as "Spare the rod and spoil the child" or "You want me to be like those other parents who don't care what happens to their children." Furthermore, this value system can lend itself to child sexual abuse. Incest perpetrators, when their actions are uncovered, sometimes describe the violations that they have committed as having been acts of tenderness or caring, using such rationalizations as "I wanted to help her learn about sexual relationships in a safe way" or "She was really starved for affection, because her mother doesn't give her any, and it just got a little out of hand" (see also Salter, 1995; Herman, 1981).

Manipulativeness

We observe that few of our clients rely entirely on verbal or physical attack to attain control. Rather, batterers employ a wide range of behavioral tactics, foremost among which is often a pattern of manipulativeness. Immediately following abusive incidents, a batterer may strive to manipulate his partner's perceptions of his actions or to create confusion about the causes or meaning of the incidents, which has been described as a form of mind control (Jacobson & Gottman, 1998). Over the longer term, his manipulativeness may take a different form: Periods of abuse are usually interspersed with times of relative calm, during which the batterer may be loving or friendly, with shows of generosity or flexibility, in an attempt to regain his partner's trust and to create the hope that he has changed. Given the traumatic effects on her of his history of abusing her, the respite and sense of hopefulness engendered by his good periods can cause serious confusion in her. He thus may be able to reengage her over and over again in a way that can be baffling to outsiders who do not understand the deep combined effects of trauma, intimidation, and manipulation, which can form strong "trauma bonds" (Dutton, 1995; Dutton & Painter, 1993; Herman, 1992).

Batterers' manipulativeness often extends to the public arena as well. The great majority of batterers project a public image that is in sharp contrast to the private reality of their behavior and attitudes (Jacobson & Gottman, 1998; Ayoub et al., 1991; Adams, 1989). They may impress others as friendly, calm, and reasonable people, often with a capacity to be funny and entertaining. The public reputation that a batterer can build may cause people to be reluctant to believe allegations of his battering, thus making it more difficult for his partner and children to obtain emotional support or assistance. Our clients shape the public image of their partners as well, describing them to others as controlling, demanding, and verbally abusive at the same time as they paint themselves as caring and supportive partners who are earnestly trying to make things at home go well. The cumulative effect of these behaviors on those outside the family is to build sympathy and support for the batterer and to isolate the battered woman by damaging her credibility.

A batterer's family members and his surrounding community generally find manipulation harder to identify than more overt tactics of abuse. For example, many of our clients use arguing styles at home that rely more on twisting their partners' words, distorting past events, and other tactics of confusion than on loud yelling or name-calling. The partner of this style of batterer may suffer from increased confusion and self-blame, and in some cases may become emotionally unstable; the batterer may then use her deteriorating emotional condition to discredit further her disclosures of abuse.

The manipulativeness of batterers can create ambivalence and disorientation for their children. For example, children sometimes say to us that they don't understand why their mother gets so angry during arguments in which their father seems calm, because they do not grasp the significance of his words or his underlying tone. Following incidents of overt abuse or violence, he may be charming and attentive to the children while the trauma of victimization causes the children's mother to be short-tempered, withdrawn, or fragile. The batterer thus can shape the children's perceptions of the incident that has just occurred, leading them to form the impression that their mother is aggressive and that the batterer is the "nice" parent. Children also appear to sometimes be confused or influenced by the positive public reputations of their battering fathers.

Manipulation is in itself a psychological risk to children. For example, experts in treating schizophrenia have found that severely contradictory messages from parents appear to play a greater role than overt abuse in engendering children's psychosis (Karon & Vandenbos, 1981). When these tactics are combined with the dynamics of domestic violence, the risks to children's mental health increase further.

Batterers are also adept at manipulating those attempting to intervene. Our clients are commonly able to lie persuasively, sounding sincere and providing an impressive level of detail while sometimes weaving together multiple fabrications. We find that it may be impossible to uncover accurate information except by reviewing police reports and child protective records, speaking with probation officers and therapists, and interviewing the battered partner and other witnesses. In a number of our cases, evaluators working for courts or child protective services have made errors due to their failure to adequately test the batterer's credibility.

Contradictory Statements and Behaviors

Assessment of batterers and their impact on families is further complicated by the contradictions typically present in a batterer's thinking and presentation. Many of our clients, for example, state that they oppose any use of violence toward women, that men should treat their partners with respect, that decision making should be "50–50," and that the needs of the children should be the priority. Some clients make forceful, articulate, and appropriate confrontations of other men in their abuser groups while themselves continuing to be abusive and violent at home. Evaluating professionals should be cautious not to assess an alleged batterer simply by asking his beliefs, as he will generally be able to tailor his statements to the response that he believes is desired. The more educated batterer is sometimes especially adept at concealing his underlying thinking.

Externalization of Responsibility

Our clients are consistent in holding beliefs that relieve them of responsibility for their abusiveness, and they exhibit patterns of justifying their actions and making excuses (see also Dutton, 1995; Edleson & Tolman, 1992). They shift blame to their partners' conduct (e.g., "She really knows how to push my buttons") and to other supposed causes such as stress, substance abuse, issues from childhood, and intolerable emotional states. This belief system leads our clients to make contradictory statements such as "I know you should never hit a woman, but there's only so much a man can take" or "I know I'm responsible for my own actions, but she pushed me too far."

The batterer tends similarly to shift responsibility for the *effects* of his actions. For example, if his partner flinches during an argument because she thinks he is about to strike out, he may ridicule her as hypersensitive or theatrical. If she becomes depressed (which is a common symptom of abuse), he may call her lazy or say, "You just want to live off my hard work." He then may use the effects of his actions as an excuse for further mistreatment of her. Our clients take the same attitude toward the effects on their children of exposure to domestic violence, attributing their difficulties to the mother's poor parenting or to inherently weak character in the children. We find that the behavioral and emotional problems of our clients' children often increase over time and that therefore a batterer's criticism of his children (and of his partner as a parent) can mount in frequency and harshness.

A critical family dynamic that we observe is that batterers tend to have some success in persuading their family members to take on responsibility for the abuse. Children may blame their mothers for the abuse, mothers may blame children, siblings tend to blame each other, and all family members tend periodically to blame themselves. Family members may accuse each other of having made the batterer angry by challenging him, failing to cater to him adequately, making too much noise, or other actions that displeased him. When a woman attempts to end a relationship to escape abuse, the batterer may tell her that she is the one causing harm to the children because she is breaking up the family (Pence & Paymar, 1993). If his abusive behavior drives his children away from him emotionally, he is likely to accuse the mother of "alienating" the children from him (see Chapters 5 and 6).

In a substantial proportion of batterers, their externalization of responsibility extends to their interactions with their children. This tendency is a risk factor for children, as "abusive parents often project responsibility for their abusive behavior onto external factors, including the child" (Milner & Chilamkurti, 1991, p. 352). We often observe our clients using excuses for their mistreatment of the children that are similar to those that they use in justifying their abuse of the mother.

Denial, Minimization, and Victim Blaming

Batterers rarely disclose their violence fully, even in the face of considerable evidence (Heckert & Gondolf, 2000; Healey et al., 1998). Our clients also deny the effects of their battering on their partners. This denial can sometimes hold firm through months of participation in a batterer program, though the existence of independent evidence such as police reports with which to confront the client can assist in breaking down denial.

Even those men who admit to some portions of their violence typically minimize their history of abuse (Lloyd & Emery, 2000; Healey et al., 1998; Dutton, 1995), reporting significantly less violence than their female partners attribute to them and particularly minimizing their threatening behaviors (Edleson & Brygger, 1986). They may characterize aggressive violence as self-defense or may lie about violent events (Adams, 1989).

In assessment of an alleged or established batterer, minimization can be more effectively misleading than denial. By expressing remorse while simultaneously portraying his victim as provocative and dishonest, a batterer is sometimes able to persuade a professional that he has been wrongly accused or that his efforts to change have not been recognized. The batterer who uses this approach often states that his partner is falsely alleging domestic violence because she found out that he was involved with another woman, he refused a reunion that she desired, she was pushed into the accusations by an overzealous advocate, or she is using her claims as a weapon in custody litigation. We have had clients say roughly the following, for example: "I did shove her a couple of times, and one time I hauled off and slapped her when she called my mother a whore, and I really regret it. But now she's saying I grabbed her by the throat and threatened to kill her, which I would never do and she knows it."

Our clients often characterize their actions as defensive in nature or as being necessary to prevent more serious harm (see also Lloyd & Emery, 2000; Healey et al., 1998; Pence & Paymar, 1993). The most common explanations that clients of ours provide include such claims as that his partner was assaulting him and he injured her when he was warding off her blows; that he was enraged by her frequent assaults against him and "finally decided to show her what it's like"; that she was assaulting one of the children and he stepped in to protect the child; and that she was attempting to drive while drunk or to act self-destructively in some other way. Further inquiry typically reveals distortions in these accounts.

Child-abusing batterers exhibit similar patterns of denial, minimizing, and victim blaming regarding their parenting. Information that we receive from child protective services often contrasts sharply with our clients' minimization of their violence, threats, or boundary violations toward children. Many of our clients distort or exaggerate their children's behavior, tending to cast them as highly troubled or destructive. Furthermore, the descriptions that we receive from partners of our clients suggest that the behavioral and emotional problems that the children do have may be largely a product of exposure to battering behavior.

Serial Battering

Batterers tend to abuse more than one woman over the course of their adult relationships (Dutton, 1995; Woffordt, Mihalic, & Menard, 1994; Kalmuss & Seltzer, 1986). Child protective services and family and juvenile courts should avoid operating on the mistaken belief that a batterer's likelihood to assault a female partner can be reduced through the ending of his current relationship. The high degree of conflict in his current relationship is probably the result of his abusiveness rather than its cause, and if he replicates these dynamics in his future relationships, his children may be at risk.

MISCONCEPTIONS ABOUT BATTERERS

Important myths about batterers are widespread, and some of these have taken hold among professionals in ways that can lead to errors in assessment or in intervention. The most common misconceptions are examined here.

Substance Abuse

We believe that the available research on batterers and substance abuse indicates that the overlap between the two is not as great as many people have assumed. Most incidents of domestic violence take place without the use of alcohol by the batterer, and roughly 80% of alcohol-abusing men do not beat their partners (Kaufman Kantor & Straus, 1990). Alcohol and most drugs do not have physiological effects that cause violence, and indeed alcohol is most likely to contribute to violence in those who *believe* that it will do so (Gelles, 1993). A large proportion of our clients, including some who are highly physically violent, show no signs of substance abuse (see also Zubretsky & Digirolamo, 1996), and those clients who do have addiction problems commit serious acts of abuse even when sober. In cases where a battered partner reports that the man is violent only when drinking, further questioning usually reveals that lower-level violence such as pushing and threatening has happened at other times. Moreover, any increases in violence associated with substance abuse should still be understood as a matter of choice: Our clients admit to us that they give themselves more permission to be violent when intoxicated (see also Edleson & Tolman, 1992) and reveal similar attitudes and decision-making processes regarding their violence whether or not they are intoxicated. Similar observations have been made regarding lesbian batterers (Renzetti, 1997). Thus, the particular constellation of attitudes and behaviors that typically accompanies battering cannot reasonably be attributed to an alcohol problem (for similar conclusions, see Zubretsky & Digirolamo, 1996).

The impact on battering behavior of recovery from addiction is mixed. A fairly small but significant number of our clients become *more* dangerous and dictatorial when they stop abusing the substance, apparently because of their increased ability to closely monitor their partners' behavior and their increased irritability. We have observed another group of abusers who exhibit a period of substantial reduction in violence during roughly their first 4 to 12 months of sobriety, but as the batterer reaches a point of feeling more secure in his recovery and therefore less consumed by it, his abusive behavior tends to reemerge. Indeed, certain concepts that batterers learn in 12-step programs sometimes become new weapons integrated into their systems of verbal abuse, such as accusing a partner of "being in denial" about her own problems or labeling her "codependent." Clients in a final group, again, fairly small, do appear to make lasting changes in battering behavior following recovery from addiction. However, it is important to note that these are men who have been participating simultaneously in a specialized batterer program with a minimum duration of 11 months. Reports of long-term improvements in overall abusiveness coming from addiction recovery *alone* are rare (Bennett, 1995), and professionals should avoid suggesting to the family members of a batterer or to the batterer himself that his recovery will increase physical or psychological safety in the home.

Although substance abuse is not causal in domestic violence, it can contribute to a batterer's frequency and severity of violence (Bennett, 1995), and the most dangerous batterers have elevated rates of heavy substance abuse (Websdale, 1999; Campbell, 1995a). Substance abuse history is thus one important factor in risk assessment.

Mental Health Problems

Most of our clients have no detectable mental health problems. The available studies suggest that aside from those who are extremely physically violent, batterers do not appear to have substantially higher rates of psychopathology than do nonbattering men (Gondolf, 1999; O'Leary, 1993; review in Tolman & Bennett, 1990). Clinicians have difficulty in reliably assigning batterers to types within a psychological typology (Langhinrichsen-Rohlins, Huss, & Ramsey, 2000), and there is no particular personality disorder or mental illness that batterers show consistently (Langhinrichsen-Rohlins et al., 2000; Sonkin, 1987). According to Gelles and Straus (1988), "90 percent [of abusive incidents] are not amenable to a psychological explanation" (p. 43). There is especially strong evidence of a characteristic absence of psychopathology in those batterers who are not violent outside of the home (Holtzworth-Munroe & Stuart, 1994).

We have had infrequent cases where a client's violence did appear to be produced primarily by a mental illness, with the following distinguishing characteristics: (a) The men's partners reported that they did not exhibit chronic patterns of controlling behavior or entitled attitudes. (b) The men showed unusually low levels of investment in justifying or rationalizing their violence, even under confrontation. (c) They had higher levels of empathy and lower levels of negative characterization with respect to their victims than did other clients. (d) They had histories of explosive behaviors with nonpartners about which they expressed remorse and embarrassment. We estimate that such men have been 1% or fewer of our clients.

A second and much larger group of men with whom we have worked have serious indications of mental illness or have already been diagnosed but also exhibit the central characteristics that make up the batterer profile. In such cases, the mental health problem should not be seen as the cause of the battering but rather as an important aggravating factor and as an obstacle to efforts at rehabilitation, analogous to the substance abuse of other batterers (see also Edleson & Tolman, 1992).

A number of subtler emotional problems are widely assumed to be causes of battering, including low self-esteem, insecurity, childhood victimization, poor impulse control, and feelings of inadequacy. Our clinical experience, however, does not support the belief that such problems are consistently present in batterers. Similarly, a number of studies have examined the role of life stress in causing battering and have found little evidence of any connection (review in Tolman & Bennett, 1990).

In an attempt to address the fact that battering behavior rarely extends outside of the family, one formulation has portrayed batterers as having profound emotional issues regarding intimacy (e.g., Dutton, 1995). However, this theory does not offer an explanation of why so many men (and women) with severe intimacy problems do not batter, nor can it account for the multiple aspects of battering behavior that have little or nothing to do with intimacy, such as a batterer's tendency to become intimidating when his authority is challenged. It also does not account for batterers' tendency to have peers who are also abusive to women (Silverman & Williamson, 1997). Cross-cultural studies of domestic violence indicate that battering occurs in a range of different structures of intimacy between partners (e.g., Mitchell, 1992; Levinson, 1989).

Psychotherapy appears to have low rates of effectiveness with batterers (Jacobson & Gottman, 1998), which we observe to result from their high entitlement and from their tendency to manipulate the therapeutic process. We have received only rare reports from partners of our clients of behavioral improvements in the abuser through participation in psychotherapy or through the use of psychotropic medication, and none of those improvements have been maintained over the long term. Furthermore, we find our battering clients to be highly resistant to using psychotropic medication regularly and responsibly.

A similar misconception about batterers involves their purported deficiencies in conflict resolution, communication, assertiveness, and anger management skills. In fact, Dutton (1995) observed that the batterer's lack of assertiveness was present only in partner relationships and not in other contexts. Another study found that skill differences between batterers and nonbatterers were small (Morrison,

Van Hasselt, & Bellack, 1987). These findings strengthen our clinical observation that batterers are generally not unable to use nonabusive skills but rather are unwilling to do so because of their attitudes. In our experience, batterer intervention specialists are in wide agreement that the teaching of conflict resolution or anger management skills to batterers is only useful if the clients' underlying attitudes are also confronted.

A particularly prevalent misconception about batterers is that they have poor impulse control. However, it is unusual to find an abuser who has a history of lost jobs due to impulsive behavior at work or other indications of low impulse control. Moreover, a complete history of a man's abusive and controlling behaviors toward his partner generally reveals some actions that require forethought or even planning. Exploration of an abuser's nonpartner relationships, his handling of his own finances, and other spheres of life generally reveals no severe history of impulsivity.

One mental health diagnosis that should be treated as a special case is antisocial personality disorder, also known as the psychopathic or sociopathic personality. This is a condition in which the person lacks a social conscience, leading to manipulative and exploitative behavior, a tendency toward violence and intimidation, and chronic law breaking. The male sociopath typically has superficial, dishonest, and abusive relationships with women, including chronic infidelity (American Psychiatric Association, 1994). Although the sociopath and the batterer are similar in their exploitativeness (Jacobson & Gottman, 1998), there are two key differences between the two personalities: (a) The sociopath exhibits his antisocial tendencies with many different people (typically including employers) and not just with intimate partners. (b) The sociopath's behavior pattern begins no later than mid-adolescence, but the batterer's problem emerges more commonly in his late teens or twenties. Antisocial personality disorder is dangerous and highly resistant to treatment, so a man who has both this diagnosis and a history of battering may be a serious risk to his partner, former partners, or children.

Generalized Violence and Criminality

The great majority of our clients, including some of the most severely or dangerously violent ones, have not had any chronic problems with violence outside of partner relationships. Studies have similarly concluded that although batterers do have a higher rate of generalized violence than do nonbatterers, the great majority of batterers restrict their violence to intimate relationships (Jacobson & Gottman, 1998; Hotaling, Straus, & Lincoln, 1990). They are not generally perceived as violent in nature by people who interact with them in other contexts; the exception to this is in certain situations where they are confronted about their battering behavior or when they perceive others as interfering with their control over their partners or children. In other situations, batterers are known for their self-control: For example, their ability to calm themselves abruptly when police arrive at the home and to behave reasonably and amicably in the presence of the officers is a standard subject of police training on domestic violence.

Class assumptions have played a role in the construction of the societal image of the batterer as a generally violent man who is poor or blue-collar, often allowing batterers who are well educated, successful, and self-assured to escape detection. Similarly, the public imagination has exaggerated the contribution to battering of the "macho," tough-guy personality style, with its stereotypic class and racial associations.

Those batterers who do exhibit generalized violence have been shown to be an increased risk to their partners and children (Campbell, Soeken, McFarlane, & Parker, 1998). Men in this category can exhibit less concern for the consequences to themselves of their actions, are less restricted by their own guilt, and can be familiar with particularly destructive methods of violence (including weapons use). The presence of a pattern of generalized violence therefore does need to be taken into account as one factor in assessing a batterer's dangerousness.

Race, Cultural, and Class Stereotypes

Battering has been established to be a serious problem in the great majority of racial and cultural groups that have been studied in the modernized world (Heise et al., 1999; Levinson, 1989). Within the United States, rates of battering are high among all racial groups (Tjaden & Thoennes, 2000) and do not appear to differ dramatically between different races and cultural groups when class is controlled for (Silvern, Karyl, & Landis, 1995; review in Hampton, Carrillo, & Kim, 1998, and in Koss et al., 1994); for example, Latino couples are no more male dominated or approving of violence than are Anglo couples (review in West, 1998). There is, however, a general dearth of research on batterers of color (Kanuha, 1996), forcing us to rely primarily on clinical experience in discussing the relevance of race and culture.

In our experience, professionals handling domestic violence cases —perhaps especially child protective service providers but also judges, therapists, custody evaluators, and others—have been prone to make errors based on cultural and class assumptions. These assumptions often come to our attention through the professional's statement that the family in a particular case "comes from a culture where domestic violence is considered acceptable." Such a view confuses and obscures the fact that modern cultures are made up of complex cross-currents, with values constantly being debated and undergoing shifts. To summarize a culture's view of domestic violence in one phrase is culturally insensitive; moreover, values among men in any given culture can be in sharp conflict with those among women. In addition, even in cultures where men's right to control females is largely accepted among both men and women, abusers still have higher than average levels for their society of beliefs in their right to exert power (review in Heise et al., 1999). Visible individuals and groups working in opposition to domestic violence exist throughout the world; at least 53 countries now have laws against domestic violence and 41 have criminalized marital rape (Heise et al., 1999). In short, we are unaware of evidence indicating that any culture has a broad consensus explicitly condoning domestic violence.

In more sensitively discussing the influence of racial, cultural, and class factors on battering behavior, we must begin by stressing the high level of implicit support for domestic violence in *mainstream* culture in the United States, including among the white, educated, and economically privileged sectors of society. For example, college students given a scenario involving domestic violence by a man tend to blame the woman and to relieve the man of responsibility; this tendency increases the more the scenario portrays a high degree of intimacy in the relationship, with few research subjects believing that the man is responsible for his actions (Summers & Feldman, 1984). Another study found that over 25% of college males studying undergraduate psychology believe that it is appropriate for a man to beat a woman whom he believes to be sexually unfaithful and that over 10% believe it is appropriate to beat a female partner who repeatedly refuses to have sex (Silverman & Williamson, 1997). In addition, batterers can read cultural messages in the failure of some police departments or courts to take domestic violence offenses seriously or to hold batterers accountable for their actions; for example, sentences for crimes related to domestic violence are generally lower than those for comparable violent crimes among strangers (Gender Bias Study Committee, 1989). Batterers may take similar lessons from the reluctance of police to take action regarding spousal rape (Bergen, 1996).

Moreover, international studies are helpful in considering further the importance of race and ethnicity in patterns of battering. Overall, the level of domestic violence in the United States is comparable to that of other societies (Straus & Gelles, 1990), appearing to be among neither the highest nor the lowest; for example, domestic violence rates in Puerto Rico have been found to be higher than the U.S. average but those in Cuba much lower (Kaufman Kantor, Jasinski, & Aldarondo, cited in West, 1998; see also Levinson, 1989). The best predictors of level of battering in a society have been found to be economic and social factors, including the level of economic inequality between men and women and the level of restriction on women's economic rights (such as the right to inherit land or money); the extent of husband dominance in family decision making; the level of access by women to divorce; and the overall level of violence in the society (Heise et al., 1999; Mitchell, 1992; Levinson, 1989). Rates of partner abuse appear to be lower in societies where women have more power and authority outside of the family as well as inside (Heise et al., 1999). Thus, a global perspective reinforces our view that battering cannot be explained in terms of racial or ethnic factors in themselves.

Battering is also not the province of a particular socioeconomic class. Although most studies suggest that poorer families have a higher incidence of domestic violence (e.g., Bachman, 2000; Straus, Gelles, & Steinmetz, 1980), there are also findings that rates are elevated in the wealthiest families (review in Stark & Flitcraft, 1988), that men of higher occupational status have higher rates of chronic offending (Woffordt et al., 1994), and that women at both the highest and lowest economic strata find it the most difficult to get away from abusive partners (Woffordt et al., 1994). A higher level of education does not appear to make a man less likely to batter (review in Hotaling & Sugarman, 1986), and a batterer's level of education does not significantly affect his likelihood to physically abuse children (Suh & Abel, 1990).

The above points are not meant to suggest that cultural literacy and class sensitivity are irrelevant to professionals addressing domestic violence. Batterers' styles do vary by culture, so that the particular spheres of greatest control, the most likely excuses for abuse, and even the forms of violence used follow some cultural generalizations (Levinson, 1989). Cultural literacy is important in understanding how a particular man may construct the rationalizations for his actions and what some of the moments or situations of greatest danger may be for his partner and children (Haj-Yahia, 1996) and therefore also in designing effective services for batterers (Carrillo & Tello, 1998).

Similarly, the challenges faced by a battered woman are culturally specific, including what kind of support (if any) she can expect to receive from relatives, police, clergy, and other key institutions, and how her own cultural and religious beliefs shape her perceptions of her options (Bonilla-Santiago, 1996; Haj-Yahia, 1996). There is evidence, for example, that religious participation increases the ability of African American women to avoid abusive relationships (Raj et al., 1999). An immigrant woman may face language barriers when she attempts to get assistance, or her legal status may present her with the additional fear that the batterer will have her deported. Considering class issues, the higher rates of domestic violence found among low-income families may reflect the additional obstacles that poor women face to leaving rather than a greater propensity of poor men to batter.

In our clinical experience, although we do observe some racial, ethnic, and class variations in the tactics and justifications used by batterers, we find the commonalities stronger than the differences. Our clinical experience with batterers involves primarily white, African American, Caribbean, and Central American men, as well as some Portuguese and Cape Verdean individuals. The class makeup of our clients has been fairly representative of the United States, with higher incomes among our self-referred clients and those mandated by courts in wealthier areas.

Lack of cultural awareness can lead to underreactions and overreactions by professionals. The belief that domestic violence is the norm in certain cultures can cause child protective workers to overlook potentially dangerous situations, just as the belief that men from certain groups are likely to be batterers may lead to a prejudicial court response or cause child protective services to remove children from a home prematurely. Class assumptions can have similar effects; we observe, for example, that both courts and child protective services sometimes underreact to the well-educated, economically comfortable batterer (see also Adams, 1989).

We do see indications that some better-educated batterers may rely less on physical violence and draw more on sophisticated techniques of psychological abuse that they have at their disposal. These observations are consistent with findings that, at lower levels of violence, more privileged men are just as likely to batter as are low-income men (Hotaling & Sugarman, cited in Moore, 1997). However, this style of abuser may be at less risk of arrest, because his incidents of physical battering tend to be lower in frequency and severity. Overgeneralization should be avoided, however, as we have also worked with upper- and middle-class clients who were violent to the point of terror and with working-class clients who used low levels of violence and high levels of psychological abuse.

As with culture, the obstacles faced by a battered mother are specific to her class position. A poorer woman may have few job options, her friends may be unable to take her and her children into their already crowded houses, and her relatives may not have money to lend. A wealthier woman may find the contrast between her life-style and the conditions in a battered women's shelter overwhelming and may find her children resentful toward her if she takes them out of their comfortable surroundings.

Two final points need to be made regarding race, culture, and class. First, we observe clinically that cultural mores play a role in shaping the strengths and weaknesses of a batterer's parenting (as they do anyone's) and interact with his battering problem in complex ways. (Research on the parenting of batterers that examines cultural variations is virtually nonexistent at this point.) Second, class and cultural expectations affect how able children feel to disclose the abuse to outsiders and to process their emotional reactions to it. For example, wealthier children may be socialized more strongly to avoid harming the family's reputation and may also assume that they would be disbelieved if they disclosed the abuse. Immigrant children may be afraid to disclose any personal information to those perceived as authorities.

SUMMARY

Domestic violence perpetration involves a definable and identifiable pattern of attitudes and behaviors. Batterers share key characteristics, each of which has important implications for the experience of children in the home. The battering problem has unique etiology and dynamics and cannot be reduced to any other cause such as substance abuse, mental illness, or violent personality type. Effective assessment and intervention with families affected by domestic violence requires a grasp of the central elements of the battering pattern and of the dynamics that it may set in motion in a particular family. Cultural and class awareness are also indispensable, for the social context in which the parents live shapes their behaviors and their real and perceived options, which in turn shape the children's experience.

2

Power Parenting
The Batterer's Style With Children

Having reviewed the behavioral and attitudinal characteristics of domestic violence perpetrators, we can now examine batterers' typical style as parents. We divide this discussion into two sections, looking first at overall tendencies in batterers' interactions with children and then specifically examining the risk of child abuse. As we will indicate, the predominant weaknesses in the child rearing of batterers in large part follow predictably from the central elements of the profile that we have already elucidated in Chapter 1.

TYPICAL CHARACTERISTICS OF BATTERERS AS PARENTS

Both our clinical experience and published studies reveal a set of recurring themes in the parenting of batterers that are present at substantially greater rates than in the parenting of nonbattering men. However, we do not find these *parenting* characteristics of batterers to be quite as consistently present as the behaviors and attitudes that batterers exhibit *toward their partners*. For example, a portion of batterers are fairly dependable in showing kind behavior toward their children, but no batterer is dependable in these respects toward his partner.

Although there is a spectrum of parenting behaviors by batterers, one cannot say that any batterer is a fully responsible parent. Whether or not it is the batterer's intention, exposing children to domestic violence has multiple negative effects on them, including inherently damaging their relationships with their mother. The batterer's abuse of the children's mother should thus be seen as reflecting on his parenting (see also Jaffe & Geffner, 1998) and as indicative of other weaknesses that are likely to be present. Professionals wishing to assess or to intervene in the parenting of batterers can expect that one or more of the following problems will be present in the parenting of the great majority of these men.

Authoritarianism

To the extent that our clients involve themselves in the discipline of their children (which varies greatly), they tend to be rigid, authoritarian parents (see also Margolin, John, Ghosh, & Gordis, 1996; Walker & Edwall, 1987). They often expect their will to be obeyed unquestioningly, taking an intolerant view of any resistance or arguing from their children. They demonstrate a limited ability to accept feedback or criticism from family members or to make the kinds of adjustments in parenting decisions that responsible parents are frequently called on to make in order to effectively meet the needs of the children. This rigidity can contribute to developmental problems for children, who need to be able to struggle with their parents as part of the process of identity formation (Bukatko & Daehler, 2001).

Similar observations were made by Holden and Ritchie (1991), who found that batterers were more frequently angry at their children than were nonbatterers, spanked their children more than twice as often, and were more likely to spank their children "hard." The authors also found that batterers tended to react to conflicts involving their children with "power-assertive" responses more often than did nonbattering men. Other researchers have observed that batterers tend to swing unpredictably between authoritarian and permissive parenting (Roy, 1988) or between authoritarian parenting and showing no interest in their children at all (Adams, 1991).

Children exposed to domestic violence are very often at emotional risk because of the traumatic effects of the violence itself, and thus poor parenting by a batterer can be felt more deeply than might be the case in other circumstances. For example, Holden and Ritchie (1991) found that children exposed to domestic violence were particularly likely to have behavioral problems if their fathers had high rates of irritability. Margolin et al. (1996) found that a father's authoritarian treatment of the children has more pronounced negative effects if he also abuses the children's mother. Thus, in assessing the effects on children of a batterer's parenting style—as in custody evaluation, for example—the history of domestic violence should be taken into account.

The batterer's tendency to authoritarian parenting follows from a number of aspects of his profile. Because of his tendency to be controlling, he may expect his children to adhere uncritically to his authority; in particular, sons may be the special targets of his strict control (Margolin et al., 1996), although a recent study found that girls of battered women in shelter had experienced harsher verbal treatment from their fathers than had boys (Cummings, Peplar, & Moore, 1999). Because of his entitlement and self-centeredness, the batterer may expect the rewards and public status of being a father without the difficulties and sacrifices that are involved. Authoritarian discipline affords a quick way to solve problems without the time-consuming complexities that arise from serious involvement in children's thoughts, feelings, and conflicts. The dictatorial style also appeals to the aspect of the batterer that sees the children as personal possessions with whom he can do as he sees fit.

The batterer's authoritarian outlook can stunt the development of his own parenting skills. Men's willingness to "accept that wives can mentor them in nurturing skills" is a factor in their development as effective parents (Pollack, 1998, p. 123), but batterers tend to be much less open than are nonbattering men to the parenting influence or training of their partners (Adams, 1991). We often find that our clients insist that their approach to raising boys in particular is superior to that of their partners, yet rigid and unsupportive parenting styles have been found to be as damaging for boys as for girls (Pollack, 1998).

In addition to being harmful in itself, rigid parenting and lack of empathy for children have been linked to risk for child abuse (review in Milner & Chilamkurti, 1991). There are indications that abusive parenting is in part a product of a parent's belief system:

> At-risk and abusive parents' more frequent reliance on power assertion (i.e., verbal and physical force) techniques may not reflect simply a skill deficit. . . . Matched comparison parents appear similar in their awareness of different discipline techniques. The more frequent use of physically punitive techniques . . . appears to reflect their perceptions of the wrongness of child transgressions and their belief that power assertion is effective in gaining control of their children's behavior. (Milner & Chilamkurti, 1991, p. 359)

These factors may contribute to the high rates of child abuse observed in batterers, which we discuss below.

Underinvolvement, Neglect, and Irresponsibility

Batterers tend to be underinvolved and neglectful parents (usually in combination with periods of authoritarian involvement) and to be less physically affectionate with their children than are nonbatterers (Holden & Ritchie, 1991; Crites & Coker, 1988). The prevailing view among our clients is that their children are part of their domain of authority, yet they consider the work of caring for the children to be the responsibility of the mother. They commonly perceive children as a hindrance or annoyance and may arrange pretexts to be away from home much of the time in order to evade parenting responsibilities; for example, quite a number of our clients over the years have admitted to provoking fights with their partners in order to create an excuse to leave home to participate in another activity. Batterers are sometimes unwilling to make any compromises or sacrifices from their individual desires in order to meet family responsibilities (Adams, 1991), although we find them sometimes less reluctant to contribute financially than in other ways.

Our clients are not reliable in knowing the names of their children's schoolteachers or daycare providers, knowing the details of medical conditions or the names of doctors, or being able to describe their children's interests, strengths, or ambitions. Batterers' lack of knowledge about their children often reveals itself in behavioral expectations that are not appropriate to children's ages, most commonly taking the form of expecting children to behave like mature adults (Jacobson & Gottman, 1998). Moreover, fathers appear to be largely unaware of the effects on children of exposure to domestic violence, effects that are commonly observed by mothers and by teachers (Sternberg, Lamb, & Dawud-Noursi, 1998).

We find that the batterer tends to take an interest in his children when it is convenient for him or when an opportunity arises for public recognition for his fathering. One client of ours who was rarely available to help his children with their homework nonetheless boasted of the academic award that his son eventually won. Another man who was chronically verbally harsh with his daughter about how "uncoordinated" she was and who would ridicule her for her "unrealistic" athletic ambitions was observed by his wife jumping up and down by the side of the soccer field when his daughter played well, telling the other parents, "I've always told her she could do it if she'd just keep working at it."

On the occasions when a batterer chooses to focus attention on his children, he may be powerfully present, interacting with energy and humor and spending money freely on them. Our clients describe these events to us as evidence of what good fathers they are. These interactions can have a potent influence on children's feelings, especially given that the battered woman may not have such entertaining times with them because of her own trauma, the batterer's denial of money for her to spend on the children, and the fact that she carries the primary burden of their daily care. Indeed, the batterer's lack of availability can increase his value in the children's eyes: They may become excited over opportunities to be with him and aware of the importance of taking advantage of times when he is in a good mood. He thus may be able to establish a superior position as a parent partly through his neglectful tendencies. As child protective workers often comment, children tend to eagerly accept positive attention from a neglectful (or abusive) parent, forgetting for the moment their past disappointments and resentments. Partners of our clients sometimes describe their distress at seeing their children repeatedly disappointed by the batterer; as one woman said, "He promises all the time to do things with them or get them things, but it rarely happens."

A batterer's level of commitment to his children cannot be assessed on the basis of his statements or his expressions of emotions, such as the shedding of tears while talking about them or the proud showing of photographs. Such displays can be products of manipulativeness or of self-centeredness rather than of genuine connection to the child, and we have observed that our clients make recurring promises to become more consistently involved with their children, promises that they typically fail to fulfill (except during a period of litigation). Assessment of a batterer's potential as a parent therefore needs to rely largely on what his actual past performance has been, which varies considerably from batterer to batterer. In this context, it is also important to keep in mind that lack of attention to the child by the parent is one risk factor for child abuse perpetration (review in Milner & Chilamkurti, 1991).

Undermining of the Mother

Battering is, by its nature, undermining of a mother's authority, and it can have far-reaching effects on her ability to parent her children (see also Hughes & Marshall, 1995). Even if the batterer does not overtly undermine the mother, children absorb messages from the batterer's behavior that can shape their responses to their mother's parenting. The contemptuousness that batterers typically use in arguing with their partners, for example, can indicate to the children that their mother deserves to be insulted and that it is not necessary to speak respectfully to her. Children may learn from the batterer's verbal abusiveness that it is appropriate to yell at their mother or to call her names, and they may absorb specific approaches to deriding or degrading her. In fact, among the most common complaints from partners of our clients regarding the batterer's impact on the family is that the children mimic the batterer's precise treatment of her.

The children may also absorb from the batterer the message that physical violence toward the mother is acceptable, as long as the provocation is deemed adequate. Many teenage and preteen children of battered women assault them physically (Dutton, 1992; Holden & Ritchie, 1991), particularly boys (Johnston & Campbell, 1993b; Carlson, 1990), illustrating how potent this modeled behavior can be. We have also observed that children can digest the view that the mother is herself to blame for how she is treated, and they in turn shift responsibility to her for their own conduct toward her.

Although these undermining effects of battering in themselves can account for many difficulties in family functioning, a large proportion of batterers reinforce these effects with a more conscious pattern of undermining behaviors. These can include overruling the mother's parenting decisions, ridiculing her in front of the children, telling the children that she is an incompetent or unsafe parent, and many other tactics. These tactics tend to further the batterer's overall goal of dominating the family, by making his authority the only strong one in the family. At the same time, our clients often complain to us that their children do not respect their mother, claiming, for example, "I am stuck being the disciplinarian because they won't listen to her." We explore these family dynamics in more depth in Chapter 3.

Self-Centeredness

As in his orientation toward his partner, the batterer may tend to be selfish and self-referential in relationship to his children. When a couple first has children, the batterer is often unwilling to modify his lifestyle in order to take their needs into account (Adams, 1991) and tends to be insensitive to their feelings and experiences (Jacobson & Gottman, 1998). The tendency of batterers to be intolerant of crying babies has been a recurring theme among partners of our clients and was also noted by Jacobson and Gottman. Over time, at its most problematic, a batterer's self-centeredness can lead to a reversal of roles in which he expects his children to meet his needs rather than vice versa. Many of our clients maintain poor emotional boundaries with children, burdening them with too much information about their worries about money or health, frustrations at work, and other adult concerns. A batterer even may seek emotional support from the children—particularly girls—on the specific subject of his feelings of emotional injury by their mother, a situation that can have important implications for family dynamics.

The batterer's expectation that the children should meet his needs can take several forms. He may expect his children to abruptly make themselves available when he finally decides to spend time with them. He may believe that they should give up their independence to meet his needs (Walker & Edwall, 1987) or should be available to keep him company. We frequently observe a postseparation dynamic in which a batterer uses litigation to pressure for increased visitation, or even for custody, only to leave the children watching television or in the care of relatives most of the time. Our clients also reveal their expectations that any noise or playing in the house should stop if the man is feeling tired or irritable, that family members should attribute great importance to his minor successes or frustrations, and that the children should be physically affectionate with him whether or not they wish to be. When any of these needs is not met to his satisfaction, he may sulk or become retaliatory. In many of the families with which we work, mother and children alike are conditioned over time to cater steadily to the batterer to avoid criticism or intimidation.

Another manifestation of self-centeredness is the investment that some batterers show in having the children reflect well on them in public as extensions of themselves. Our clients are commonly eager to show photographs of their children, referring to them as "my little girl" or "my little boy," even when our other interactions with the client have demonstrated to us that his interest in his children is chronically low. Batterers often are "unable to paint a picture of their children as separate individuals" and "appear to view their children not as people with internal states and emotional needs, but rather as objects to be governed by others"; in addition, "the fathers' distortions of reality and inability to comprehend the children's developmental needs further impair the father-child relationships" (Ayoub et al., 1991, pp. 199, 205). Furthermore, our clients tend to take personal credit for their children's successes, at the same time as they hold their partners responsible for any failures (see also Ayoub et al., 1991).

Some batterers play particularly pathetic or self-destructive roles, and we have found the recurring problem of children who have become preoccupied with the possibility that their father will commit suicide, die in a car accident, or damage himself with a drug or alcohol overdose. Although the batterer may have genuine problems with depression or with substances, there is often a theatrical aspect to the way in which he presents his distresses to the family that has the effect of making his feelings the family focus and diverting attention from his abusiveness.

In cases where the batterer is more involved as a parent than is typical, perhaps taking primary care of the children while the mother works, it is nonetheless important to assess the extent to which this involvement focuses on the children's needs as opposed to his own. It is also valuable to ascertain whether the mother was forced by the batterer to be away working when she actually wanted to be with her children, because this is not an uncommon scenario in domestic violence cases.

As we described in Chapter 1, the self-centered orientation that batterers typically have toward their partners and often toward their children is not necessarily the result of a narcissistic personality type. Thus, psychological evaluation of the batterer by itself will not give an adequate picture of his ability to focus consistently on his children's needs.

Manipulativeness

The tendency of batterers to be manipulative partners often is paralleled in their behavior toward their children. Our clients are commonly able to create confusion in children regarding the nature of the abuse in the home, which family members are responsible for it (leading children to blame their mothers or themselves), and who is the kinder or more concerned parent. After separation, battered women in our cases raise concerns about manipulation of the children by the batterer with greater frequency than any other single aspect of his parenting. Chapter 3 explores in detail the effects of these dynamics on family functioning.

Ability to Perform Under Observation

The professional assessment of batterers' parenting is made more complicated by their typical ability to perform well under observation. The contrast between the public and the private behaviors of most batterers can extend to their parenting. While in the presence of friends or relatives or while in a professionally supervised interaction, many batterers may behave in a gentle, caring, and attentive way. An average-length social engagement with friends or a 1- to 2-hour supervised visit will generally not require many of the skills nor the capacity for focusing on the children's needs that are called for in day-to-day parenting, so the weaknesses in a batterer's parenting may not be evident to friends of the family or to professionals performing observations.

It can be helpful to evaluators to be aware of children's typical reactions to participating in professionally observed interactions with the batterer. Children who live with abuse or with exposure to abuse may develop an acute awareness of which kinds of situations represent greater danger and may learn to read intuitively the shifts in the abuser's mood or attitude. In our experience, it is widely recognized among both clinicians and child protective workers that some children are fairly relaxed and comfortable with an abusive parent as long as there are outsiders present. Indeed, for some children, their most positive memories involving the abusive parent may involve times of being in public or in social situations; batterers can sometimes exhibit their most charming and humorous behaviors while being observed and thereby elicit a happy, enthusiastic response from their children, who may be hungry for this quality of interaction with their father. Thus, evaluators should be cautious not to overinterpret children's positive reactions to their battering fathers under supervision.

EFFECTS ON CHILDREN OF EXPOSURE
TO DOMESTIC VIOLENCE

There is a high likelihood that children living with a batterer will witness the violence (review in Kolbo et al., 1996), and they are more aware of the violence than their parents realize (Erickson & Henderson, 1998). A substantial number of children witness sexual assaults against their mothers by the batterer (Campbell & Alford, cited in Wolak & Finkelhor, 1998). Murders of women by batterers are often witnessed by children, or children are present in the immediate aftermath (Langford et al., 1999). Batterers have been widely reported to be cruel to pets or to kill them (Lerner, 1999), which we consider important in the light of the strong attachments that children form to pets.

However, professional assessments of the parenting of batterers sometimes overlook the most evident problem—the batterer's exposure of his children to domestic violence. By contrast, other parenting choices that involve exposure of the children to disturbing or unsafe conditions, including substance abuse, are generally treated as relevant. The tendency to make an exception for domestic violence may result in part from a failure to view the batterer as fully responsible for his conduct, thus implicitly (and sometimes explicitly) holding the mother equally responsible for the children's exposure to violence (see Chapter 6).

Emotional, Behavioral, and Developmental Effects

Several studies indicate that children find violence between their parents to be among the most disturbing events involving their parents' relationship (review in Cummings, 1998). Children exposed to domestic violence are more aggressive with peers (including a tendency to bully and insult them) than are other children and have many more behavioral problems in general (Graham-Bermann, 1998); the increased rate of assaultiveness to nonfamily members is particularly marked among boys (Hotaling et al., 1990). Children exposed to domestic violence spend less time with friends, worry more about the safety of their friends, are less likely to have a best friend, and have lower-quality friendships than do other children (Graham-Bermann, 1998); they also tend to show negative effects on a range of measures of mental health (McCloskey, Figueredo, & Koss, 1995) and to show significantly elevated rates of behavior problems, hyperactivity, anxiety, withdrawal, and learning difficulties (Gleason, 1995). They may avoid being at home (Roy, 1988), yet they also tend to take on the role of attempting to protect their mothers (Walker, 1989; Roy, 1988) and even to involve themselves physically in fights in efforts to protect the abused parent (Peled, 1998).

Children may internalize various effects, sometimes with long-term consequences. For example, children of battered women often feel burdened with guilt from believing that their behavior caused past violence toward their mother (Jaffe, Hurley, & Wolfe, 1990) and anxious that they might cause her to be beaten again (Roy, 1988). Conflicts over children sometimes lead to violence (Hughes & Marshall, 1995), and children's awareness of this fact can cause profound guilt. Children's eating and sleeping routines may be disrupted by violence (Jaffe, Wolfe, & Wilson, 1990).

The level and nature of the *emotional abuse* of a mother by a batterer is an important factor in children's level of distress (Cummings, 1998) and is a strong predictor of children's social behavior and adjustment problems (Graham-Bermann, 1998). Children of battered women are exposed to at least twice the frequency of parental arguments that other children witness (Holden, Stein, Ritchie, Harris, & Jouriles, 1998), and the level of verbal abuse toward the mother strongly predicts which men will batter (Bennett, Goodman, & Dutton,

2000; Tjaden & Thoennes, 2000). These findings indicate that children exposed to battering behavior are growing up in an emotional climate that is dramatically different than that of nonviolent homes.

Some writers have suggested that the negative effects on children of domestic violence are primarily a result of a high level of interparental conflict (e.g., Johnston & Campbell, 1988). However, multiple studies have shown that violent conflict causes more extensive long-term problems and more immediate negative reactions from children than do even high levels of nonviolent conflict (review in Margolin, 1998) and that children exposed to domestic violence are more affected than are other children by verbal conflicts between their parents (Adamson & Thompson, 1998).

Studies from abroad of children exposed to domestic violence have reached similar findings regarding emotional, behavioral, and learning problems, increased likelihood to suffer other forms of abuse, and high likelihood to witness the violence. Children of battered women around the world are also more likely to be malnourished and to have health problems and less likely to have been immunized (review in Heise et al., 1999).

Few studies have examined how race or ethnicity may affect children's responses to domestic violence. Two studies comparing the reactions to domestic violence of white and of African American boys have found that white boys show more externalizing behaviors, and one study found higher overall symptoms in Hispanic children than in other children of battered women (review in Margolin, 1998).

The batterer, as the primary perpetrator of violence and of psychological aggression in the home, should be seen as responsible for the exposure of the children to the effects reviewed here. Therefore, these effects are a reflection on his parenting capacity, "because battering a child's parent ignores the needs of the child, sets a poor example of conflict resolution, reflects negative attitudes toward women, and emphasizes the use of power to forcefully get one's own needs met at the expense of someone else" (Jaffe & Geffner, 1998, p. 384).

Traumatic Bonding

In many cases, one of the principle responsibilities of an evaluator is to assess the level of bonding between a batterer and his children. Such a determination is complicated by the fact that abuse of any kind, including direct child abuse, does not necessarily lead to distant, superficial, or overtly fearful relationships. In fact, as the literature on traumatic bonding demonstrates, systematic abuse—particularly of a kind that involves cycles of intermittent fear and kindness—can lead to the formation of unusually strong but unhealthy bonds and can foster the victim's development of potent dependence on the abuser (Dutton, 1995; James, 1994; Dutton & Painter, 1993; Herman, 1992).

A few central dynamics of traumatic bonding should be highlighted. First, one of the effects of abuse is to create a potent longing in the victim for kindness and understanding and for relief from the fear or terror experienced (Dutton & Painter, 1993, 1983; Herman, 1992). A person who is able to provide soothing treatment at the right moment will tend to be perceived by the victim as a rescuer and so to be looked upon with gratitude. In traumatic bonding, the person who brings the soothing relief is the same one who perpetrated the abuse. Following an incident of abuse, for example, an abuser may apologize for what happened, express concern for how the victim is feeling, and speak in a calm and warm tone. The typical response in victims of abuse is to feel thankful for the kindness, to be eager to forgive, and to form a belief that the abuser actually cares deeply for him or her. Once this cycle has been repeated a number of times, the victim may come to feel grateful to the abuser just for stopping the abuse each time, even if no real kindness or attentiveness follows. This has been demonstrated to be a normal response to abuse-related trauma in males and in females (Herman, 1992) rather than a masochistic trait in females as was sometimes assumed previously, and the intermittency of the abuse has been demonstrated to be a critical reason for the strength of trauma bonds (Dutton & Painter, 1993). According to Herman (1992),

> Survivors of domestic or political captivity often describe occasions in which they were convinced that they would be killed, only to be spared at the last moment. After several cycles of reprieve from certain death, the victim may come to perceive the perpetrator, paradoxically, as her savior. (p. 77)

The dynamics by which hostages become bonded to and protective of their captors even while being terrorized and mistreated have come to be known as the "Stockholm Syndrome," which has also been applied to battered women (e.g., Graham et al., 2001).

Second, the victim is likely to come gradually to confuse love and abuse just as the perpetrator does, though for different reasons; the fact that loving behavior so often closely follows or precedes incidents of mistreatment causes the two to become traumatically linked in the victim's psychology (Dutton & Painter, 1993). This confusion can be augmented by explicit statements by the perpetrator, such as "I'm doing this for your own good." For example, an incest perpetrator may begin an incident of abuse by apologizing for a previous violation and perhaps offering an excuse for it. The apology creates a moment of trust on the victim's side, along with some hope that her experience might be understood, which the perpetrator then exploits to lead into another violation. A similar dynamic can take place for children of battered women, even if they are not themselves direct targets of abuse. For example, many of our clients have strong tendencies to be kind to the children following assaults on their mother, sometimes unusually so, so that the children's trauma from witnessing the abuse of their mother becomes psychologically interwoven with positive attention from the batterer (which they may be particularly eager to receive because of its scarcity).

Third, witnessing the abuse of others has some dynamics distinct from being abused directly, even though many of the effects are similar. The witness of abuse can become aware that one path to relative safety is to maintain a close bond with the abuser. Children of battered women sometimes sense that they can be at risk themselves if they are perceived by the batterer as being allied with their mother, whereas they can keep largely out of harm's way by remaining in his good graces. We have observed that children in these circumstances sometimes experience tremendous cognitive dissonance from allying with the abuser, which they attempt to relieve by taking on the batterer's distorted view of the mother. The consequent damage to the mother-child relationship has important implications, to which we will return below.

Traumatic bonding leads the child to become increasingly focused "on the needs, wants, and emotional state of the abusive adult[, which] is her best shot at maintaining safety for herself," while simultaneously causing the child to lose focus on developing his or her abilities or engaging with the world (Whitten, 1994, p. 35).

Resilience in Children Exposed to Domestic Violence

Children are not affected uniformly by their exposure to domestic violence (Jaffe, Wolfe, & Wilson, 1990). Several factors in the lives of children can affect their resilience, including their development of talents and interests (such as athletic, scholastic, or artistic capabilities), their access to close relationships with trustworthy adults, their ability to escape self-blame, and the strength of their peer relationships (review in Wolak & Finkelhor, 1998; Roy, 1988). Despite the negative influence that battering has on boys, some sons of battered women grow up to be nurturing, nonviolent fathers (Jaffe & Geffner, 1998). Children's resilience to any type of traumatic event has been linked to the presence of a good parent or parentlike figure in their lives (Margolin, 1998), which for children exposed to domestic violence points to the importance in most cases of their relationship with their mother.

Because children's capacity for resilience is well established, it is important for professionals to be aware of how the violence to which batterers expose their children may be compounded by surrounding behaviors that reduce their chances for recovery. A batterer who isolates his children will make them less likely to develop close peer relationships. A batterer who undermines the children's relationship with their mother is likely reducing their chances of having a positive relationship with a nonviolent adult. A batterer who verbally abuses children about their athletic abilities (which is an active problem in two of our current cases) or who attempts to sabotage the development of their personal strengths in other ways reduces their access to sources of pride and to social connections that could foster their recovery. Thus, professionals who wish to foster resilience in children need to be attentive to reducing the batterer's ability to further disrupt their healthy development.

CHILD ABUSE

Alongside the concerns that we have raised so far in this chapter about the parenting styles of batterers is the greatly elevated risk of direct physical, sexual, or psychological abuse. The first two categories of child abuse by batterers have been the subject of multiple research studies, but the equally important area of psychological abuse by batterers (and the emotional climate that such abuse creates) still awaits extensive scholarly attention (Graham-Bermann, 1998).

Physical Abuse

An extensive collection of published studies indicates that batterers are several times more likely than are nonbattering men to physically abuse children. This risk was established perhaps most persuasively by Straus (1990), in a large-scale study (involving over 6,000 subjects) that used a high threshold of physical abusiveness, defining it as whether the man "frequently" assaulted children. Straus reported that 49% of batterers physically abuse children, whereas only 7% of nonbattering men do so; the most frequently and severely violent batterers have 10 times the rate of child physical abuse that nonbattering men do.

Several other studies support these findings. Bowker, Arbitell, and McFerron (1988), working with a sample of battered mothers recruited through advertisements, found that 70% of batterers physically abused children. Rates of child abuse by batterers did not vary by race or religion, but they were higher in families with higher income. Other factors associated with likelihood of child abuse were high husband dominance, level of violence toward the mother, frequency of marital rape, and number of children in the family. Regression analysis demonstrated that these factors were better predictors of child abuse than were any of the background characteristics of the fathers or the mothers, including the father's own history of suffering child abuse.

Suh and Abel (1990) reviewed case files of 300 women who had entered a battered women's shelter. Forty percent of the women had reported that the batterer had physically abused their children. Among the physically abused children, 42% had received bruises, 22% had suffered broken bones, and 33% had suffered broken noses. Batterers who abused alcohol were significantly more likely to physically abuse children than were other batterers.

The risk of physical abuse of children by a batterer rises with the severity and the frequency of his violence toward his partner (Straus, 1990). Child protective workers have commented to us that in their cases involving the most dangerously and brutally violent batterers, nearly all of the families report that the batterer has physically assaulted one or more of the children. Thus, a detailed history of the domestic violence allegations is important to any evaluator assessing risk of physical abuse of the children by the batterer. In addition, batterers are a risk to kill children, especially if they murder or attempt to murder the mother; in more than one in eight domestic violence homicides, the batterer kills one or more children (Langford et al., 1999). We find that some evaluators do not consider the risk of murder of children by a batterer.

To the best of our knowledge, no published study examines *post-separation* physical abuse of children by batterers. However, we do not see any reason to expect that abuse would decline after separation. Batterers' increased statistical risk for child physical abuse follows predictably from the behavioral and attitudinal profile of the batterer, examined in Chapter 1. Although the batterer's child abuse may arise in part from tensions related to his relationship with the adult victim,

it cannot be safely assumed that these issues will lessen after separation. In fact, we observe that many batterers' motivation to intimidate
their victims through the children *increases* when the couple separates,
because of the loss of other ways to exert control. In addition, the batterer's partner is no longer present to monitor his behavior toward the
children. If there is litigation involving custody or visitation, her
reports of physical abuse of the children by him may be dismissed by
the courts as a divorce tactic, which may leave him feeling free to
behave with impunity.

By contrast, there are indications that the parenting of battered
women often improves after separation (Schechter & Edleson, 1998;
Holden et al., 1998). The reasons for this appear to be that separation
allows a woman to begin to recover from the traumatic effects of being
battered and that her parenting is strengthened from escaping the
chronic undermining of her parental authority by the batterer. However, these reasons for improvement generally would not apply to
batterers.

Physical Harm to Children Incidental to an Assault on the Mother

The available studies of batterers' physical abuse of children focus
on intentional harm. However, there is an additional important category of physical assault of children by batterers that occurs acciden-
tally or recklessly during an assault on the mother (Jaffe, Wolfe, &
Wilson, 1990; Roy, 1988; Penfold, 1982). We receive reports from the
partners of our clients of assaults against the mother while she is holding a child in her arms, leading to injury of the child; injuries to the
mother during pregnancy that harm the fetus, cause premature delivery, or lead to miscarriage (see also Stephens, Richardson, & Lewin,
1997; review in Helton, McFarlane, & Anderson, 1987); objects
thrown in anger at the mother that hit a child; and blows intended for
the mother that hit a child, which in older children is especially likely
to occur when a child attempts to intervene physically to protect the
mother (Roy, 1988). Battering during pregnancy is common (review in
Gazmarian et al., 1996), and multiple studies have found that battering contributes to increased rates of low birth weight and to overall
lower average birth weights (review in Gazmarian et al., 2000; international review in Heise et al., 1999). Some partners of our clients
report that during pregnancy, their abusive partners target their
abdomen for blows (observed also in Gelles, 1990). A recent study
found battering linked to premature labor and to fetal distress
(Cokknides, Coker, Sanderson, & Addy, cited in Heise et al., 1999).

Thus, this category of violence to children is an important area of examination for professionals who are evaluating the history of a batterer's parenting.

Psychological Abuse

We have already cited evidence that the battering of a mother is in itself psychologically abusive to her children. However, we find that many of our clients also engage in additional forms of psychological abuse of the children (see also Walker & Edwall, 1987), and battered women report far more chronic and harsh criticism of children by their partners than do nonbattered women (Adams, 1991). The serious short-term and long-term effects on children of psychological abuse have been noted (e.g., Berlin & Vondra, 1999; Kashani & Allan, 1998). Some batterers are capable of extraordinary psychological cruelty toward their children without hitting or sexually abusing them, and our experience indicates (consistent with the research findings) that the implications for children are no less profound than are those of the more traditionally recognized forms of abuse. At the same time, verbal abuse to family members is more common among parents who physically abuse children (review in Wolfe, 1985) or perpetrate incest (see Chapter 4), and so psychological abuse should be recognized as a risk factor for other forms of child maltreatment.

Much of this maltreatment appears to be intended primarily to hurt or to intimidate the mother. One of our clients, for example, admitted that he had reacted to his anger at his wife one day by cutting his teenage daughter's prom dress to shreds with scissors. Like many batterers, he was aware that cruel behavior toward his children could be at least as painful and intimidating to his partner as violence toward her would be. (This particular client had never used a high level of violence against his partner, thus illustrating why the so-called "low-level batterer" cannot be assumed to be a low-level risk to children.) In another case, presented recently at a conference, a batterer killed the family's pet rabbit one day by striking it repeatedly against the side of the house in the presence of the child, who subsequently suffered serious emotional effects from witnessing the event. Furthermore, when the child later made reference to her father about his having killed the rabbit, he denied having done so, saying that the rabbit had simply died; thus, the child was left struggling with her sense of reality, compounding the trauma.

Our experience suggests that the more caring and responsible a mother is, the more effectively a batterer can control her by harming her children emotionally. Over our 15 years of practice with batterers, one of the most steadily present and poignant aspects of our interviews with the partners of our clients has been their description of the batterer's emotional maltreatment of the children. Recurring themes have included ruining events of major importance to the children, such as birthday parties and Christmas celebrations; cruel verbal put-downs, including references to issues that the batterer knows are the areas of greatest emotional pain; repeated rejection; overt favoritism between children; and public humiliation. We have not observed any clear correlation between the severity of these behaviors and the batterer's level of physical violence toward the mother; however, we do see indications of a correlation with his level of *psychological* abuse of the mother (see Chapter 7). Our clients tend in many ways to replicate their abusive style with the partner in their relationships with the children.

Sexual Abuse

Because of the complexity of the issues involved in examining the overlap between battering and incest perpetration and because this overlap has received considerable research but little analysis in the published literature, we devote Chapter 4 to this subject.

Some additional points that apply to all three forms of child abuse need to be made in closing this section. First, research evidence demonstrates that children who are the targets of more than one form of abuse (e.g., both physical and sexual abuse) suffer greater consequences than do those who experience just one form (Saakvitne, Gamble, Pearlman, & Lev, 2000) and, more specifically, that children who both suffer child abuse directly and witness the abuse of their mother show greater difficulties than do those who only witness abuse (McCloskey et al., 1995; Hughes, Parkinson, & Vargo, 1989). Thus, children who both are traumatized by exposure to domestic violence and are subjected to one or more direct forms of abuse are likely to experience a deepening of the effects of these experiences.

Second, custody evaluators sometimes dismiss the concerns that a battered woman expresses about her children's visitation with the batterer, concluding that she is unduly afraid that the batterer will replicate behaviors that he has used toward her in interacting with the children. However, both research evidence and clinical experience indicate that a batterer's behavior toward the children's mother in fact *is* an important predictor of how he is likely to treat children.

Third, it is also true that some batterers do draw fairly sharp lines around their abusiveness of their partners, holding themselves to higher standards in their treatment of their children and making efforts to keep the children from being exposed to the dynamic of abuse. Such batterers may have a better potential than do others to be responsible fathers in the long term. However, it is always advisable to proceed with caution, because some batterers who do not use the children as weapons while the couple is together begin to do so after separation, as other avenues of control or intimidation of the partner are closed off. Batterers routinely claim to evaluators that they have been careful not to expose the children to the violence, even in cases where this is not true. Moreover, any batterer has shown serious irresponsibility toward his children by battering their mother (Jaffe & Geffner, 1998), and the implications of such irresponsibility for future parenting need to be carefully weighed.

THE BATTERER AS ROLE MODEL

As an adult in a home where children are being raised, the batterer naturally exerts an important modeling influence on the children. In homes where domestic violence occurs, there are eight times as many physical threats as in nonviolent homes, five times as many control tactics, and four times as much sexual coercion. Boys exposed to domestic violence show much higher rates of aggressiveness and bullying toward peers, and both boys and girls show signs of learning to meet their needs by manipulating, pressuring, and coercing others (Graham-Bermann, 1998). Overall, according to Graham-Bermann,

> Research on battered women would suggest that the behavior of children raised in woman-abusive families reflects the entire complex of behaviors, meanings, intentions, and actions by those whose purpose is subduing and controlling the women. These behaviors are conveyed to the children through direct modeling and reinforcement. (p. 33)

Besides providing a general model of aggression, intimidation, and selfish pursuit of one's own interests, batterers more specifically model the behaviors and attitudes that lead to domestic violence, along with a surrounding set of beliefs and values. We explore both of these types of influence below.

Teaching Domestic Violence

Exposure to domestic violence markedly increases boys' likelihood of battering their own partners when they reach adolescence or adulthood (Silverman & Williamson, 1997; review in Hotaling & Sugarman, 1986; Straus et al., 1980) and of using other types of demeaning, psychologically abusive, and aggressive behaviors toward partners (Choice, Lamke, & Pittman, 1995; Wallerstein & Blakeslee, 1989; Roy, 1988). Men who witness domestic violence in childhood also have higher rates of committing sexual assault (review in Koss et al., 1994).

The process of children's identifying with the aggressor is a recurring theme in the literature on children of battered women (e.g., Graham-Bermann, 1998). A teenage boy who identifies closely with his battering father or who is placed in the batterer's custody may run an increased risk of replicating his father's attitudes and conduct. Teen sons of batterers are commonly involved in abusing their dating partners or in fighting over a girlfriend with other males (Roy, 1988). A court's decision to place children in the custody of a battering father can inadvertently encourage them to identify with him (McMahon & Pence, 1995).

Girls who are raised in homes with domestic violence may form their images of acceptable male behavior from observing the batterer and therefore may not believe that nonviolent or respectful men exist. Batterers' typical ability to convince children that their mother is to blame for the violence may increase the likelihood that a girl will blame herself if she is abused by a male partner as an adult. Women's self-blame, which most batterers work actively to promote, has been identified as an important obstacle to leaving batterers (Dutton, 1992). Women who were exposed to domestic violence as children are less likely than are other women to seek assistance if they are abused as adults (review in Doyne et al., 1999). A number of studies have found that girls exposed to battering have elevated rates of experiencing abuse as adult women (review in Hotaling & Sugarman, 1986).

The Batterer's Impact on Children's Belief Systems and Values

Most public and written discussions of the impact of domestic violence on children focus on emotional, behavioral, and learning ability effects. Equally important, however, are the effects that batterers have on their children's *belief system*, including how their experiences of his behavior shape their world view (Augustyn, Parker, McAlister Groves,

& Zuckerman, 1995). We will briefly examine some of the salient beliefs that children of battered women may develop over time.

Victims of violence are to blame for the violence. Both from the example that the batterer sets and from his explicit statements, children can absorb the view that their mother is causing her own abuse. This lesson in turn teaches children that they can harm others and blame the victim, as long as that person "provoked" them, was acting "stupid," or failed to "shut up when I told her/him to shut up" (see also Doyne et al., 1999; Hurley & Jaffe, 1990). Children exposed to battering can also learn more generally that hurting other people is not wrong (Arroyo & Eth, 1995). These values can be exhibited through children's behaviors at school or in the neighborhood and often are revealed clearly when children offer victim-blaming explanations for their destructive behaviors. On the other side of the coin, children may learn that they do not have the right to object to being mistreated by others unless they are completely blameless themselves. The absorption of this belief may contribute to the observed tendencies for sons of batterers to perpetrate abuse as adults and sometimes for daughters of batterers to have difficulty escaping violent relationships, as discussed above.

The use of violence is justified to impose one's will or to resolve conflicts. Children exposed to domestic violence may learn that physical aggression is an acceptable means to gain control over others (Doyne et al., 1999; Jaffe, Hurley, & Wolfe, 1990). This belief may be an important aspect of the increased aggression observed in children of battered women toward peers, particularly in boys (Hurley & Jaffe, 1990). Moreover, the lesson can be reinforced by children's observation of court responses. For example, children who are obligated to have visitation with a batterer over their objections are likely to interpret the court's actions as approving of the father's violence and disapproving of the child's wish to avoid his abuse. They may observe that the parent with the most power wins the court conflicts (Jaffe & Geffner, 1998), thereby confirming their sense that the abuse of power is both justifiable and desirable.

Boys and men should be in control, and girls and women should submit. Children exposed to domestic violence can develop rigid beliefs about gender roles (Hurley & Jaffe, 1990; Roy, 1988), whether or not these are explicitly promoted by the batterer, because of the subtle messages underlying their experience in the family. These include beliefs about what a "real boy" is like. Sons of batterers have a strong tendency to absorb their father's entitlement and manipulativeness with regard to females, even if they disagree consciously with his actions. We find, for example, that many of our clients whose fathers were batterers describe having been bitterly resentful regarding his violence when they were young, yet they abuse their own partners as adults because of the attitudes that they absorbed. Other beliefs about sex roles for both males and females can be shaped by exposure to battering (e.g., Silvern et al., 1995). Girls may come to believe, for example, that victimization is inevitable (Jaffe, Wolfe, & Wilson, 1990). For both girls and boys, "Particularly disturbing are the politics of power between men and women that invite children to adopt the view that father's violence toward mother can be rationalized and accepted" (Hurley & Jaffe, 1990, p. 472).

Abusers do not experience consequences for their actions. Children are often aware of the legal system's failure to hold the batterer accountable and of his ability to escape social criticism by persuading others that his version of events is the accurate one (Pickering et al., 1993). Aggression is particularly likely to be learned by children when they observe that it brings the actor benefits and does not lead to negative consequences (Bandura, 1978), and this has been specifically observed in the context of children's exposure to domestic violence (Arroyo & Eth, 1995).

Women are weak, incompetent, stupid, or violent. We find negative attitudes toward females rampant in both sons and daughters exposed to domestic violence (see also Johnston & Campbell, 1993b; Roy, 1988). This can be true even for those children whose mothers most courageously and forcefully resist the abuse; the exposure to battering and to the batterer as parent can inculcate the above attitudes in many ways, both subtle and overt, even if their mother does not fit this image. The exposure to denigration of females damages the self-esteem of daughters (Pickering et al., 1993). Boys who witness domestic violence appear to develop more strongly negative attitudes regarding women than do boys who are abused directly by their mothers (Liss & Stahly, 1993). (Notice that a combination of all of the effects discussed so far may account in large part for the tendency of children exposed to domestic violence to enter into dating relationships in which they are abusive or abused; Markowitz, 2001; Doyne et al., 1999.)

Fathers are better parents for teenage boys than are mothers, and teen boys need to escape their mother's influence. Some of our clients repeatedly promote this belief with their teenage boys, who then may echo such statements to custody evaluators; we hear this frequently from teen boys with whom we work. There is little evidence to support this assertion (Kelly, 1993), and teen boys who maintain close relationships with their mothers appear to have better outcomes than those who do not (Pollack, 1998). We have been involved in cases where the above belief became self-fulfilling, as it sabotaged the mother's efforts to effectively parent her teen boys.

Anger causes violence.   Children exposed to battering can learn to associate angry feelings with violence (Roy, 1988) and may hear the batterer using his anger as an excuse. As a result, they sometimes become afraid of their own anger or that of other people, at the same time as they may believe that their behavior can be blamed on anger.

These are a few examples of the problematic beliefs that children may hold as a result of having a batterer as a parent. Learned attitudes have been demonstrated to play a central role in why some boys who are exposed to domestic violence grow up to abuse women as adults (Markowitz, 2001; Silverman & Williamson, 1997). We consider it important that interventions with children exposed to domestic violence include a component that assists children to unravel and analyze the beliefs that they have acquired (see also Wagar & Rodway, 1995), thus contributing to repairing mother-child and sibling relationships damaged by these beliefs and assisting children to avoid recreating the dynamics of domestic violence in their adult relationships (see related recommendations in Chapter 9).

CHILDREN'S OUTLOOK ON THE BATTERER

Children's feelings toward their battering fathers tend to be marked by ambivalence (Peled, 2000). Children typically find the batterer to be a source of disappointment, bitterness, and confusion but also see him as a source of entertainment and of relief from the tensions in their relationships with their mothers. They may fantasize about assaulting him even while simultaneously desiring a closer connection to him (Roy, 1988). Aspects of a positive relationship with him may be combined with unhealthy attachments caused by traumatic bonding and by his erratic availability. Children may identify with the batterer because of the appeal of being on his side, given his power and control in the family (Jaffe & Geffner, 1998; Wallerstein & Blakeslee, 1989;

Roy, 1988), and may feel sorry for him if he is arrested or if the family separates from him (Peled, 2000; Erickson & Henderson, 1998). Children of batterers tend in general to minimize or to rationalize their fathers' violence (Peled, 1998). These cross-currents are illustrated in a case example provided by Hurley and Jaffe (1990): "Alan's worst fear was that he would become like his father. At times, he was extremely protective of his sister and, at other times, aggressive and intimidating" (p. 474). Many of our battering clients have expressed profound resentments to us regarding the behavior of their battering fathers when they were growing up, yet these men nonetheless reproduced those behaviors in their own adult relationships.

We have observed a tendency in some service providers and court personnel not to recognize the depths of both the positive and the negative feelings that children can have toward their battering fathers, preferring to focus only on one or the other in a way that may not be helpful to children. The complexity of a batterer's behavioral tactics and personal characteristics often leads to an equally complex outlook on him on the part of his children.

Children who have positive adult alternatives to the batterer, such as a close relationship to their mother, sometimes distance themselves from the batterer, especially after separation. Batterers often externalize responsibility for this alienation by alleging that the mother has caused it, ignoring the multiple ways in which their treatment of the children's mother or of the children directly has driven them away emotionally.

SUMMARY

Batterers typically exhibit important problems in their parenting. These can include a heightened risk of physical, sexual, or psychological abuse. In addition, various stylistic problems typical of the parenting of batterers that may not rise to the level of abuse nevertheless can have profound consequences for children and for their development. These include tendencies to authoritarianism, neglect, role reversal, and undermining the mother's parenting. These parenting weaknesses can have sharpened effects on the children because of being combined with the trauma that they already face from their exposure to acts of violence. Batterers' approach to children appears to follow predictably from their behavioral and attitudinal profile as outlined in Chapter 1.

In addition to the emotional effects that batterers have on their children, the batterer's modeling shapes the belief systems of children in the home, including their outlook on abuse in relationships, personal responsibility, violence and aggression, and sex-role expectations. We believe that there is a need for a higher level of attention to this critical aspect of a batterer's impact on his children.

The batterer's style, both as partner and as parent, can have powerful implications for the functioning of the family as a whole, presenting additional psychological risks to children. It is to this subject that we turn in Chapter 3.

3

Shock Waves
The Batterer's Impact on the Home

The typical behavior of batterers, both as partners and as parents, can have far-reaching effects on all aspects of family functioning (Hurley & Jaffe, 1990). In fact, a batterer's parenting cannot properly be spoken of apart from his other behaviors because his full pattern of conduct has important implications for family dynamics, as we will see. The effects on children of this damage to family bonds have not been the subject of extensive examination, yet they may be among the principal causes of the symptoms so widely demonstrated to accompany exposure to domestic violence. Few studies have addressed the impact of domestic violence on family functioning (Hanks, 1992) or the "emotional climate" of homes where battering occurs (Graham-Bermann, 1998), although excellent clinical descriptions exist (e.g., Elbow, 1982).

Family dynamics in the presence of domestic violence are shaped by a complex weave of factors involving the relationship between the parents, the relationship of each parent to each child, and the relationship of the family to the outside world. The following scenario, which combines aspects from a number of our cases, describes two days in a home with a battering father. The scenario illustrates the patterns of interaction that battering engenders and will be used as a reference point throughout this chapter.

Roger, 36, and Marsha, 34, are married. Their son Kyle is 11, and daughter Felicia is 8. On Sunday morning, the children wake

excited about a long-anticipated afternoon canoe trip. After break-
fast, Marsha asks her son to help with the dishes, and he gets mad,
saying, "My friends are waiting for me. Why do I have to do the
stupid dishes? Why can't you or Felicia do them?"

Roger steps in and says to Marsha, "You tie that boy down
with too many chores. He needs to be active. Go on out, Kyle."
Kyle says pointedly to Marsha, "I told you this was stupid,
Mom." His father winks at him, and Kyle runs outside. Marsha
gives Roger a dirty look, then asks Felicia for help with the dishes.

Roger leaves the kitchen, but later he finds a moment when he
thinks that Felicia is out of earshot and says angrily to Marsha,
"What was that look you gave me earlier? I don't need that shit
from you!" An argument ensues about Kyle, and Roger finally
yells, "You don't understand boys! You're messing him up completely. You want to handle things your way, go ahead. I'm not
going on any stupid canoe trip." He stomps upstairs and slams the
door.

An hour later, Roger has still not emerged, and Marsha has to
tell the children that the canoe trip is off. Felicia bursts into tears
and says, "This wouldn't have happened if you hadn't argued with
him! You know how mad he gets. Why did you have to do that?"

Later, Felicia wants help organizing her butterfly collection
and asks her father. He yells at her to leave him alone. After lunch,
Roger finally comes downstairs and goes outside to join Kyle and
his friends in a game of touch football. He jokes as if nothing has
happened. After the game, one of Kyle's friends says, "I wish I had
a dad that was as much fun as yours." Roger then leaves to play
golf for the afternoon.

After dinner, when the children are in their rooms, Marsha
asks Roger if he could either help pick up the house or take care of
his mother's birthday card. He says, "Don't bother me with this
stupid stuff," and an argument rapidly escalates to yelling and
name-calling. Marsha is louder than Roger in the argument, as his
style is to use logic and cold sarcasm. Roger finally becomes
enraged, however, and knocks over two kitchen chairs, smashes a
glass against the wall, and shoves Marsha against the refrigerator
so that she falls to the floor. He continues yelling as he goes out
the front door.

When Roger returns a short while later, police are at the house
following a neighbor's call. The police ask if there has been any
violence, and both Marsha and Roger say no, just some arguing.
Roger tells the police that Marsha did most of the yelling. Because

Marsha does not have visible injuries, the police do not arrest Roger. The children hear all of these events from upstairs. A few minutes after the police have left, Felicia begins to repeatedly ask Marsha, "What happened?" and refuses to go back to bed until her mother answers her. Marsha finally yells at her to get back in her room "or you'll be sorry."

In the morning, Marsha tells Roger that she can't take the fighting anymore and that she wants him to look for a separate place to stay. He refuses to leave, saying that he paid for the house and that if she doesn't like it, she should be the one to move. He says that he should report her to the Department of Social Services for being a lousy mother and that if they break up, he will get custody of the children. Marsha and Roger are unaware that the children can hear pieces of this argument from upstairs. The children leave for school and both parents go to work.

Kyle acts up in class that day and is sent to the principal's office. The principal says to Kyle, "I'm very disappointed to see you going back to your old ways, young man, since you've been doing better for a while now. This better be the last time, or you'll be suspended."

Felicia is sent to her school nurse complaining of a stomach ache. She is crying and the pain is getting worse, so the school calls Marsha, who leaves work to take Felicia to the doctor. The pediatrician finds nothing wrong, saying that Felicia perhaps ate something that didn't agree with her.

At home, Felicia falls asleep. Marsha calls her therapist, describing the incidents of the night before. They talk about the stresses that Roger is under and how Marsha could help him feel better. The therapist says, "I'd like you to think about why you feel the need to provoke Roger, when you know what it can lead to. It seems to be a way to punish yourself."

When Roger gets home that night, he brings presents for both children and announces that he is taking the family out for dinner and ice cream. He tells Marsha that he is sorry that he lost his temper but "let's not dwell on it," and gives her a hug and a kiss in front of the children. She stiffens and looks away, which the children notice, but gradually she interacts more cordially with Roger, who is fun and charming all evening. Before bed that night, Kyle says to his mother, "I don't understand why you have to be the way you are with Dad. He tries so hard to make things go well."

Roger helps Felicia get ready for bed that night, and while they are alone together, he says to her, "I'm sorry that Mommy yelled at you last night. She shouldn't do that. She needs to work on her temper, and I'm going to get her to see a therapist. Don't you worry about it, she just has some problems."

Felicia has a bad dream that night and comes to her parents' bed, but Roger tells her angrily that she is too old for that. She returns to her room and stays awake alone, frightened. When Roger is asleep, Marsha slips out of bed quietly and goes to be with Felicia. Two days later, Kyle gets in a fight with another boy at school and is suspended.

We explore below multiple dynamics illustrated by this scenario.

UNDERMINING OF THE MOTHER'S AUTHORITY

As we introduced in Chapter 2, battering undermines a mother's authority, commonly involving both effects that are inherently undermining and additional behaviors by the batterer that are more explicitly and intentionally undermining. We examine both of these aspects here.

Inherent Undermining Effects of Abuse

Battering in itself undermines a mother's parenting in several ways. The batterer's conduct provides a behavioral and attitudinal model for children that can outweigh the more constructive messages that they may receive from their social surroundings. This model's most specific effect is to teach children a negative and disrespectful outlook on their mother. The batterer's violence and threats, for example, communicate to the children that their mother's physical integrity need not be respected. During an assault, children may observe that their mother feels afraid and powerless; they may observe her efforts to defend herself but also see that these attempts are largely ineffectual, and they may even take in the fact that the more she attempts to fight back, the more seriously she gets hurt. In the aftermath of violence, their mother's shock, depression, or withdrawal is likely to be evident to the children, and they may perceive her as downtrodden. In all of these ways, children's view of their mother is shaped by the battering (see also Pickering et al., 1993).

The verbal abuse that accompanies most assaults can contribute further to forming children's image of their mother. Foul and degrading language, name-calling, and blaming of the victim accompany most incidents of battering, and children are exposed to the belittling and contradicting of their mother (Hughes & Marshall, 1995). The batterer also may threaten his partner with further harm if she does not do as she is told. This combination of verbal abuse and violence often contains important implicit messages to children that their mother caused the batterer to assault her through her stupidity, selfishness, or failure to obey his instructions. Thus, children may learn that verbal or physical abuse of their mother is justified when she is behaving in a way that is not desired, that she is stupid, inferior, or worthy of ridicule, and that she is far less powerful than is the batterer.

The aftermath of an assault can introduce additional elements to the children's learning process. They are likely to be upset and emotionally vulnerable following a violent incident and therefore may be particularly subject to influences on their interpretation of what took place. In the overwhelming majority of assaults, there will be no consequences for the batterer, which may tend to confirm for the children that he is both the more powerful party and the more justified one. Even in the minority of cases where police are called, meaningful consequences for the batterer do not necessarily ensue. Well-intentioned school personnel or human service providers are sometimes overly concerned with protecting the children from loyalty conflicts and so will use neutral phrases such as "the violence that happened between your parents"; such language can serve to obscure the batterer's responsibility for his actions, perhaps making it easier for children to blame their mothers or themselves.

The great majority of incidents of domestic violence, however, never come to the attention of police or school personnel, and thus children's private experiences within the family most often shape what lessons they take from the violence. They may find that over the days subsequent to the assault, their parents make no mention of the incident (Peled, 1998), strengthening the children's impression that a shameful and secret event has occurred. They may feel ashamed of their father's violence, but they are likely to be just as ashamed of their mother's degradation or humiliation or of what they believe to be her role in causing the violence. They also may perceive her as passive, because children of a battered mother are often unaware of ways in which she may be attempting to stop the abuse.

Children's interactions with their parents in the days following an act of violence further inform their view. During this period, their mother is likely to be struggling with a mixture of shock, rage, and fear and may be experiencing posttrauma symptoms such as nightmares, flashbacks, or depression. Thus, the children may find her cold and withdrawn, short-tempered, and emotionally volatile. Under these circumstances, any difficulties that they may have in interacting with her can reinforce their earlier impressions that her character was a central cause of the violence, and they may accept the batterer's view of their mother as crazy or unfit (McMahon & Pence, 1995). By contrast, the batterer may make a concerted effort to win the children's loyalty and may be markedly attentive and positive with them. He may joke and play, spend money on them, or take them out to do things, as Roger exhibited in our opening scenario. Many batterers are able to engage in childlike, light-hearted play, which the mother often has difficulty doing because of the effects of battering and verbal abuse (Walker, 1979). Thus, it is not uncommon for children to see the batterer as the fun parent (Erickson & Henderson, 1998) and to blame their mother for the parental conflicts and even for the battering (Jaffe, Wolfe, & Wilson, 1990).

The undermining of a battered mother's authority thus has multiple aspects, including (a) the violence itself, (b) the verbally abusive and victim-blaming messages that the batterer gives before and during the violence, and (c) the dynamics of the aftermath. All three of these aspects can lead the children of a battered woman to gradually acquire the batterer's view of her and to begin to describe her in terms similar to ones that he would use. This battererlike language can be especially marked among teenagers. We observe this tendency even in those children whose role in the family is to be on the battered woman's "side," who may state, for example, that the reason why they need to protect their mother is because of her incompetence or immaturity.

Deliberate Undermining

The preponderance of our clients augment the inherently undermining effects of battering with deliberate tactics designed to control the children's loyalties and to govern their perceptions. Chronic undermining is significantly more common with battering than with non-battering men (Adams, 1991). Some batterers control their partners' parental authority as part of their overall dominance and may punish their partners for questioning their authority over the children (Ptacek, 1997). In addition, we observe that children of a battered woman have some natural tendency to sympathize with her, and our clients sometimes appear to be aware that a battered woman's close relationship to her children can be a great source of strength, validation, and social connection for her, and in the long run may help her to escape the abuse; thus, the batterer may feel the need to take active steps to shift the children's leanings. Finally, some of our clients have negative opinions about women in general and for this reason wish to minimize maternal influence over the children's development.

Our opening scenario illustrates typical undermining behaviors used by batterers, beginning with direct interference with the mother's ability to create structure and to teach responsibility. Roger explicitly intercedes with Marsha to relieve Kyle of his household responsibilities, thereby encouraging Kyle to see him as the kind parent and Marsha as overly strict. Roger's interference also lays the groundwork for Kyle to respond to his mother with resentment or defiance the next time that she attempts to hold him to his responsibilities. In practice, we find that batterers create tension between mothers and their children in just this way. The batterer may then stand aside from the resulting conflicts or may even step in as the mediator, "to help the children and their mother work it out," as a number of our clients have reported.

In our scenario, Roger definitely overrules Marsha's decision, using an authoritative tone of voice. From witnessing such superseding by the batterer, children may grasp that their mother is second in command, with the batterer free to delegate responsibilities to her or to rescind them from her. We have observed that children thereby learn to prolong conflicts with their mother until they can involve the father, thus lessening her ability to manage their behavior.

It is important to note that the batterer's overruling of the mother does not necessarily take the direction of his being the more permissive parent. He may forbid them freedoms or privileges that she feels they are ready to take on. Some batterers are invested in restricting the extent of the children's social contacts and so may supersede maternal decisions in order to keep them home (see also Jaffe, Wolfe, & Wilson, 1990). The batterers most inclined to isolate their children appear to be those who have the greatest concern that the children may disclose abuse to outsiders and those who rely heavily on the children for companionship or support.

Continuing with the scenario, we next see Roger wink at Kyle approvingly for insulting his mother. Kyle is thus rewarded for behaving disrespectfully and is emboldened. Future efforts that Marsha may make to require Kyle to address her appropriately may be unsuccessful, as he assumes that his father will not permit her to impose consistent consequences. One effect of this dynamic is that the child can be drawn into participating in the psychological abuse of the mother, armed with the father's power by proxy (see also Walker, 1979). It is generally true that aggressive behavior that meets with praise or approval is more likely to be repeated (Bandura, 1978).

We find that preteen and teenage boys, who are often experimenting with social roles regarding their relationship to females, are especially subject to the batterer's influence. By being rewarded for their inappropriate behavior toward their mothers, they are in effect being trained to abuse women, though this is not necessarily the batterer's intent. In effect, preteen and teen boys sometimes begin to practice abusive behaviors on their mothers, imitating behaviors that they have witnessed in their fathers (Johnston & Campbell, 1993b). Indeed, boys who are exposed to batterers are more than twice as likely as are other boys to physically assault their mothers (Carlson, 1990). We have observed that our teen clients gain a certain thrill from discovering their power over their mothers in this way, while simultaneously tending to experience guilt. They then sometimes attempt to relieve their cognitive dissonance by further lowering their image of their mothers and by developing other justifications for their treatment of her. These boys can begin to exhibit ways of talking and thinking about their mothers that are closely parallel to adult battering styles.

Moving now to Roger's bedtime conversation with Felicia on the second night, we see him communicating to her that her mother is not a competent parent, is out of control, and is not treating her well. Similar statements that clients of ours have made to the children include describing the mother as a drunk or a drug addict, saying that she is having sex with other men, telling them that their mother does not love them or that they were conceived by accident and weren't wanted by their mother, and stating that their mother is lazy and lives off of the batterer's hard work. One client of ours told the children that because of the mother's promiscuity, he could not be certain that he was their biological father. Although the batterer's statements to the children about their mother tend to be fabrications, their potential emotional destructiveness is probably equally serious in cases where they contain elements of truth.

A number of additional tactics that our clients or their partners report with some frequency but that are not reflected in our scenario include ridiculing or humiliating the mother in front of the children; swearing at her, calling her names, or insulting her; laughing at her; and being unusually nice to the children when they are in conflict with her. These actions serve as attitudinal and behavioral models for the children, so that a battered mother often finds herself left to manage multiple forms of rude and uncooperative behavior on the part of her children (Pickering et al., 1993). Compounding her difficulties, the batterer may explicitly tell her that she is a bad or incompetent mother (Hughes & Marshall, 1995), and the children may hear these statements.

We have observed that the inherently undermining effects of battering, often combined with more deliberate undermining tactics, can lead to dynamics in the family that cause the mother to appear incompetent and ineffective as a parent while the batterer presents to outsiders as able to take charge of the children's behavior appropriately (see also Pickering et al., 1993). Furthermore, the mother's fear of replicating the father's abusive or authoritarian parenting style may lead her to be afraid to act with appropriate parental authority (Bilinkoff, 1995).

Partner violence sometimes follows conflicts regarding the children (Hughes & Marshall, 1995), further undermining the mother's authority and her ability to have a voice in parenting decisions. Mothers who attempt to protect their children from emotional or physical mistreatment by the batterer put themselves at risk of violence (Roy, 1988), and many restraining order affidavits describe violence or threats by the batterer when the mother attempts to intercede on behalf of her children (Ptacek, 1997).

Undermining After Separation

Separation or divorce can begin an important new phase in the father's undermining of the mother's authority. In our observations, batterers are commonly retaliatory in the aftermath of a breakup, and interfering with the mother's parenting can be an important tactic. Furthermore, many batterers respond to separation by intensifying their own desire to justify past actions and to deny their abusiveness. In some cases, a client of ours wishes to prove to the woman and to outsiders that he is the more psychologically healthy person and points to her difficulties with her children (which may be largely of his causing) as evidence of her incompetence, instability, or need for his assistance. Some batterers are interested in pursuing custody litigation and so wish to strengthen their parenting position and to weaken the mother's.

Postseparation undermining tactics that we encounter are numerous, so we will review only selected ones here. The most common behavior of this kind among our clients is to create an atmosphere in their homes that is largely or entirely lacking in discipline. During periods when the children are in his care, the batterer may allow them to eat unhealthful foods steadily, permit them to stay up late at night watching movies or playing video games, and ignore any homework responsibilities. He may go out of his way to involve the children in activities that he knows upset or worry their mother, such as driving with the children not wearing seat restraints, taking them to a shooting range to learn weapons use (we have had several cases of this), or showing them movies that are frightening, violent, or sexual. When children who have enjoyed this kind of catering and freedom return to their mother's home, they feel increased resistance to accepting her efforts to impose structure. They may feel that now that they are home with their mother, life is once again consumed with homework, bedtimes, chores, and healthful eating.

A batterer who intends to pursue custody litigation may discuss with the children the possibility of coming to live with him. For example, Bancroft recently served as Guardian ad Litem in a case where the batterer admitted freely, with no sense of wrongdoing, that he had begun speaking about the possibility of a change in custody with his two children when they were only 6 and 8 years old, respectively. The mother's authority was steadily eroded over the subsequent years, and the children would periodically make statements to her such as "I don't have to listen to you, because Dad's going to ask for custody and I'm going to go live with him."

Although competitiveness and undermining can be dynamics in difficult separations even where battering has not occurred, the implications of such behavior become even more problematic in the context of domestic violence, given children's increased need for safety and security in their relationships with their mothers (see Chapter 5).

When a batterer is no longer present in the home because of parental separation, the past undermining of the mother's authority can become even more apparent as the father is no longer available to enforce discipline. For example, we find that partners of our clients are more likely to be physically assaulted by their children after parental separation than while the batterer is still in the home. Children may feel suddenly freed from having to constrict themselves around the batterer; although this freedom has healthy aspects, it also can lead to serious problems for the battered mother in managing the children's erupting behavior. In many cases, the batterer is then able to use the effects of his undermining of her authority, combined with the effects of his absence, to make a case in court for why the children need to be in his custody because the mother cannot control them. This dynamic is visible when children return home from visits with the batterer, at which time they "may quite typically 'erupt' while in the mother's care after having to contain their impulses and feelings while with the father" (Walker & Edwall, 1987, p. 146).

Perhaps (at least in part) as a result of the dynamics produced by the batterer's undermining, battered mothers have roughly twice the rate of physically abusing children that nonbattered mothers do (Holden et al., 1998; Straus, 1990). Although the increased risk is much lower than for batterers, who are seven times more likely than are nonbatterers to physically abuse children (Straus, 1990), it nonetheless indicates that battered mothers often need assistance in reestablishing parental authority and in using nonviolent methods of discipline.

EFFECTS ON MOTHER-CHILD RELATIONSHIPS

The undermining of the mother's parental authority is just one aspect of a batterer's potential interference with his partner's ability to maintain close relationships with her children. Distance and tension between battered women and their children are common (Erickson & Henderson, 1998) and come from myriad sources. These tensions spring from the batterer's style both as partner and as parent; here as elsewhere, the batterer's entire pattern of conduct needs to be seen as interwoven with his parenting, because his behavior can cause profound disruptions in relationships between the mother and the children, between him and the children, and between siblings.

Direct Interference With Her Parenting

Returning to our scenario, we encounter a scene on the second night when Felicia has a nightmare and attempts to climb into her parents' bed for security but is sent away by Roger. Roger's behavior illustrates what we have observed to be the single most common form of direct interference by our clients in their partners' parenting: preventing the mother from holding or comforting a crying or frightened child or in other ways forbidding her to provide parental care. We have had widespread reports from the partners of our clients of being blocked even from picking up a crying *infant;* in a recent custody evaluation performed by Bancroft, the batterer (a college professor) stated that his former partner had been "spoiling" their 11-month-old baby boy by going to him when he cried in the night and "fawning over him." A batterer can become particularly irate when his partner attempts to comfort a child who has been frightened or hurt *by him,* as he sees such assistance as implicitly criticizing his conduct. Such interference can contribute over time to the children forming the impression that their mother is not a dependable parent or does not care about protecting them.

Battered mothers can begin to lose control of the parenting process before they are even pregnant, as they tend to have less power than do nonbattered women over decisions regarding birth control and are more likely to have unwanted pregnancies (Goodwin et al., 2000) and to have more children (McKibben, De Vos, & Newberger, 1989). Findings from a Nicaraguan study suggest that the increased number of children in homes where battering occurs may be a result rather than a cause of the domestic violence, because almost all of the battering began early in the marriage (Ellsberg, Pena, Herrera, & Liljestrand, cited in Heise et al., 1999). Studies from many countries have shown that women are less likely to use contraception if they fear that their husbands will react violently to their doing so (review in Heise et al., 1999).

We have often remarked over the years on the frequency with which battered women report difficulties with their early mother-infant bonding. Although this may result partly from depression or other posttrauma effects of the battering, much of the cause may be concrete and direct. We have had cases, for example, of batterers who forbid mothers from breast-feeding, declaring it distasteful.

Our clients' reactions to pregnancy and childbirth can be understood in the light of their underlying outlook, particularly their typical expectation of being the center of attention. During pregnancy, the focus of attention in a couple necessarily shifts to the expecting mother. This marked shift in the dynamics of a relationship are received poorly by a large proportion of batterers, who demand continued labor and caretaking from the mother, refuse to increase their own contribution, and feel jealous of her attention to the coming child (see similar observations in Campbell, Oliver, & Bullock, 1998). Pregnant battered women receive noticeably lower levels of emotional support from their partners than do nonbattered women (Curry & Harvey, 1998). Furthermore, because of their sexual entitlement, some of our clients resent the physical changes that pregnancy brings, wanting their partners to remain thin and sexually available (see similar discussion in Straus et al., 1980).

The effects of these dynamics have been recognized increasingly by medical personnel. Several studies have examined the high rate of battering of pregnant women (review in Gazmarian et al., 1996; Helton et al., 1987). There are no significant demographic differences between those battered women who are abused during pregnancy and those who are not (Campbell, Oliver, & Bullock, 1998). Obstetricians comment on the frequency with which abused women miss prenatal appointments, and they may observe additional warning signs of domestic violence such as inadequate weight gain (review in Heise et al., 1999), which can be due to stress or to the batterer pressuring her not to get "fat"; depression; or high anxiety (Eisenstat & Bancroft, 1999). Abused women often enter prenatal care late (review in Heise et al., 1999; Parker, McFarlane, Soeken, Torres, & Campbell, 1993). In a recent case of ours, the battering father heavily pressured the mother to have a natural childbirth and called her "bitch" in the midst of the delivery when she finally accepted an epidural.

Not all batterers increase their violence during pregnancy: About half of batterers actually decrease their violence during this period, and for another quarter, the pregnancy does not affect their abusiveness in either direction (Campbell, Oliver, & Bullock, 1998). These findings support our contention (discussed in Chapter 7) that a batterer's level of violence or of psychological abusiveness during pregnancy may be one useful indicator in distinguishing batterers who are a high risk to children, as it may demonstrate a tendency to ignore the children's well-being when wishing to abuse the mother.

Following childbirth, the demands on a mother's attention become even greater, which can engender further collision with the batterer's entitlement. A recurring statement from our clients who have infant children is "She cares more about the baby than she does about me," revealing their belief that a woman's parenting responsibilities should not reduce her availability to look after her partner.

Direct interference with the mother's parenting can continue through the years, taking various forms that include harsh and frequent criticism of her parenting, retaliation against her for failing to follow his parenting instructions, controlling the family finances and refusing to give her adequate resources to pay for the children's basic necessities (which is sometimes followed by calling her an irresponsible parent for not feeding or clothing the children properly), not permitting the children to speak to their mother when he is angry at her, and many others. Furthermore, many batterers isolate their partners socially (Dutton, 1992; Jaffe, Wolfe, & Wilson, 1990), and such restrictions on a mother's freedom can interfere with her ability to obtain medical care for her children, involve them in a social life, or take them to participate in stimulating activities. Taken together, the array of common behaviors by batterers described above represents a serious potential threat to children's healthy attachment to their mothers (see also Jaffe, Wolfe, & Wilson, 1990).

Indirect Interference With Her Parenting

Battering leaves many emotional and physical scars on a mother, any of which can make it harder for her to care for her children (review in Levendosky & Graham-Bermann, 2000; Osofsky, 1998). Widely recognized effects of beatings and of attendant psychological abuse include depression, anxiety, nightmares and sleeplessness, flashbacks, crying easily, rage, loss of self-confidence, and others (Dutton, 1992; Douglas, 1987). A mother who is struggling with the experience of being battered may find it difficult to be an engaged, energetic parent (Osofsky, 1998; Margolin, 1998), to focus attention on her children (Holden et al., 1998), and to keep track of the myriad details that child care and schooling require. Her patience may be short, and thus she may be prone to grouchiness and yelling, which can be compounded by the erosion of her authority as described above. If the batterer subjects her to heavy criticism of her parenting, as is common (Hughes & Marshall, 1995), she may develop a timid or indecisive parenting style. Battered mothers appear to have lowered awareness of their children's needs (Osofsky, 1998) and to have more frequent conflicts with their children (Holden et al., 1998).

Battering can contribute to the development of a substance abuse problem by the mother, which can in turn lead her to lose custody of her children to the state or to the batterer. One study found battered women to have 16 times the rate of alcohol abuse of nonbattered women (Stark & Flitcraft, 1988), and another found that more severe battering correlated with higher alcohol use on the woman's part (Clark & Foy, 2000). However, we observe that our clients typically claim that their partners' alcohol problems predate the abuse.

Children of battered women can target their mother for their angry resentments toward the batterer, as they often do not feel comfortable expressing their anger directly to him (Roy, 1988). This dynamic is illustrated in our scenario, with Felicia blaming her mother for the cancellation of the family canoe trip. Similar dynamics can shape postseparation interactions. A recurring theme in our work with divorced couples, for example, is that the batterer may refuse to see the children unless he is catered to regarding all the visitation arrangements, with the children then targeting their mother for their disappointment over not seeing their father. If the mother attempts to protect her children by placing restrictions on the batterer's visitation, children may resent her for that as well (Peled, 1998).

The violent and aggressive behavior that commonly appears in children exposed to batterers puts further stress on their relationships with their mothers, as it typically falls to her to attempt to find ways to manage those behaviors. This aggressiveness in children can create a loop of reactions and counterreactions between mothers and children that causes deterioration of relationships (Jaffe, Wolfe, & Wilson, 1990).

Battered mothers' fear of the batterer can cause them to change their parenting behavior with their children when in the presence of the father; in one study, 34% of battered mothers reported making such changes, as compared to only 5% of nonbattered mothers (Holden & Ritchie, 1991). These battered mothers were divided almost evenly between those who become more lenient when in the presence of the batterer and those who become more harsh.

Violence and other frightening behaviors by a batterer can make it necessary for a mother to adjust her parenting to avoid recurrences. Some of our clients have used violence against the mother when blaming her for not adequately controlling the children's misbehavior or noise level (also in Jouriles & Norwood, 1995). Such violence can cause the mother to develop overly strict rules for her children's behavior in order to protect the children and herself from the batterer's reactions (Holden & Ritchie, 1991; Walker & Edwall, 1987) or to become generally overprotective (Osofsky, 1998).

Therapists and child protective workers often comment to us on children's tendency to feel bitter toward their mothers for failing to leave a batterer or for not challenging him. Children are largely unaware of the complex obstacles involved in leaving an abusive relationship (described comprehensively in Davies, Lyon, & Monti-Catania, 1998), nor do they always realize the ways in which the batterer may retaliate against their mother on the occasions when she does assert herself. A crucial bind thus arises for the mother: Her children are likely to be resentful toward her both for what happens when she *does* resist the batterer's will, in that she is perceived as causing him to erupt, and for what happens when she *does not* do so, in that she is perceived as tolerating the abuse or as failing to stand up for the children's interests (see also Johnston & Campbell, 1993b). We observe that the great majority of children exposed to domestic violence respond to separation with potent mixed feelings; they commonly undergo an initial period of relief, but this is typically followed by their increasingly missing their father and desiring to reunite the family. They may turn resentful and critical of their mother over time for "not being willing to work on it" or for "not forgiving Dad and giving him another chance," sometimes echoing phrases that they are hearing from him. The children thus tend to resent their mother if she leaves the father and breaks up the family (Peled, 1998) but also if she fails to leave him and "puts up with" the abuse (Roy, 1988).

Because of the traumatic effects to children of seeing or hearing violence, they are in acute need of support, reassurance, and closeness from their mother in the aftermath of an assault. However, this is precisely the period during which she may be the most unavailable to them emotionally because of her own shock, physical injuries, and other effects of domestic violence (Wolak & Finkelhor, 1998; Jaffe, Hurley, & Wolfe, 1990). For the mother to be unable to nurture the children at their time of greatest need represents a significant rupture in their perceptions of her as caring and as reliable. We observe in some children of battered women a lingering sense that their mother has abandoned them and cannot be counted on to protect them. In periods between assaults, the mother may feel forced to focus on meeting her partner's needs in order to prevent the next assault, which can leave her children feeling neglected (Walker, 1979).

Particular attention should be drawn to a critical theme underlying most of our discussion of family dynamics so far: the typical ability of men who batter to shape the children's views of both parents and to condition children to misinterpret the abuse that they observe in a way that leads them to blame their mother and to minimize the abuse. One study, for example, found that exposure to domestic violence affected children's views of their mother more negatively than it did their views of their father (Sternberg et al., cited in Wolak & Finkelhor, 1998). It should also be noted that the batterer's manipulation of how he is perceived as a father is likely to have an impact on *his partner's* perceptions as well. We find, for example, that partners of our clients generally describe the men as good fathers when responding to general questions, but when more specific questions are asked, they reveal more problems in the man's parenting (see similar observations in Holden & Ritchie, 1991).

In reviewing the wide range of ways in which batterers' violence and other behaviors can damage mother-child relationships, it is important to note the finding of Holden and Ritchie (1991) that the single best predictor of behavior problems in children exposed to domestic violence was the mother's level of parenting stress, not her overall life stress. In addition, battered mothers report much higher levels of parenting stress than do nonbattered mothers, and their likelihood to use physical aggression with their children is correlated with their level of parenting stress (Holden et al., 1998). Battered mothers do not show marked differences by ethnic group in the level or nature of their parenting problems (Holden et al., 1998). *Thus, the damage that domestic violence can cause to mother-child relationships may be the most serious cause of distress for children of battered women.*

At the same time, it is important to recognize that many battered mothers manage to parent effectively despite the tremendous challenges that battering causes for mother-child relationships, continuing to respond well to their children's needs (Holden et al., 1998). A large portion of battered mothers reportedly are aware that they need help in dealing with their children (Erickson & Henderson, 1998) and may therefore be open to parenting assistance. Thus, the parenting of battered mothers shows a range of responses to circumstances, depending on factors including the severity of the batterer's interference, her strengths as a parent, and the resources available to her.

Children's Tendency to Distance Themselves

In the context of the range of dynamics that we have discussed, children of battered women can feel an impetus to draw away from their mothers emotionally (McMahon & Pence, 1995), and this may be especially true for boys (Johnston & Campbell, 1993b). We have observed both boys and girls who have exhibited a desire to disassociate themselves from their battered mother, beginning as young as age 5. This tendency appears to be more pronounced in boys who are roughly age 8 and older and in teenagers of both sexes; we find it is most prevalent of all in the teen boys with whom we have worked, who often stand out for their audible tones of contempt, derision, and shame in discussing their mothers. Children tend over time to absorb the batterer's disrespect for their mother, which can lead them to feel superior to her and ashamed to be connected to her. Furthermore, they may have well-founded fears that the batterer will retaliate against them with verbal abuse or violence if he sees them as allied with their mother. These dynamics can be exacerbated if the batterer has a history of rewarding the children for speaking inappropriately to their mother or for distancing themselves from her, as Roger did with Kyle in our scenario. The batterer may openly ridicule or shame children for being close to their mother. We have encountered this most frequently in verbal taunts that many of our clients make toward their sons, calling them "Mama's boy." In addition, children may feel that their mother has failed to protect them from their father's abusiveness, for reasons that we have explored above.

These dynamics, when taken together, can create powerful incentives for children to keep their mothers at arm's length. The resultant psychological damage to children can be grave, as they are losing the strength of their connection to the person who in most cases is their best potential source of love, nurturing, and appropriate parental guidance.

Violence by Children Against Their Mothers

As we have alluded to briefly, children of battered women have elevated rates of assaultive behavior toward their mothers (Dutton, 1992; Hanks, 1992; Holden & Ritchie, 1991), particularly preteens and teenagers and particularly boys (Johnston & Campbell, 1993b; Carlson, 1990; Straus et al., 1980). This behavior sometimes involves conscious reproduction of the father's behavior; for example, Straus et al. (1980) reported instances where children threatened to have the father hit the mother if she did not do what they wanted her to do. Roy (1988) states that about 20% of the preteen and teenage boys in her study "joined their fathers in victimizing their mothers. They identified with the aggressor and ultimately became the aggressors—a role they both loathed and admired" (p. 64). We also receive occasional reports of assaultiveness toward mothers beginning at younger ages.

In our experience, children's violence against their battered mothers appears to arise most frequently in cases where the parents have separated and one child begins to assume the batterer's role. Teenage boys can be taller and stronger than their mothers and thus may develop the capacity to be physically intimidating. In the great majority of our interviews with battered mothers who have become targets of assaults by their teen boys, we find that the boy is not only using violence but is reproducing an array of abusive behaviors that he learned from the batterer. In one of our current cases involving a 13-year-old, for example, the boy interrogates the mother about her social contacts and attempts to govern what times she may leave or not leave the house, just as his father used to do; he recently punched his mother in the leg, leaving a visible bruise. In another recent case of ours, an older teen boy threatened his mother that he would rip her arms off and throw them in the trash, which he reported to his therapist with audible pride. He stated, "My mother only wants me so that she can collect child support," and he referred to her as a "lunatic" and a "liar," reproducing statements frequently made by his father.

Teenagers' reactions are summarized by Jaffe and Geffner (1998).

Adolescents may turn against the mother in an attempt to win the approval, love, and affection of the father as they begin to identify

with the power of the abuser. They may have seen that there were no
negative consequences for the abusive use of power and control, and
they may begin to model the aggressive behaviors in their own relationships with peers and [with] their mother. (p. 387)

A transition from being the mother's protector to participating in
abusing her is sometimes observed in children at this stage of life.

USE OF CHILDREN AS WEAPONS AGAINST THE MOTHER

Among the most potentially damaging parenting choices that batterers
can make, leading to an array of unhealthy family dynamics, is the
involvement of children as arms in efforts to control or to abuse their
partners. Not all batterers draw their children into the abuse, but we
have been struck over the years by how many do (see also Erickson
& Henderson, 1998; Peled, 1998; McMahon & Pence, 1995). Our
discussions with the partners of our clients make clear to us that the
involvement of the children can be one of the most upsetting and
intimidating aspects of the battered woman's experience. It is perhaps
precisely the effectiveness of these tactics that makes them recur so
commonly in our clients' behaviors.

Children as Weapons During the Relationship

Depending on the context, most of the undermining and interfering behaviors that we have already described can be used as deliberate
weapons of abuse. A few behavioral examples from our clients include
refusing to allow his partner to enter the room where their 3-year-old
lay in bed calling for her, because he was angry that she had arrived
home late that evening from visiting her older son in the hospital; punishing his partner for refusing to quit her job by telling their young
daughter, "Mommy likes to go to her work because there is a man
there that she has sex with"; intimidating his partner into dropping her
restraining order by threatening to reveal humiliating information
about her personal history to the children; and training their 2-year-
old, who was just learning to talk, to call the mother "Mommy bitch."

Several categories of behavior by batterers involving the children
appear to figure prominently in the abuse of battered mothers. One is
direct mistreatment of the children in retaliation against her. As noted
in Chapter 2, for example, one mild-mannered client of ours admitted
in session that he had gone into his teenage daughter's closet and
destroyed her prom dress with a pair of scissors in a rage at his wife;

he was open with us about the fact that his goal was to hurt the mother. In another striking case, one of our early clients admitted that he had deliberately given the couple's infant spoiled milk to retaliate against the mother. It should be noted that both of these men had used low levels of physical violence relative to other batterers in their groups but were capable of severe psychological cruelty. A number of our clients over the years have knocked over Christmas trees, broken children's new birthday presents, caused the children to miss important events in their lives such as weddings or funerals, or have physically assaulted children, all in contexts where the batterer's focus was explicitly on abusing the mother.

Deliberate endangerment of the children can be similarly intimidating of the mother. In one of our cases, the father spun the car repeatedly in circles in a snow-covered parking lot with their infant girl in the backseat. On other occasions, this same batterer would balance the infant on the edge of a high stair, watching for the mother's fear, and then would laugh at her reaction. A large number of our clients have driven recklessly with children in the car in response to arguments. In addition to the intrinsic effects of such acts, they communicate an implied threat of more serious harm to the children in the future.

A batterer may *require the children to monitor and to report on their mother's behavior* during periods when he is away from her (see also Adams, 1989), as part of maintaining her isolation. The effect on the children is to create a grave loyalty conflict and burden, as they do not wish to betray their mother but are afraid of withholding information from their father. At the same time, they can gradually become attached to the power that this position gives them over their mother, reversing the proper parent-child roles in the family and tending to infantilize her.

Neglect of the children can also be used as a form of retaliation against the mother. For example, a client of ours who was angry that his wife asked him to contribute more to cleaning up after dinner (which he viewed as their daughters' job) responded by disappearing from the home for three days, leaving his partner to contend with the daughters' upset and worry over his long absence and with unrelieved responsibility for their five children.

A substantial number of our clients have used *threats to harm the children* in response to their partners' efforts to resist being controlled. One study found batterers to be more than four times more likely than nonbatterers to make such threats (McCloskey et al., 1995). Threats to harm children become even more sharply intimidating in cases where a batterer's past behaviors demonstrate to the mother that he is capable of carrying them out. The most common threat of this kind reported to us by partners of our clients is that he will leave the family and not provide financial support, which could leave the mother and children destitute. (On domestic violence as a cause of homelessness, see Zorza, 1991.) One partner of a client, who had left the batterer for a period of time and was now living with him again, informed us that she had allowed him to move back in after he had threatened to molest their daughter during his visitation with her. In another case, the batterer threatened on several occasions to wake up their sleeping infant if the mother did not do as she was told. These intimidating tactics sometimes escalate to threats to kill the children; we have had many dozens of reports over the years of clients of ours using this tactic, including sometimes threatening that they will kill their partners, the children, and then themselves. These threats have not always come from those batterers who have histories of the most frequent or brutal violence, yet they sometimes cause similar levels of terror (see also Adams, 1989).

Partners of our clients report that an equally terrifying use of the children as weapons is the batterer's *threatening to take her children away from her,* which can take a number of forms. One is to threaten to *report her to the state's child protective service,* alleging that she abuses the children or is alcoholic or making other claims that may or may not be true. If the child protective service does become involved, the state may place the children in foster care; child protective services often have failed to take domestic violence into account and therefore have held mothers responsible for the effects on children of the batterer's behavior (Echlin & Marshall, 1995). In some cases, the batterer leaves the home, and child protective services then place the children in his care; Bancroft was recently Guardian ad Litem in a case where child protective personnel placed a 9-year-old boy with the battering father, despite their awareness that his violence had already caused the mother to lose custody of her two teenage children by a different father. (This case is described in detail in Chapter 5.) We find that our clients sometimes present themselves to child protective personnel as concerned, somewhat detached men who simply are trying to "help her with her problems with her children." In a few cases, the batterer has appeared actually to desire that the woman lose custody of her children to the state as part of his pattern of cruelty toward her. We find that lack of awareness of the above dynamics on the part of many child protective workers sometimes can allow batterers to succeed in using the child protection system against the mother.

Kidnapping is another threat that must be taken seriously. A large-scale study of kidnapping found that the great majority of parental abductions are carried out by fathers or by their agents (Finkelhor, Hotaling, & Sedlak, 1990), and most parental abductions take place in the context of a history of domestic violence (Greif & Hegar, 1993). We have been involved in a number of cases where batterers have kidnapped children and then succeeded in winning custody of them.

The threat to take the mother's children from her by legally *winning custody* is used by many batterers (Ptacek, 1997; Pence & Paymar, 1993). In a surprising number of our cases, the batterer has succeeded in carrying out this threat. As noted in Chapter 1, batterers are more likely than are nonbattering men to seek custody (APA Presidential Task Force, 1996; McMahon & Pence, 1995; Liss & Stahly, 1993), and when they do so, they often win (McMahon & Pence, 1995). Batterers have numerous advantages over battered mothers in custody disputes, as we explore in detail in Chapter 5.

Finally, a batterer's threats to *kill the children* cannot be taken lightly. Batterers sometimes do murder children, usually in conjunction with a homicide or attempted homicide against the mother. Killings of children by men tend to take place in the context of partner violence (Websdale, 1999), and batterers kill one or more children in 10% to 15% of domestic violence homicides (Langford et al., 1999). In a well-publicized case in New England, a batterer shot four children to death in front of their mother and then killed himself—but did not attempt to kill *her*. This case illustrates the role that the batterer's desire to emotionally injure the mother can play in an assault or murder of her children.

A batterer's actions to harm children, threaten to harm them, or take them away from their mother can be sources of severe fear and emotional trauma for battered women and their children. This critical aspect of domestic violence appears to be widely underestimated for its prevalence and destructiveness.

Children as Weapons After Separation

Our clients sometimes increase their use of the children as weapons after separating from their partners, as other avenues of control or of intimidation become less available. A batterer's first goal can be to pressure his partner into a reunification or to retaliate against her, and children can be an effective vehicle toward either goal (Straus, 1995; Adams, 1989). Clients of ours have told their children such things as "Mommy went to court and got an order that says if I go to the house,

I will get put in jail," "I'm not living with you because your mother is angry at me," and "Your mother is having sex with another man right now, and that is why she doesn't want me in the house." We have rarely had a client admit to his children that the separation resulted from his violence or abusiveness. Through distorting events in this way, some batterers can lead children to blame their mother for the separation and to pressure her to allow their father to return (Hart, 1990a). Children typically miss abusive fathers during separation and wish for their return to the home (Peled, 1998), except in the case of the most terrorizing batterers. This disruption and tension in a mother's relationship with her child can exacerbate the fear and ambivalence that most battered women feel when attempting to leave a batterer. Dozens of partners of our clients have reported to us that they have returned to the batterer after a period of separation because of pressure from their children.

Batterers can use children as vehicles for communicating with their former partners, a tactic that becomes particularly important if the woman has obtained a restraining order or has taken other steps to indicate that she wishes that the batterer not contact her. One client of ours had said to his wife prior to separation, "I love you, and that's for life. If I can't have you, no one else will, and we're going to die together." After separation, he said to the children, "Tell your mother I will always love her." The children had no awareness of the implications of this message.

Preexisting problems in the parenting behavior of a particular batterer tend to intensify after separation for reasons that we have discussed above, including the retaliatory tendencies common in batterers and the absence of supervision by his former partner. Thus, issues such as the undermining of her authority, efforts to turn the children against her, or threatening to take the children away from her can become more pronounced in this period. To these he also may add inconsistency in visiting with the children, retaliatory or intimidating custody and visitation proceedings, and exorbitant expenditures or promises in order to curry the children's favor. If the mother attempts to begin a new relationship, he may use the children to interfere by turning them against the new partner, making a groundless child abuse report, or filing for custody. It is common for batterers to threaten to take the children away from the battered woman by proving her to be an unfit mother (Doyne et al., 1999). Threatened or actual litigation regarding custody or visitation can become a critical avenue for the batterer to maintain control after separation (Shepard, cited in Straus, 1995).

THE BATTERER'S IMPACT ON OTHER ASPECTS
OF FAMILY FUNCTIONING

A few important additional ways in which batterers can affect patterns of interaction within their families call for our attention. We find little discussion of these dynamics in the existing literature regarding the effects on children of exposure to domestic violence.

Sowing of Divisions

Batterers can cause divisions among family members in a range of ways, adding to the divisive impact of the typical sources of family tension that we have already reviewed (see also Johnston & Campbell, 1993b; Roy, 1988; Davidson, 1978). The reason why some batterers appear to be invested in creating divisions in their families can perhaps best be illustrated by observing what tends to happen if they do *not* do so. In cases where mothers and children succeed in remaining unified against a batterer, supporting each other and refusing to act as agents of the abuse, he can lose much of his ability to control and to manipulate family members. In such a family, the mother may increase her self-esteem and self-confidence through her healthy relationship with her children and through her successes as a mother; we have spoken to a number of battered women who state that their relationships with their children were an important factor in their being able ultimately to leave the abuser. Some batterers appear to be aware that their access to power and control is threatened if this kind of solidarity exists within the family, and they take steps to prevent alliances from forming.

Unfortunately, our experience indicates that whether or not this is a deliberate goal, the behavior of the majority of batterers with children does prevent family unity. Although we occasionally hear clients of ours complain that their families have "turned against" them, we find much more commonly that families of batterers experience factionalism and mutual resentment (see also Walker & Edwall, 1987), except in cases where the batterer is not the children's legal or emotional father. Our observations are echoed by Johnston and Campbell (1993b), who state that families affected by domestic violence commonly have "a great many splits and alignments among the family members, and children's alliances keep shifting from one parent to the other" (p. 293).

Among the most overtly divisive behaviors is the strong tendency in batterers to use *favoritism* toward one of the children (review in

Peled, 2000). This dynamic was illustrated in our opening scenario, where Roger rejected Felicia's requests for help with a project but then joined Kyle in a game with his friends. In a recent case of ours, the mother described how the father would arrive home from work to two children who were very excited to see him, "and he would give all his attention to our son and brush off our daughter like she was a mosquito." She reported further that the daughter was only permitted to spend time with her father when he wanted to nap, at which time he would allow her to sleep by his side.

Our clients may favor either boys or girls, although we observe that the former is somewhat more common. When the favored child is a boy and there are also girls in the family, the favoritism often takes an overtly sexist form, with father and son bonding in superiority to females (Johnston & Campbell, 1993b). When the favored child is a girl, the father-daughter relationship can sometimes take on a romantic aspect in which the mother is in part replaced as the father's partner; in these cases, we have heightened concern about the possibility of boundary violations by the father. We also have observed that batterers may use favoritism in a constantly shifting way, so that which child is in the father's good graces keeps changing.

Favoritism can have deep and long-lasting divisive effects even in the absence of domestic violence. We are familiar with cases where adult siblings in their thirties or even older are still struggling in their relationships with each other from the effects of parental favoritism in childhood. When combined with the effects of exposure to domestic violence, the implications become even more worrisome.

We have observed a number of other tactics used by our clients to turn family members against each other. One involves lying to family members about statements that others have supposedly made about them, as with our client who told his children, "Your mother said she is sick and tired of looking after you and wants to put you up for adoption." Another client said to his daughter, "Your brother told me he thinks your haircut looks stupid, but I think it's nice." Several of our clients have deliberately betrayed confidences from private discussion between the parents, such as the man who said to his son, "Mommy said she thinks you just don't have a head for math." We have also noticed that batterers sometimes feed family members' resentments toward each other rather than assisting children to work out their conflicts. Finally, batterers in some of our cases have punished children collectively for the misbehavior of one child, fostering mutual blaming. Many of these behaviors are strikingly similar to divisive tactics used by incest perpetrators, who appear to have similar motives for wishing to turn family members against one another (Leberg, 1997). Divisions among siblings have been noted as a dynamic in families where incest occurs (Giaretto, 1980).

Battering also can contribute to divisions among siblings in ways that are not necessarily conscious or intended on the part of the batterer. Violence among siblings is more common in homes where there is domestic violence (Suh & Abel, 1990; Hurley & Jaffe, 1990), is particularly common in boys, and is likely to occur even where the children are not themselves targets of abuse and regardless of class differences (Hotaling et al., 1990). Those children who most identify with the batterer are especially likely to abuse younger siblings (Hanks, 1992). Some children may take the role of protector of their mother while others identify more with the aggressor, contributing to factionalism. In sum, relationships between siblings exposed to domestic violence "are marked by high levels of sibling rivalry and jealousy, with punishment, intimidation, exploitation, and scapegoating passed down the sibling hierarchy from eldest to youngest" (Hurley & Jaffe, 1990, p. 473).

Scapegoating One of the Children

Providers specializing in child abuse or substance abuse have recognized for many years the prevalence of scapegoating in the families with which they work (e.g., Satir, 1972). They attribute this phenomenon largely to the fear that family members may have of acknowledging the abuse, perhaps even to themselves. In families where the abusive parent is perceived as having disproportionate power, family members have additional reason to channel their resentment, fear, and blame onto one of the children. In family systems terminology, the scapegoated child is known as the "identified patient," who appears to be selected unconsciously by other family members for his or her vulnerability.

We find that such scapegoating is common among families where there is battering (see also Wagar & Rodway, 1995). In our experience, the battered mother herself is sometimes drawn into this pattern of blaming one child and can lack awareness of the family dynamics that have led to the child's inferior status and acting-out behaviors. Both human service and juvenile court personnel comment on the frequency with which domestic violence turns out to be an underlying dynamic in families that present at first as being involved with services because of a "problem child." We find that our clients can contribute strongly to such scapegoating, which places the family and community focus on the "bad" child and diverts attention from the batterer's conduct.

The Impact of Chronic Fear and Emotional Deprivation

Underlying the patterns of interaction that we have been discussing is the impact on the children of chronic fear (Jaffe, Hurley, & Wolfe, 1990), which can deepen and solidify unhealthy dynamics. Fear may lead family members to react with anger and panic toward anyone who is perceived as upsetting the batterer, whether by misbehaving, standing up to him, or simply attracting too much attention to themselves. Children living with chronic fear may experience blurring of their identities with that of the batterer, as they strive to convince both him and themselves that they share his interests, style, and preferences in order to avoid being endangered by him. This kind of identification with the aggressor is widely recognized as a symptom of abuse-related trauma (Dutton & Painter, 1993). In some circumstances, however, fear can be a unifying force, especially in cases where the batterer uses terror tactics, and periods when a family is highly divided may alternate with times when mother and children support each other.

The presence of emotional deprivation can play a similar role in heightening the effects of other dynamics. Battering in a family shifts the locus of attention from the children to the batterer, which can result in children chronically failing to get their needs met. This deprivation in turn can increase the batterer's ability to manipulate the children, as their eagerness for his attention and approval are sharpened. A sense of emotional scarcity in a family can contribute to children perceiving each other as competitors rather than as allies.

Role Reversal

Finally, we want to underline the many ways in which a batterer may cause role reversal between mothers and children, with a number of examples already provided earlier. Over time, the progressive parentification of children and infantilizing of the mother can lead to a situation in which the mother competes with her own children for the batterer's occasional kindness and attention and family members jockey for position to avoid being the target of his rage, insults, or violence. Children may act both as protectors and as controllers of their mothers (Roy, 1988), often feeling responsible for managing their fathers' rage (Doyne et al., 1999; Johnston & Campbell, 1993b) and for taking care of their younger siblings (Jaffe, Wolfe, & Wilson, 1990). There are extreme cases in which the mother becomes psychologically paralyzed over time (e.g., Jones, 1994, on the Hedda Nussbaum case) and the batterer's position becomes that of absolute ruler, often with the children acting as his agents.

RESILIENCE IN MOTHER-CHILD
AND IN SIBLING RELATIONSHIPS

We have observed that resilience occurs not just in individuals exposed to domestic violence but in their relationships as well. The destructive patterns that batterers and battering can create between mothers and children alternate "with patterns of caring, rescuing, nurturing, playfulness, and cooperation" (Hurley & Jaffe, 1990, p. 473), and mothers sometimes succeed in finding ways to increase their parenting effectiveness in response to their awareness of the effects of domestic violence (Levendosky, Lynch, & Graham-Bermann, 2000). Some mothers and children remain close and unified despite the batterer's abuse, and some siblings maintain reliably supportive relationships. To our knowledge, however, the resilience of these relationships has not been the focus of any study.

Similarly, children's resistance to the batterer has not been the subject of any study of which we know, although it was examined to a limited extent by Roy (1988). We have encountered many cases in which children and mothers have made escape plans together, have lied to the batterer to protect each other's freedom and safety, or have called the police during violent incidents. We also have encountered numerous examples of mothers and children supporting each other well in resisting the batterer, in avoiding self-blame, and in recovering from frightening or injurious incidents. We have had a small number of cases in which families have unified to successfully drive the batterer from the home. Even the act of maintaining their own thoughts and opinions can be a profound act of resistance by family members, given the investment of many batterers in controlling the actual views and beliefs of family members (Straus, 1995).

Based on our experience, we have identified the following factors that can contribute to the resilience of familial relationships and the maintenance of healthier family dynamics: (a) a mother who is an unusually competent and caring parent, is able to combine kindness with strong discipline, and does particularly well at shielding her children from the effects of the batterer's abuse; (b) mothers and children who receive particularly good support from friends, relatives, their religious organization, or other community resources; (c) a batterer who is not a skilled manipulator or whose violence is obvious and extreme and who therefore is less successful at causing mutual blame, self-blame, and other divisive and unhealthy dynamics; (d) a batterer who is highly neglectful and uninvolved in any aspect of parenting or who abuses his children directly, physically or sexually (although this behavior can also lead to the *most* divided families, depending on the batterer's ability to manipulate some family members while terrorizing, violating, or ignoring others); and (e) a family that receives an especially constructive response from law enforcement, courts, or child protective services, in a way that holds the batterer fully accountable for his actions and that offers support to mothers and children to help them remain close.

Our battering clients whose families remain unified present themselves as victims of a family effort to "gang up" on them and rarely recognize their role in driving family members away from them. After separation, those families who remain the most unified and who have the greatest degree of psychological health among mothers and children appear to be among those most vulnerable to being labeled as having "parental alienation," which can result in forced visitation for the children with the batterer or even a change to being in his custody (see Chapters 5 and 6).

Unless actively undermined by the batterer's postseparation behavior, mother-child relationships tend to improve over time once the batterer is no longer residing with the family (Peled, 1998). Service providers can contribute in many ways to the resilience of these relationships (see Chapters 5 and 9).

SUMMARY

Battering can have a far-reaching impact on patterns of interaction within a family. Many of the symptoms demonstrated to occur in children exposed to domestic violence may result largely from these disruptions in family functioning rather than being entirely the product of traumatic witnessing of assaults. Professionals wishing to intervene in families affected by domestic violence and to offer assistance to children can strengthen their effectiveness by paying attention to such critical issues as the undermining effects on the mother's parental authority, the children's absorption from the batterer of negative views of their mother, and the divisions among family members that abuse tends to engender. Thus, fostering children's long-term recovery and well-being involves both assisting them to heal from the emotionally traumatic effects of the incidents that they have witnessed and intervening to help them to repair and strengthen their bonds with their mothers and with each other. Both child protective personnel and custody evaluators can avoid serious errors by ensuring that dynamics resulting from domestic violence (including important postseparation ones) have been taken into account.

We wish to finish with a word of caution. Professionals who become aware of the implications of domestic violence for children and families sometimes respond with increased impatience or criticism of battered mothers who do not leave the batterer. Such responses can be the product of an inadequate understanding of the complexities of leaving a batterer, including the potential *increased risk to children* from the batterer if she does so. Chapter 5 examines in detail the post-separation role that batterers tend to play as parents and the continued challenges faced by battered mothers in attempting to protect their children.

4

The Batterer as Incest Perpetrator

Lundy Bancroft and Margaret Miller

Although numerous published studies have found an overlap between domestic violence and incest perpetration, there is a notable lack of published analysis of this phenomenon. For example, a recent comprehensive overview of research on domestic violence (Jasinski & Williams, 1998) did not mention this overlap, and another recent review of risk factors for sexual abuse did not mention battering as a possible perpetrator characteristic (Milner, 1998). We have been able to find only one publication regarding evaluation of sexual abuse allegations that recommends considering a history of violence on the part of the alleged perpetrator as a factor (Thoennes & Pearson, 1988a). We believe that careful examination of the connection between these two forms of abuse sheds important light on practice issues faced by professionals both in domestic violence and in child sexual abuse.

REVIEW OF STUDIES

Multiple studies demonstrate that the mothers of incest victims are likely to be battered by the perpetrator. Other studies indicate that daughters of batterers have unusually high rates of incest victimization. These two sets of studies taken together suggest that exposure to batterers is among the strongest indicators of risk of incest victimization.

Paveza's case-controlled study (1988) involved 34 families in which father-daughter incest occurred and 68 control families. The project began by examining 103 variables, which were eventually reduced to the 4 that were found to have the best predictive value. One of these top 4 predictors was the father's violence to the mother, and two others were the level of dissatisfaction in the marriage and the distance between mother and daughter, both of which can also be connected to domestic violence (see Chapter 3). Paveza reported that daughters of batterers were 6.5 times more likely than were other girls to be victims of father-daughter incest.

Truesdell, McNeil, and Deschner (1986) surveyed 30 mothers of incest victims attending group treatment for incest at a metropolitan child welfare office. Seventy-three percent of the mothers reported at least one incident of physical abuse of them by the perpetrator, mostly in the milder category of violence involving pushing, grabbing, or shoving.

McCloskey, Figueredo, and Koss (1995) identified children who had been exposed to domestic violence and measured various possible effects, one of which was incest victimization. The study was made up of 166 battered mothers and 199 nonbattered mothers, recruited from a large number of independent sources to avoid bias. Mothers who had been battered reported incest perpetration by the batterer against one or more of their children in 9.6% of the cases. Only one nonbattered mother reported incest, representing 0.5% of the control cases.

Sirles and Franke (1989) examined 193 families who were participating in an intake process at an incest treatment program to study factors influencing whether mothers believed or disbelieved their children's reports of incest. As an incidental finding, the study reported that physical abuse of the mother was present in 44.3% of the cases.

Herman (1981) studied 60 women who were psychotherapy patients with various clinicians in private practice. Forty of the women were survivors of childhood incest and 20 were not. Among the incest survivors, 50% (20 of the women) reported that their mother had been beaten by their father during their childhood; in the comparison group, 20% reported such violence. The violence was described as serious but not extreme and, "though terrifying to the mothers and children, did not exceed clear limits" (p. 74).

Roy (1988) interviewed 146 children aged 11 to 17 who had been exposed to domestic violence, a majority of whom were residing with their mothers in shelters. None still lived with the batterer. Of the girls, 28% reported that they had been sexually abused by their fathers, and another 3% who did not disclose had documentation of sexual abuse in their case files. None of the boys reported sexual abuse by their fathers.

Although the above studies vary widely in their sample sizes and methods of selection and assessment, the picture that emerges is quite consistent, with roughly half (ranging from 44.5% to 73%) of incest perpetrators also battering the children's mother and exposure to domestic violence emerging as an important risk factor for incest victimization.

An additional study by Johnston and Campbell (1993b) observed that many batterers in their study had "poor boundaries" in their relationships with their younger daughters, including interactions that appeared romantic and involved "mutual seductiveness" (p. 287), although the authors did not raise concerns about these observations as possible indicators of incest.

These studies taken together suggest that the incest-perpetrating batterer tends to be highly psychologically abusive to the child's mother but may use a level of physical abuse that is in the middle or low range compared to other batterers (Truesdell et al., 1986; Herman, 1981), although a high rate of incest perpetration also has been observed among more severely violent batterers (Roy, 1988). Our clinical experience confirms the impression that the incest-perpetrating batterer more commonly uses low levels of physical violence, although we have also worked with a few highly violent perpetrators. Thus, risk of child sexual abuse by a batterer does not seem to be directly correlated to his level of physical violence toward the mother, whereas such a correlation does exist for the risk of child physical abuse (Straus, 1990; Bowker et al., 1988). Rather, the sexually abusing batterer appears to stand out for his high entitlement, self-centered expectation that children should meet his needs (role reversal), high level of manipulativeness, and perception of his children as owned objects, as we discuss below. There is not strong evidence that race or class are major factors in likelihood to sexually abuse children (review in Finkelhor, 1994). Finally, although batterers have been found to be much more likely than nonbatterers to perpetrate incest, those who do so remain a small minority. Subtler forms of boundary violation by batterers may occur in an larger percentage of cases, however.

THE PREDATORY CHILD MOLESTER
VERSUS THE INCEST PERPETRATOR

The research on child sexual abuse reveals important distinctions between incest perpetrators and other child sexual abusers, although these contrasts often have been overlooked by other writers and practitioners. The predatory child molester, for example, is an offender who tends to have a strong sexual preference for children (Barbaree & Marshall, 1989), with limited interest in adult sexual relationships. He tends to prefer male victims. He is often known to prey on children with whom he has a minimal relationship, perhaps taking advantage of a position of trust as coach, priest, or scoutmaster. He may have many dozens of victims over his career of molesting (Abel et al., cited in Becker & Quinsey, 1993). He may have a history of generally violent or antisocial behavior (Prentky, Knight, & Lee, 1997). He is more likely than is the incest perpetrator to use force during his offenses (Barbaree & Marshall, 1989).

The incest perpetrator, on the other hand, does not appear to have as elevated a rate of sexual preference for children as does the predatory child molester (Prentky et al., 1997; Barbaree & Marshall, 1989). The incest perpetrator commonly has normal adult sexual interest and involvement that may co-occur with his offenses against a child. This is consistent in turn with the fact that he tends to have a higher level of social competence than does the predatory child molester (Prentky et al., 1997). He tends to prefer female victims, though he may also offend against males. He tends primarily to offend against children with whom he has a relationship of caretaking or of substantial familiarity and trust. He thus averages a far smaller number of victims (fewer than two) over his lifetime than does the predatory child molester (Abel et al., cited in Becker & Quinsey, 1993). Incest perpetrators do not show significantly elevated rates of psychopathology, while extrafamilial child sexual abusers do (Serin, Malcolm, Khanna, & Barbaree, cited in Milner, 1998). The incest perpetrator does not differ in socioeconomic status from nonoffenders, whereas the predatory child molester has some increased likelihood to have lower socioeconomic status (Barbaree & Marshall, 1989). Finally, he is less likely than is the predatory child molester to use force against a child (Bresee, Stearns, Bess, & Packer, 1986).

Further distinctions exist among child sexual abusers. For example, a subgroup of predatory child molesters does prefer female victims; this group averages 20 victims over a career of offending, versus 150 victims for the predatory child molester who prefers male children and 1.8 victims for the incest-only perpetrator (review in Myers, 1997a). Incest perpetrators have been divided into the "Aggressive-Dominant" style and the "Passive-Withdrawn" style (Groth, 1982), although we have observed that a batterer/incest perpetrator can present with either of these styles. Salter (1995) further distinguished between sadistic and nonsadistic offenders. Regrettably, the term *pedophile* is commonly used to refer to any of the above styles of perpetrator (including the incest perpetrator) in much of the literature on child sexual abuse. This tendency to blur distinctions may be one of the reasons for the wide-spread failure to recognize the particular similarities between incest perpetrators and batterers (and for common errors in evaluations of incest allegations).

SHARED TACTICS OF BATTERERS
AND INCEST PERPETRATORS

Careful analysis of the abusive tactics and attitudinal characteristics both of batterers and of incest perpetrators can bring into logical focus the connection between these two forms of abuse. We will concentrate on those characteristics of incest perpetrators that provide ready parallels to the characteristics of batterers that have been discussed in previous chapters. We begin by examining several tactical similarities. (In the following discussion, we commonly will refer to the incest victim as "she" because of the higher rates of female victimization, but this should not be taken to deny the existence or importance of male victims of incest by batterers.)

Psychological Abuse and Control.   Psychological abuse and control typically play a large role in the behavior of an incest perpetrator toward his victim and toward other family members (Leberg, 1997; Salter, 1995; Herman, 1981). The perpetrator often subjects the victim to harsh and frequent criticism and to other forms of verbal abuse such as insults, invalidation, and ridicule. The abuser tends to alternate between times of treating her as lovable and attractive and times of verbally degrading her (Salter, 1995). This pattern is typically established for an extended period of time before any sexual violations take place. In some cases, the verbal abuse is directed primarily toward another family member, and the victim's awareness of that abuse causes her to fear becoming the target herself. The perpetrator often exercises authoritarian control over the victim through social isolation, a dictatorial parenting style, and a controlling style of involvement in "the minute details of each family member's life" (Maltz & Holman, 1987, p. 17; see also Herman, 1981).

The perpetrator may favor the victim over other children in the family (de Young, 1986; Herman, 1981). Many perpetrators use their victims as confidantes, which they often combine with presenting themselves "as if they need to be taken care of [so that] their victims feel sorry for them" (Maltz & Holman, 1987, p. 17). Incest perpetrators are described as sometimes preparing for a violation by first engaging the victim in an open emotional discussion with an adult tone, involving for example ways in which he feels hurt or rejected by the victim's mother (Herman, 1981), thereby drawing her into a secret alliance with him.

Preparation of the Victim. The tendency of the great majority of batterers to be nonviolent—and even charming and attentive—in the early period of a relationship is widely recognized in the literature on domestic violence and has been a clear pattern among our clients. The period of kind and loving treatment of the partner is then typically followed by a gradual mounting of verbal abuse, criticism, and control. A similar preparation of the victim is recognized in the literature on incest perpetration, where it is known as "grooming" (e.g., Leberg, 1997; Salter, 1995). The perpetrator may begin this period by lavishing special attention on the victim, buying her gifts, or allowing her forbidden treats (de Young, 1986). According to Stern and Meyer (1980), "The gradual evolution of molestation weighs heavily against reporting," especially as the child is "made a partner in a conspiracy of silence through bribes, threats, and affection" (p. 83). In the context of domestic violence, the child's vulnerability to sexual abuse may be increased by his or her fear of the batterer as a result of previous witnessing of his violence.

Preparation of the Social Environment. As is true with batterers, incest perpetrators are known to discourage assistance to their victims through tactics of shaping public perceptions of themselves and of their victims (Leberg, 1997). The perpetrator projects an image of himself that does not fit with public perceptions of what a sexual abuser would be like, showing himself to be humorous, outgoing, kind, and good with children. The abuser's public persona can make it difficult for those who know him to believe that he could commit a sexual offense (Faller, 1988). At the same time, he may strive to create a negative public perception of the victim so as to prepare people to discount any possible disclosures that she may make.

Preparation of the Family Environment. An incest perpetrator may put particular focus on damaging the mother-daughter connection (Leberg, 1997), just as we have observed so commonly among our battering clients. A recurring theme in the incest literature is the poor relationship between mothers and incest victims (e.g., Paveza, 1988; Herman, 1981; Giaretto, 1980), although the perpetrator's role in causing these tensions is rarely examined.

Like batterers, incest perpetrators have been observed to sow divisions among siblings (for example by using favoritism to create mutual resentments), and "the child molester's efforts to isolate the victim from others not only has a profound impact on the victim's well-being but also affects how everyone in the family gets along" (Leberg, 1997, p. 25). Herman (1981) observed that although most of the brothers of incest victims in her study were not molested by the perpetrator, they were commonly physically abused by him.

The Imposition of Secrecy.   Like batterers, incest perpetrators are widely reported to threaten their victims regarding the consequences of any disclosure of the abuse (review in Myers, 1997a; de Young, 1986), sometimes including threats of violence and commonly involving the threat that the child will be separated from one or both parents (Herman, 1981); they also use other strategies to enforce secrecy (Salter, 1995). Professionals need to be aware of the high risk of retaliation against a child who reveals sexual abuse, just as is necessary with a child who reveals that his or her mother is being battered.

Discrediting of Disclosures.   Both groups of abusers commonly respond to disclosures by characterizing their victims as dishonest, hysterical, or vindictive (Herman, 1992). One client of ours said of the incest allegations, "She was angry at me because I wouldn't buy her a Nintendo, and she told me she was going to get me back for it." Another client whose daughter had made detailed and credible disclosures of sexual abuse stated to us, "She falsely accused her grandfather of molesting her when she was 9 years old, and he was so old he could hardly walk, so he couldn't possibly have done what she said. And she accused someone else before that."

Manipulation.   The majority of the literature on incest victims and much of the literature on offenders portrays the perpetrator as highly manipulative (e.g., Leberg, 1997; Salter, 1995; Maltz & Holman, 1987). Indeed, most incestuous violations do not involve the use of force (Herman, 1981) but rather rely primarily on manipulation (Salter, 1995). The perpetrator typically attempts to confuse the victim about his intentions and to create a sense that he is motivated by caring. Following a violation, he may persuade the victim that she is at fault for what took place (or at least shares responsibility) because she "led him on" or "seduced" him or because she colluded with him in maintaining secrecy, even though she may have been coerced into doing so (de Young, 1986).

SHARED ATTITUDES OF BATTERERS
AND INCEST PERPETRATORS

As is true of battering, evidence exists that attitudes and perceptual distortions play an important role in incest perpetration (Becker & Quinsey, 1993; Herman, 1981), as they do in sexual offending in general (Rapaport & Burkhard, 1984). Many of these beliefs and distortions are similar in both groups of abusers.

Entitlement. Groth (1982) observed that for many incest perpetrators,

> Sexual access to his daughter is experienced as part of his narcissistic entitlement as the head of the family. . . . The husband occupies the dominant role in the family and maintains a position of power by keeping his wife and children financially dependent on him and socially isolated from extrafamily relationships. (p. 222)

Hanson, Gizzarelli, and Scott (1994) and Salter (1988) also identified the perpetrator's belief in his paternal entitlement as a cause of incest. According to Leberg (1997), "Depending on the circumstances, the incestuous father will often claim it is his right to have some sexual activity with his daughter because he works so hard to pay the bills and 'to keep the family together'" (p. 30). Stern and Meyer (1980) observed clinically that one category of incest perpetrator "feels that his daughter belongs to him and that this fact gives him license to use her sexually" (p. 84), and the perpetrator's view of the child as an *owned object* is also discussed by Salter (1995). Several studies show that sexually aggressive men in general have elevated rates of attitudes that support sexual assault, including an array of myths and entitlements (review in Koss et al., 1994), and child sexual abusers and rapists score equally high on their endorsements both of rape myths and of beliefs that support child sexual abuse (Pithers, 1999).

Salter (1988) identified paternal jealousy toward daughters as a warning sign for incest, providing a case example in which a father threatened to shoot a 15-year-old baby-sitter who had molested his daughter, but the girl told the child protective workers that the baby-sitter "just did what my father does to me" (p. 234).

Continuing the parallel with battering, we observe that the incest perpetrator has a marked tendency to be *self-centered* with respect to his children (see also Bresee et al., 1986) and to believe that he is entitled to be waited on both by his children and by their mother (Herman, 1981), apparently in large part because of his sense of entitlement or ownership. This can lead to role reversal with his children, as he expects them to meet his needs for attention, ego gratification, and intimacy (Justice & Justice, cited in Truesdell et al., 1986).

Externalization of Responsibility and Victim Blaming.   As is true of batterers, incest perpetrators often claim that their offenses are caused by a loss of self-control or by provocation by the victim, thereby distracting attention from the consciousness and planning that typically go into their offenses (Salter, 1995, 1988), from their awareness and manipulation of children's needs and vulnerabilities (Pithers, 1999), and from the underlying thought processes and values that may drive both the offenses and the surrounding behaviors (Salter, 1995). Perpetrators also sometimes claim to have been seduced by the child, and regrettably, some professionals have supported this view (e.g., Gardner, 1987).

Furthermore, incest perpetrators are known to blame the child's mother for their actions. The examples that we have encountered most commonly in our cases include (a) the father's claim that he turned to the child for sex or affection because the mother was physically rejecting him and was not meeting his needs (see also Salter, 1988; Giaretto, 1980) and (b) the claim that the mother was rejecting the child and that he was therefore attempting to give the child some of the caring and affection that the mother was denying her. Other excuses used by perpetrators include alcohol, work problems, or a general claim of being a victim of life circumstances (Salter, 1988). One study found that perpetrators of sexual abuse appear to claim much higher rates of childhood sexual victimization than they have actually experienced; when researchers informed perpetrators that a polygraph was going to be administered, the rate claiming to have survived child sexual abuse themselves dropped from 70% to 29% (Hindman, cited in Leberg, 1997).

Confusion of Love and Abuse.   Like batterers, incest perpetrators commonly describe their offenses as resulting from the caring or love that they feel for the victim. A perpetrator may assert that the contact was beneficial for the victim (Maltz & Holman, 1987)—for example, as a way of introducing her to sex (Herman, 1981)—and that he "treats her better than other men would" (Stern & Meyer, 1980, p. 84). Perpetrators may make comments to the victim such as "You know you like this" or other statements that justify the abuse or suggest that it is good for the child (see examples in Salter, 1988).

Objectification. In order to be able to engage repeatedly in violations, an incest perpetrator appears to need a strong ability to shield himself from the child's distress. As with our battering clients, incest perpetrators show strong capacities to defend themselves against empathy for the fear, confusion, emotional pain, and (sometimes) physical pain that they are causing (Pithers, 1999; Salter, 1988), even in cases where the child's anguish is evident to them (Elliott et al., cited in Pithers, 1999).

The Sexualization of Domination. The tendency among child sexual abusers to find subordination sexually arousing has been postulated as a cause of their behavior (Finkelhor & Lewis, cited in Pithers, 1999). This observation appears to have particular relevance to the incest perpetrator, who has been shown typically not to have a dramatically elevated rate of sexual attraction to children per se (see above) and who therefore is perhaps more accurately described as having a sexual attraction to power and domination. This tendency has also been observed in batterers, who have high rates of committing sexual assaults against their partners (Campbell, 1995b; review in Bowker, 1983). Our clients show other signs of finding domination sexually appealing, such as several who have lost interest in sex when their partners refused to be submissive in the overall relationship.

A number of additional parallels exist between batterers and incest perpetrators, including denial and minimization regarding the history of offenses (Becker & Quinsey, 1993); skillful dishonesty, particularly with respect to the ability to make convincing denials regarding abuse allegations (Leberg, 1997; Faller, 1988); some increased likelihood of substance abuse (Becker & Quinsey, 1993); and some likelihood of encouraging the mother to abuse substances (Leberg, 1997). Taken together, the similar behavioral and attitudinal profiles of batterers and of incest perpetrators suggest that the overlap between the two types of abusive behavior may be rooted in a shared fundamental power orientation toward family relationships.

IMPLICATIONS OF THE OVERLAP
FOR PROFESSIONAL RESPONSE

Examining battering and incest perpetration together in the above way can shed some light on the professional response to each. For example, we observe that professionals in both areas sometimes focus narrowly on specific severe acts of violence or of sexual violation, disconnected from their context of surrounding tactics and behaviors by the abuser. Incest victims, like children exposed to domestic violence, may be suffering as much from the abuser's pattern of controlling, manipulative, or intimidating behaviors (as described above) as from the incidents of actual assault or inappropriate touching, and approaches to recovery have to take these patterns into account (Salter, 1995). Similarly, efforts to bring about change either in batterers or in incest perpetrators cannot succeed if they address only a man's specific offenses without adequate attention to his thinking and conduct in daily life, including his patterns of psychological abusiveness and controlling behavior (Pence & Paymar, 1993). The mental and emotional processes that lead both to domestic violence and to incest perpetration do not begin in the minutes or even the hours prior to an assault but rather operate over periods of years. Approaches that teach batterers to defuse conflicts or teach incest perpetrators to dissipate sexual energy, for example, but that fail to address exploitative attitudes such as entitlement and objectification fail in the long term because the underlying modes of thought eventually overwhelm the prevention strategies being taught. Thus, the most sophisticated programs both for abusers (e.g., Pence & Paymar, 1993) and for incest perpetrators (e.g., Pithers, 1999) focus largely on confronting controlling and psychologically abusive behaviors, restructuring entitled attitudes, and developing victim empathy.

Courts and child protective services need to be aware that even in cases where physical violence or sexual violations are believed to have stopped, equally serious problems in the abuser's behavior may be continuing. Efforts to assist victims to heal, to intervene with offenders to bring about change, or to structure continued contact between abusers and their children need to take these contextual issues into account.

SEXUAL ABUSE ALLEGATIONS IN CUSTODY AND VISITATION DISPUTES

Sexual abuse allegations in custody and visitation disputes, which often are accompanied by allegations of domestic violence, have been the subject of a great deal of controversy and research. Studies of the incidence of sexual abuse allegations in custody disputes have found them very low, present in about 2% of cases (McIntosh & Prinz, 1993; Thoennes & Tjaden, 1990). However, some professionals believe that false allegations are widespread and increasing and that they are used as a tactic in custody disputes (e.g., Green, 1991; Gardner, 1991, 1987). To our knowledge, no studies exist to support this view. The largest study, performed for the Association of Family and Conciliation Courts, found that child protective services validate sexual abuse allegations arising in custody and visitation disputes just as frequently as those arising at other times (Thoennes & Tjaden, 1990), despite the fact that child welfare workers may themselves be skeptical of such allegations. False allegations were brought both by mothers and by fathers. Other studies, with smaller samples and more problematic sampling methods, have found a somewhat higher rate of unsubstantiated allegations during custody disputes compared to other circumstances, but even these studies have found more than half of the allegations to be well-founded, and most of the unsupported ones appear to researchers to have been brought in good faith (Hlady & Gunter, 1990; Jones & Seig, 1988; Paradise, Rostain, & Nathanson, 1988; Jones & McGraw, 1987). Furthermore, McGraw and Smith (1992) found that more thorough investigations led to validation of a much higher percentage of cases (see also Carnes, Nelson-Gardell, Wilson, & Orgassa, 2001). This is a critical finding because alleged abusers are sometimes able to persuade courts or custody evaluators not to examine evidence or to perform superficial investigations by appealing to mistaken beliefs about the prevalence of false allegations.

Alleged incest perpetrators use various tactics to discredit disclosures and to avert a thorough investigation, including emphasizing the lack of physical evidence (which evidence is actually unusual even in confirmed sexual abuse cases) (Myers, 1997b); using misleading claims about the findings of research on children's memory and suggestibility (review in Myers, 1997a, and in Reed, 1996); taking advantage of lack of knowledge among professionals about the frequency of delayed disclosure (de Young, 1986); similar use of lack of knowledge about the frequency of retraction, which occurs for many reasons including pressure for secrecy from the perpetrator and the "often unsettling reactions of others to the complaint" (de Young, 1986, p. 553; see also Myers, 1997a); and similar lack of familiarity with children's typical difficulty in disclosing sexual abuse to professionals (DeVoe & Faller, 1999). Many appellate courts have ruled that mildly leading questions are necessary to elicit accurate information from children and so do not automatically discredit the evidence (Myers, 1997a). Faller (1988) studied cases in which the perpetrator *confessed* to sexual abuse and found that in one third of cases, the child's disclosure contained one or more of the following factors commonly believed to indicate false accusation: (a) The child lacked emotion when describing the abuse; (b) the child's description lacked a credible childlike perspective and level of knowledge regarding the events; or (c) the child's description lacked detail. Fifteen percent of the confessed cases contained two of these items or all three. Finally, we have noticed throughout this literature that discussions of suggestibility tend to look only at how children can be led to falsely allege sexual abuse and not at the ways in which they may be led to falsely deny it.

Alleged perpetrators can sometimes find that the process of psychological evaluation works to their advantage. Psychological evaluators cannot distinguish reliably between incest offenders and nonoffenders (Becker & Quinsey, 1993; Hall & Crowther, 1991), and clinical evaluation is especially poor at predicting future sexual offenses against children, scoring only slightly better than chance in assessing which men would reoffend and which would not (Hall, 1988). Psychological testing fared no better in predicting future sexual offenses against children (Hall, 1988). At the same time, psychological testing of the mother who brings the allegation is sometimes used to discredit her reports, as she may be described by the evaluator as angry or bitter about the divorce, hypervigilant, or paranoid. Such evaluations rarely take into account the normative psychological responses of mothers whose children are sexually abused (Newberger, Gremy, Waternaux, & Newberger, 1993).

Accused perpetrators can sometimes gain custody when a court decides to punish a mother for a sexual abuse allegation that is determined to be false (Myers, 1997a). The label of "false allegation" may apply equally to cases where the child recants, refuses to answer questions in an evaluation, or confirms to the evaluator that she made the alleged statements to her mother but states that they were misinterpreted. A batterer may attempt to use any of these circumstances to gain custody, even though none constitutes a deliberately false allegation. (In fact, any of the above can occur in cases where the allegation is true; see DeVoe & Faller, 1999; de Young, 1986.) There are also credible reports of cases where judges or custody evaluators refuse to examine the evidence of sexual abuse yet declare that the allegation is false (Myers, 1997a; Rosen & Etlin, 1996). The Sexual Abuse Allegations Project (Thoennes & Pearson, 1988b) concluded that "global generalizations" about the validity of sexual abuse charges should not be made based on the presence of a custody dispute or the timing of an allegation (pp. 284–285).

SUMMARY

Children (particularly girls) exposed to batterers are at significantly increased risk of incest victimization, although the risk of physical abuse happens to be much higher. The published studies indicate that a batterer is at least four times more likely than is a nonbatterer to perpetrate incest, with some studies finding a risk increased by nine times or more. Batterers and incest perpetrators reveal numerous similarities in their behavioral and attitudinal profiles. Both groups show low rates of psychological or sexual dysfunction and high tendencies to the formation of exploitative relationships.

Furthermore, the family dynamics that are known to result from incest are strikingly similar to those arising from exposure to domestic violence. An incest perpetrator may undermine mother-child relationships, sow other kinds of divisions within the family, and succeed at enforcing secrecy through manipulation and intimidation of the victim. In families in which both incest and domestic violence occur, the mother's own victimization may be an obstacle to her ability to protect her daughter or son. Mental health and legal professionals can strengthen their responses to children affected by these two kinds of abuse by attending to these shared dynamics.

5

Impeding Recovery

The Batterer in Custody and Visitation Disputes

When a batterer and his partner separate, an important new phase opens in his role as a parent. As a period of separation begins, a number of questions regarding the children have to be sorted out by the family members: How much time will their father be spending with them? How much control will the children and their mother have over when and how the children spend time with him? How will it be for the children to spend extended periods of time with the batterer without the presence of their mother and without access to her? Given that separation tends to occur amid potent bad feelings in both parents, how will it be for the children to spend unsupervised time with a batterer who is involved in particularly high levels of anger and resentment?

In many cases, one concern overarches all of the questions above: Where will the children's primary residence be, and who will be governing the key decisions affecting their lives such as schooling, medical care, and religious education? Batterers seek custody more frequently than do nonbattering fathers (APA Presidential Task Force, 1996; Liss & Stahly, 1993) and can have important advantages over battered women in custody litigation (as we will discuss later). The stress of a custody dispute can contribute to turmoil and division within families and can deepen a battered mother's traumatic symptoms, with resultant implications for her children. In addition, in the absence of a thorough investigation, the court often finds itself in the position of having to evaluate the accuracy of domestic violence allegations with very limited evidence, sometimes making such determinations on the basis of misconceptions about batterers and their victims. The arena of custody and visitation litigation may be the aspect of domestic violence victimization that has been least examined and reformed.

In cases where the battered woman appears to have severe parenting problems of her own, child protective services may also be involved, adding an additional complication to determinations about the children's future: If the mother is not a safe parent for the children at present and the father offers to care for the children, should the state or province place them with him? Is such a placement preferable to putting them in foster care with people to whom they have no deep emotional or legal connection?

All of these questions have to be sorted out in the context of the impact that domestic violence has had on the functioning of the family. Problems in the batterer's parenting style can become even more pronounced after separation, with increases in the undermining of the mother's parenting and in other types of irresponsibility toward or mistreatment of the children. Many children show behavioral signs indicative of recovery once the batterer is out of the home, and mothers' aggression toward their children drops significantly (Holden et al., 1998), progress that renewed contact with the batterer could undermine. Decisions about how best to meet the children's needs thus become urgent and complex when a battered woman and a batterer separate.

Finally, the possibility remains that the children will continue to be exposed to domestic violence. Indeed, the level of violence may even increase: Married women living apart from their husbands experience nearly four times the frequency of physical assaults, sexual assaults, and stalking than do those who are still living with the abuser (Tjaden & Thoennes, 2000). When a woman is attempting to end a relationship, batterers are particularly likely to be violent (Websdale, 1999; Adams, 1989) or to attempt rape (Bergen, 1996).

We begin our examination of these questions with a case example from our custody evaluation practice that illustrates the range of elements that will be addressed in this chapter. (Certain minor identifying facts have been altered.)

Hilda Verne became involved with Jerry Pendergast while she was still married to Gregory Verne, and she ultimately left her marriage to be with Jerry. Hilda and Gregory's two children, Travis (8 at the time she left the marriage) and Cameron (6), continued living with Hilda but visited regularly with Gregory. Hilda and Jerry eventually had a child of their own, Nick Pendergast, and two years later had a daughter, Victoria Pendergast.

Over roughly the next two years, Jerry began to show signs of being violent to Hilda, and the violence escalated. When Nick was four years old, Jerry choked Hilda by the throat in Nick's presence, with Victoria also in the home but outside of the room. Police were called, and observing the marks on Hilda's neck, they arrested Jerry. Some months later, Jerry was convicted of the assault and placed on probation. Jerry was also increasingly assaultive toward Hilda and Gregory's son Cameron, once banging his head against a table and another time dragging him down a flight of stairs by his leg. Travis and Cameron reported the violence in their home to Gregory, who told Hilda that he was going to seek custody of their boys. Hilda agreed to give up custody voluntarily and sought services for herself. Following Gregory's report about Jerry's violence to Cameron, the state's child protective arm, the Department of Human Services (DHS), became involved with the case. However, DHS withdrew from the case when Hilda relinquished custody of Travis and Cameron, despite the presence of other children in her home.

When Nick was 6 and Victoria was 4, Jerry was again arrested and convicted for an assault against Hilda, and because of his probation, he was incarcerated for eight months. Upon his release, he moved to another town and did not seek visitation with Nick and Victoria until a year later. At that time, he moved back to the area, went to court, and was granted visitation with the children overnight on alternating weekends. After visits with Jerry began, Nick's behavior at his mother's home became increasingly difficult; he would arrive home after visits saying negative things about Hilda, including stating that she had falsely accused his father of violence. The tensions regarding Nick's behavior escalated to a point where Hilda and he were in chronic conflict and Hilda felt unable to manage him. During one incident, Hilda grabbed Nick hard by the arm and left a large black and blue mark. She reported the incident to school personnel and contacted DHS herself, admitting to her abuse of Nick and seeking services. Upon hearing of this incident, Jerry went to court and filed for custody of Nick, and Bancroft was appointed Guardian ad Litem (GAL).

During the GAL's evaluation, Jerry denied any history of domestic violence toward Hilda or toward any past partners, stating that

Hilda had invented all of the allegations. He stated that he had tried numerous times to leave the relationship and that each time he did so, Hilda would fabricate an allegation of domestic assault, or threaten to do so, in order to intimidate him so that he wouldn't leave. He stated that Hilda had fabricated similar allegations against her former husband Gregory. He explained the year hiatus in his contact with the children following his release from jail by saying that he feared that if he sought visitation, Hilda would retaliate against him by inventing further incidents of violence and thus he might be returned to jail. He stated that he had parted amicably with past partners and that his siblings still kept in touch with one of those women, Deanne, and considered her a friend.

The GAL was able, through Jerry's siblings, to track down Deanne, who said that Jerry had once punched her hard in the eye and that she had been left with blurred vision for a long time thereafter, for which she had sought medical attention. She expressed concern that her relationship with Jerry's siblings would be damaged by her making these disclosures to the GAL. The GAL also succeeded (with considerable difficulty) in reaching another former partner, who hung up the phone abruptly when asked whether Jerry had been violent in their relationship and did not answer further phone calls.

The GAL was able to speak to Gregory Verne, who denied that Hilda had ever accused him of assaulting her. He stated that his relationship with Hilda had remained a cooperative one despite mutual bad feelings. However, he also stated that their son Cameron was still experiencing emotional difficulties resulting from Jerry's violence toward him and toward his mother. The GAL was also able to obtain police records and DHS records that gave further evidence of Jerry's history of battering Hilda. DHS personnel stated that Hilda had cooperated with services and appeared serious about improving her disciplinary style with Nick. Finally, the GAL spoke with Nick's former therapist, who said that Nick had participated well in therapy for several sessions but then had started making statements such as "My dad says I don't have to tell you anything" and had gradually stopped being willing to discuss issues from either home. He now was refusing to attend therapy at all, saying, "My dad says no one can make me go."

In observing Nick with his mother, the GAL noted that Nick was openly disrespectful toward and uncooperative with her and that he would smile at the GAL as if expecting approval for these behaviors. At the same time, Nick twice had abrupt periods in which he would grab onto his mother, hold her tightly, and tell her that he loved her, exhibiting insecurity.

Based on the above facts, the GAL recommended that custody remain with the mother, that the father's visits be shortened somewhat (from two overnights to one), and that the mother continue her serious participation in services. As one important element, it was also recommended that the father be required to support Nick's return to therapy and that the therapist be attentive to any signs that Jerry was undermining the therapeutic relationship and/or undermining the mother-child relationship. The court followed the GAL's recommendations with respect to custody but did not implement the recommended therapy for Nick, nor did it address the GAL's concern that the father appeared to undermine the mother-son relationship on an ongoing basis. DHS again closed the case.

Approximately 6 months later, a new crisis erupted. Hilda had continued to find Nick's behavior unmanageable and had finally requested to Jerry that he take Nick for a few days so that she could have a respite. Jerry accepted, and he then went to court to seek custody of Nick on an emergency basis, saying that Hilda could not care for him appropriately. DHS was contacted by the court and reinvolved in the case. Hilda explained in court that she had only been looking for a respite, not for a change in custody, and that she needed additional services to help her control Nick. The court, however, assigned custody to DHS. DHS spoke with the GAL and learned the background of the case, including Jerry's history of violence toward multiple partners and his violence toward Cameron. DHS nonetheless opted to place Nick in his father's care, where he remained for the subsequent 60 days (constituting the standard DHS assessment period). At the end of that period, largely because of intervention by domestic violence specialists within the DHS system, Nick was returned to Hilda's custody. Nick showed symptoms of trauma from his long separation from his mother (during which only a handful of visits with his mother were permitted). At the GAL's recommendation, DHS did assist the mother in placing Nick in therapy at a clinic specializing in child trauma and issues of exposure to domestic violence. The new therapist set as a priority the strengthening of the mother-son relationship and assisting the mother in reestablishing parental authority.

CREATING A CONTEXT FOR CHILDREN'S HEALING

Divorce or separation can be a deeply distressing experience for children, with long-term implications for their well-being (review in Kelly, 1993; Wallerstein & Blakeslee, 1989). We observe that this distress can be compounded in cases where the children have previous exposure to domestic violence and to the disruptions in family functioning that it engenders, and thus we consider it appropriate to speak of these children as *dually traumatized*. (The children also may carry additional traumatic effects from having been the direct targets of physical, sexual, or psychological abuse, which children of batterers experience at elevated rates, as discussed in Chapter 2.)

The long-term prospects of children in these circumstances are tied to their ability to heal from these dual sources of trauma. This healing depends in turn on access to an environment that is conducive to emotional recovery. A number of studies have explored a range of issues involving resilience in children (review in Heller, Larrieu, D'Imperio, & Boris, 1999). Hetherington, for example, found that divorced children in low-conflict environments were better adjusted than were children of high-conflict couples that were still married (cited in Kelly, 1993).

The following elements are critical to the creation of a healing environment for children of battered women following divorce or separation.

A Sense of Physical and Emotional Safety in Their Current Surroundings. The establishment of both the actuality and the sensation of safety is a first and indispensable step toward any process of emotional healing from trauma (van der Kolk & McFarlane, 1996; Herman, 1992) and is likely to be especially important for children whose previous experience has included fear and danger.

Structure, Limits, and Predictability. We have observed that domestic violence can create a sense of chaos in children's home environment, as they feel unable to predict what will happen at any given moment. Although some of our battering clients build visibly toward incidents of violence, others can erupt at any time without warning signals. A batterer's disciplining of his children tends to alternate between harshness and leniency (Holden & Ritchie, 1991), and the mother's authority is undermined by the battering (Hughes & Marshall, 1995). We therefore find it evident that in order for healing to take place after divorce or separation, children need structure, limits, and predictability as a counterweight to the dynamics with which they have lived previously.

A Strong Bond to the Nonbattering Parent.   The quality of children's relationship with a nurturing parent has been established to be among the best predictors of their thriving and of their ability to recover from marital conflict or parental psychopathology (Furstenberg & Cherlin, 1991; review in Johnston, Kline, & Tschann, 1989). Furthermore, children's postdivorce adjustment is tied largely to the "overall quality of life" in the custodial home, including the creation of a "nurturant, protective milieu" (Wallerstein, 1991, p. 353). These identified needs are accentuated for children who have experienced profound and chronic emotional distress or trauma, where a strong bond to a caretaking parent has been shown to be critical for recovery (review in Heller et al., 1999; additional studies in Graham-Bermann, 1998). Traumatized children need to be with a parent who is able to "acknowledge, recognize, and bear witness to the child's pain" (James, 1994, p. 60). Research indicates that children's sense of security is critical in their responses to domestic violence and in their potential for resilience (Cummings, 1998) and that a strong mother-child relationship is an important contributor to resilience in children of battered women (Jaffe & Geffner, 1998; review in Jaffe, Hurley, & Wolfe, 1990). Assisting the healing of mothers' relationships with their children is thus a critical aspect of promoting postdivorce recovery in children exposed to domestic violence (Erickson & Henderson, 1998). One prominent divorce researcher has observed that joint custody that is imposed over the mother's objections can interfere with the healthy flourishing of mother-daughter relationships (Wallerstein & Blakeslee, 1989), and we have observed such interference both with daughters and with sons in domestic violence cases.

In order for mother-child bonds to be strong and healthy following exposure to a batterer, we believe that the following elements are necessary: (a) The children must feel that their mother can now protect them; (b) the children must recover their respect for her; and (c) the children must feel that the surrounding social environment supports them in being close to her, countering any efforts by the batterer to shame them regarding their closeness to her.

Not to Feel Responsible for Taking Care of Adults.   Children exposed to domestic violence can come to feel burdened with responsibility for the protection and care of their mother, father, or siblings. Specific elements that we recommend toward relieving this burden include adults using good judgment in deciding how much information to share with the children about adult lives and concerns, and the children coming to feel that their parents and siblings are healing from the emotional injuries that they suffered prior to and during the parents' separation. Interventions by courts and child protective services need to make allowance for the mother's healing needs, in order to assist children in being less preoccupied with her well-being.

Contact With the Battering Parent (if it can occur with adequate protection for children's physical and emotional safety).   In our experience, few children prefer to stop all contact with their battering fathers (although this does occur in some cases, usually where the batterer's violence has been extraordinarily terrifying or where he has abused the children directly). We find that children generally wish to be able to continue to express their love for their father, to have him know them, and to be able to tell him about key events in their lives. They also may want reassurance that he is not in overwhelming emotional distress. However, this contact must not interfere with the other healing needs that we are discussing here, including the strengthening of mother-child relationships.

A Strong Bond to Their Siblings.   Overall level of family support is important in fostering resilience (Heller et al., 1999). As we saw in Chapter 3, children exposed to domestic violence often have unusually high levels of tension in their sibling relationships. Healing damaged relationships with siblings and drawing strength from sibling connections that have not been damaged severely can be important to recovery in children exposed to battering.

These characteristics of a healing environment should serve as a frequent reference point in examining the most constructive responses to batterers as parents after separation, including the structuring of custody and visitation.

BATTERERS' POSTSEPARATION CONDUCT
WITH CHILDREN

In Chapter 3, we discussed a number of postseparation issues in the parenting of batterers, involving ways in which they may further or intensify their undermining of the mother's authority and other ways in which they may interfere with mother-child relationships. A number of additional dynamics need our attention here.

Levels of Postseparation Involvement

Some of our clients avoid involvement in their children's lives after separation, either to escape responsibility for spending time with them or to avoid paying child support. Based on reports from mothers, the effects on the children of these disappearances vary, depending largely on how afraid the children were of their father and how much interest in them he had taken previously. Some children reportedly show only brief sadness or concern about the father, whereas others remain distressed by his absence for an extended period of time. Some former partners of our clients state that the batterer's disappearance has been an important source of emotional reinjury to the children.

A second group of batterers in our observation conduct themselves either fairly responsibly or quite responsibly with the children after separation. We have interviewed former partners of our clients who have been separated for 5 years or more and who report that they have not had major postseparation problems with the batterer as a parent and whose children are primarily positive about their relationship with him. Some of the characteristics that we observe in these batterers include the following: (a) They generally do not have histories of having chronically or deliberately undermined the mother's authority or of having used the children as weapons against her *while the couple was still together;* (b) they used somewhat lower levels of psychological abuse toward the mother while the couple was together than did other batterers, though their levels of physical violence varied; (c) they were more accepting than were other batterers of the end of the relationship; and (d) they show stronger abilities than do most other batterers to focus on the children's needs rather than perceiving the children as extensions of themselves.

A third category of batterers, which in our experience is the largest group, are those who remain involved with their children after separation and who continue or worsen the patterns of inappropriate parenting behavior that they exhibited while the family was still together. These behaviors can be intensified by the batterer's desire to curry favor with the children in order to be the preferred parent and in order to overcome any resistance the children may have to spending extensive time with him. We find that in a majority of our cases where the couple is divorced or separated, concerns about psychological manipulation of the children by the batterer are raised by the mother.

Competitiveness With the Mother

After a relationship ends, many of our battering clients attempt to establish that they are competent and caring parents and that their former partners are not. We observe that parenting can become an arena through which the batterer attempts to prove to friends and relatives that he was the more psychologically healthy member of the couple, striving thereby to discredit his former partner's reports that he was abusive. We have had numerous clients over the years make statements to us to the effect that "You'll see what happens now that we've broken up; her life is going to fall apart, because I am the one who has been holding her together." One way a batterer can attempt to make this prediction come true is by creating as many difficulties as possible in the parenting life of his former partner.

The negative effects on children of competitiveness between divorced or separated parents are believed to be potentially serious even in the absence of battering (Wallerstein & Blakeslee, 1989). We find these behaviors by batterers to represent a sharpened psychological risk to children attempting to recover from the effects of exposure to domestic violence.

Inconsistency

A substantial portion of our divorced or separated clients exhibit ambivalence about the extent of contact that they desire with their children. We find that the more self-centered batterer makes such decisions with little regard for the needs or feelings of his children, focusing instead on what degree of involvement with the children feels good to him. At the same time, we find that the high level of entitlement typical to such a client can lead him to the belief that his lack of involvement should not decrease his parental rights or authority. We thus have the phenomenon of the batterer who disappears for months or even years from the children's lives, often failing to pay child support over that period, but then resurfaces and seeks a court order granting him visitation for 48 hours on alternating weekends. We find that such requests can be looked upon favorably by family courts, who are reluctant to limit participation by a father who is now showing interest. However, in the context of domestic violence, the following factors should be taken into account, based on our experience: (a) Batterers who disappear from their children's lives tend to be high in selfishness and self-centeredness, with resultant increased risk to damage mother-child relationships (as in the case example that opened this chapter);

(b) batterers who are inconsistent parents tend to remain so, and thus the children may grow close to him only to lose him again, setting back their healing process; and (c) granting extended visitation privileges to a batterer following a disappearance can reinforce his belief that he will not be held to a reasonable standard of parental responsibility. For the above reasons, batterers who resurface after long absences need to be reintegrated slowly and carefully into their children's lives.

Interference With Children's Participation in Therapy

We receive recurring reports from our clients themselves, from their former partners, and from therapists regarding the sabotaging of the children's therapeutic relationships by the batterer, as occurred in the case example earlier in the chapter (see also Peled, 2000). Agencies that offer group counseling for children exposed to domestic violence are reporting a mounting problem with batterers' succeeding through the legal system in preventing their children from attending the group (e.g., D. Gaudette, personal communication, October 11, 2001). The tactics reported to us most commonly involve pressuring and influencing the children regarding their participation. Some examples include telling them that therapists try to get children to say bad things about their fathers so that the father can be taken away from them completely, telling them that therapy is "stupid," saying that therapy is for people who are crazy, and pressuring boys to perceive therapy as feminine in nature and therefore as undignified for a boy. Clients of ours also have threatened therapists with lawsuits if they see the child, have made repeated harassing calls, or have even threatened physical harm to the therapist. In one case, three different therapists had refused to work with the child out of fear, as the batterer had successively threatened each one.

Based on our observations, we can identify a number of factors that motivate batterers to interfere with children's therapy. The primary reason appears to be that batterers wish to avoid accountability for their actions as parents; the direct involvement with the children of an independent professional can interfere with a batterer's ability to discredit concerns raised by the mother about his parenting. In addition, some batterers may perceive, more or less correctly, that the children's participation in therapy or in a psychoeducational group leads them to be more questioning of the batterer and more difficult for him to manipulate or to intimidate.

One concern about therapy increasingly expressed by our clients is that their children will be persuaded falsely by a therapist that incidents of mistreatment (such as sexual abuse) have occurred. We have reviewed much of the literature on children's memory and suggestibility (see Geddie, Beer, Bartosik, & Wuensch, 2001; review in Banyard, 2000; review in Reed, 1996; Doris, 1991; Zaragoza, 1991) and find the following points to be of critical relevance to our discussion here: (a) Some children can be caused, through misleading questions, to provide inaccurate information. However, most studies find that only a minority of children can be led to give false information, even among pre-school-age children, and that it is easier to lead them about peripheral details than about central information. There is no evidence that children can be easily persuaded that a traumatic event has occurred, especially one involving betrayal by a trusted caretaker. (b) Children vary by age and by personality in their ability to be guided into making false statements through the use of leading questions. In most cases, this process appears to have more to do with the child's desire to cooperate than with the inculcation of a memory, which suggests that subsequent nonleading interviews may be able to clarify earlier errors. (c) There continues to be important evidence, including from recent studies, of the relative soundness of most memories that children report in noncoercive circumstances, and investigatory methods are available to assess whether children's earlier statements have been coerced. (d) Children give more accurate information in response to specific, nonleading questions than to more general and open-ended questions, so the concept of "leading" needs to be carefully defined in order to avoid rejecting appropriate questions. (e) Finally, methods are available to increase the accuracy of information collected through interviewing children and to reduce their vulnerability to suggestion.

The ongoing debates regarding memory in adults, particularly recovered memories of childhood trauma (review in Banyard, 2000, and in Courtois, 1999; see also Pope, 1996, and Williams, 1994a, 1994b), have sometimes carried over into court cases involving children's memories of events that they have never forgotten. This represents a confounding of two distinct bodies of research that are not interchangeable.

Finally, we observe from our own cases that a thorough investigation sometimes reveals extensive evidence of the accuracy of a child's allegations in cases where the batterer claimed that the child's memory had been inculcated. Thus, it appears that many batterers may be concerned more about accurate statements that may be elicited by a therapist than about inaccurate ones. At the same time, our experience indicates that concerns about ethics and practices of some therapists are indeed warranted.

Use of Visitation to Gain Access to the Mother

A batterer may use visitation as a way of creating opportunities for contact with his former partner (Sheeran & Hampton, 1999; McMahon & Pence, 1995; Adams, 1989), so that he can pressure her for a reunion, harass or intimidate her verbally, or assault her (Liss & Stahly, 1993; Walker & Edwall, 1987). Some of our clients have used visitation to gain information from the children regarding the mother's address, place of employment, or routines. Assaults and murders sometimes occur during exchanges for visitation (Websdale, Sheeran, & Johnson, 1998; McMahon & Pence, 1995); in one recent publicized case, a woman was murdered in the parking lot of a supervised visitation center following a scheduled visit (Sheeran & Hampton, 1999).

The Batterer in Unsupervised Visitation

In the overwhelming majority of cases with which we have been involved or about which we have learned through our research, family courts have granted men who batter unsupervised visitation with their children. Even in cases where supervised visitation is imposed, the requirement is generally temporary. We have yet to encounter a case where unsupervised visitation was conditioned on reliable evidence that the batterer had overcome his battering problem (see Chapter 8); in cases where some period of supervision is imposed, it is generally lifted based on the batterer's conduct *in the supervised visits*, which is not a reliable measure of safety (see Chapter 2).

The parenting of batterers in unsupervised contexts poses multiple risks to children (Hart, 1990a). We observe that some of these are continuations of existing problems in the parenting of batterers (see Chapters 1 through 3) and others are fomented or exacerbated by the postseparation attitudes and behaviors typical of our clients. The risks, which are detailed in Chapter 7, include the exposure of the children to new acts of violence, their use as weapons by the batterer for post-separation reprisals, direct mistreatment by the batterer, and many others.

Various combinations of the above factors can lead children to feel unsafe during visitation, and their anxiety sometimes continues after they are returned to their mother's care or reemerges in anticipation of subsequent visits. As one battered mother that we interviewed stated, "By the time they are back to sleeping well at night and feeling relaxed again, it's almost time for the next visit, and they start to get anxious again." The underlying goal of making it possible for children to feel safe, which is a crucial aspect of the context of recovery, can thus sometimes be compromised through unsupervised visitation. Children also can be made to feel responsible for the batterer and guilty regarding his emotional distress; for example, we have had a number of cases where the batterer tells the children that he cries frequently when he is apart from them (the same tactic is described in Erickson & Henderson, 1998).

Because of the complexity of the dynamics involved, children's orientation toward unsupervised contact with their battering fathers is often one of marked ambivalence. The partners of our clients describe the period prior to a visit as tending to involve a mixture of excitement and anxiety. The lack of structure and supervision that are common in visitation with batterers can be exciting for children, while simultaneously engendering insecurity. Exposure during visitation to an atmosphere of high negativity regarding their mother (and sometimes regarding women and children in general) can create confusion. In our experience, overexposure to sweets, video games, violent movies, or other stimuli that may be restricted in their custodial home can lead children to experience visitation in an addictive way, in that they may use such stimuli to anesthetize themselves to the fear and insecurity of being in the batterer's care. The batterer's exposure of the children to violence in media may be especially important, because such violence has been found to trigger children's feelings regarding battering that they have witnessed previously (Eron, Huesmann, & Zilli, cited in Graham-Bermann, 1998).

In many of our cases, we have observed a gradual decline in children's interest in visitation over a period of several months to a few years, as the initial sources of excitement become less potent and the upsetting aspects of irresponsible or undermining parenting by the batterer become more distressing to the children. However, batterers can often succeed at persuading courts that the children's mother is responsible for their mounting reluctance to visit.

Finally, we wish to make note of what we have found to be a dearth of research on the behavior of batterers during unsupervised visitation. This is an important gap to fill, in order to test and expand clinical observations.

Effects on Children of Unsupervised Visitation

Children's behavioral and emotional functioning often improves when a battered woman separates from a batterer (Holden et al., 1998). Battered women's service providers with whom we have spoken observe that these gains sometimes fade once children begin to have visitation with the batterer, particularly if the visits are unsupervised, with a resurgence of their symptoms and of their level of conflict with their mothers. Jaffe and Geffner (1998) observe that this decline can gradually lead to withdrawal and to a sense of resignation in the child if a proper protective plan is not put in place regarding custody and visitation.

As discussed in Chapter 2, some children react to the violence that they have witnessed and to the self-centered or aggressive parenting style of the batterer by becoming increasingly rejecting toward him and reluctant to participate in visitation. This outcome, and the painful internal loyalty struggles that children experience when deciding to reject their fathers in this fashion, could perhaps be prevented by requiring proper supervision during paternal visits (Liss & Stahly, 1993).

The Batterer in Supervised Visitation

In our experience, because of the manipulative style of many batterers, supervised visitation does not guarantee children's emotional safety and well-being unless the supervision is vigilant and is performed by a professional trained in the parenting of batterers and in the dynamics of domestic violence. We have been involved in cases where batterers at supervised visitation centers have passed messages to children through notes written in the margins of books, where a batterer/incest perpetrator took advantage of a momentary lapse in the supervisor's attention to take pictures of the child's rear end, where an incest perpetrator continued pressuring the child for kisses in supervised visitation, where various verbal messages were passed to the mother through the child, and various other risks both to children and to their mothers.

In less structured forms of supervision, the risks of manipulation are even greater. In a case in which we are currently involved, the supervisor has lengthy conversations with the batterer/incest perpetrator during visits. The existence of these conversations means that the supervisor is not fully focused on the child's safety and means that the father is receiving the opportunity to develop a relationship with the supervisor that could compromise her neutrality and vigilance. We have been involved in several other cases in which such conversations led the supervisor to become increasingly sympathetic to the abuser and hostile to the battered mother. In a similar case of ours, family members who were appointed to supervise visits appeared to be directly involved in shaming the child regarding his disclosure of sexual abuse and in pressuring him to recant.

The Batterer and Child Support

Batterers are less likely than are nonbatterers to pay child support fully and consistently (Liss & Stahly, 1993). They often avoid paying altogether, especially if they do not intend to seek custody (Jacobson & Gottman, 1998). Women may be afraid to press for child support because of the danger of physical assault by the batterer (Kirkwood, 1993), and the batterer may explicitly threaten to hurt her if she pursues payment (Ptacek, 1997). The woman may also fear that the batterer will retaliate with actions for custody or for increased visitation if she seeks child support; we have found this fear to be realized in several cases in which we have been involved. The impact on the battered woman and on her children of his refusal to pay child support or to pay at an appropriate rate needs to be understood in the context of his overall history of economic abuse, which is common with batterers (Pence & Paymar, 1993), and how that history has affected the family.

In one of Bancroft's first custody evaluations, the batterer was seeking custody of a 3-year-old girl yet admitted openly that he had three children from a previous relationship for whom he paid no child support and whom he made no effort to visit "because they moved to New Mexico and it was too much of a pain." Unfortunately, we find that custody and visitation evaluators do not typically consider the batterer's history of responsibility in paying child support as a relevant factor in assessing his level of parenting commitment and his capacity to prioritize his children's needs.

BATTERERS' MOTIVATIONS FOR SEEKING CUSTODY OR INCREASED VISITATION

Studies suggest that batterers are more likely than are nonbattering fathers to seek custody, especially of sons, and are as likely as are nonbattering fathers to prevail (APA Presidential Task Force, 1996; Liss & Stahly, 1993; Walker & Edwall, 1987). Our professional experience tends to confirm these patterns, and here we will make some observations on the reasons why batterers exhibit increased likelihood to pursue custody or to use legal action to attempt to expand their visitation schedules.

Distorted Perceptions of Their Victims. Batterers generally have a contemptuous outlook on their partners, which can be sharpened by separation. For example, numerous clients of ours have expressed their conviction that their partner's decision to leave the relationship was evidence of the woman's immaturity, weak commitment to the relationship, or lack of concern for the children, as with the client who told us, "Obviously, it's no big deal to her if our children come from a broken home." Our clients almost universally minimize the role of their abusiveness in causing the end of the relationship.

Distorted Perceptions of Themselves. We find it nearly universal among batterers to have little sense of the seriousness of their own abusiveness and of its effects on their children. Their tendency to self-centeredness can sometimes lead to grandiose or romanticized self-images. Furthermore, we encounter cases where the batterer is in denial about the marked improvement that has occurred in the children's emotional, social, and scholastic functioning following the reduction in their exposure to him.

Desire to Impose Control. For some batterers, custody litigation is an important arena through which they seek to reimpose the control and domination that the end of the adult relationship has weakened (McMahon & Pence, 1995; Walker & Edwall, 1987). Entitled attitudes can feed this desire for control, as many batterers believe that they should have ultimate authority over decisions involving the children.

The Desire to Retaliate. We observe that many of our clients who seek custody of their children reveal under questioning that their motive is to hurt and to frighten their former partners (see also Doyne et al., 1999); in our experience, custody actions can be uniquely effective for this goal. Also, the costs of custody litigation can be devastating to a mother's financial position and can eliminate many opportunities for her children to improve their living conditions or to participate in enriching activities.

The Desire for Vindication. Partly to refute claims of abuse, our divorced or separated clients tend to have a strong drive to prove that they are more emotionally healthy than are their former partners. These men sometimes pursue custody as a way to gain social validation (see also Doyne et al., 1999). Our clients who win custody do interpret their victories as validation of their perspectives, and children unfortunately appear to interpret an award of custody to the batterer in the same way.

Their View of the Effects of Battering on Their Former Partners. It is common for battered women to suffer from depression, substance abuse, hypervigilance, emotional lability, sleep disturbances, and many other problems (Dutton, 1992; Douglas, 1987). Because batterers almost universally fail to recognize the impact of their actions on their partners, they view these symptoms as inherent problems in the woman and as reasons why she should not be given responsibility to care for the children (Dalton, 1999).

The Desire to Gain Economic or Legal Concessions. A number of our clients have admitted that they filed for custody in order to gain a bargaining chip to trade off against alimony, child support, or conjugal assets. Many battered mothers report to us that they accepted settlements that left them and their children in poor economic circumstances in order to keep custody of their children. Batterers also sometimes may use custody actions to coerce their former partners to drop criminal charges (Adams, 1989).

Other Reasons for Wishing to Intimidate. Several clients of ours have initiated actions for custody upon learning that their former partners had begun new relationships or upon being accused of child sexual abuse.

Avoidance of Child Support. We have had a small number of cases in which the batterer's attempts to win custody appeared to be motivated primarily by the desire to avoid having a child support obligation.

BATTERERS' ADVANTAGES IN CUSTODY DISPUTES

Batterers win custody of their children with greater frequency than is generally realized. Although it is widely believed that family courts have a bias in favor of mothers, custody studies have demonstrated that since the 1970s, fathers have been at a marked advantage in custody disputes (Gender Bias Study Committee, 1990; Weitzman, 1985). There is a general reluctance among family courts in the United States (Walker, 1989) and abroad (Eriksson & Hester, 2001) to consider a man's battering as a reflection on his parenting or as a factor in determining custody. The partners of our clients often state that the fear of losing custody is a major factor in their decisions to postpone leaving the batterer; this is particularly true for those women who do not have any proof of the history of violence (such as arrest records) or whose batterers have the economic resources to pursue litigation.

A battered mother faces multiple disadvantages in custody litigation, many of which are related to the history of domestic violence. We review here the central reasons why batterers are so often able to prevail.

The Effects of Domestic Violence on Family Dynamics.   As examined in Chapter 3, battering tends to undermine a mother's parental authority and to create multiple tensions between mothers and children. The difficulty that battered mothers may have in controlling their children's behavior can be exacerbated in the immediate aftermath of a separation by the father's absence from the home; children may target the mother for their anger regarding the parental separation, and they may feel free to behave as they choose now that the batterer's authoritarian presence is gone. Custody evaluators may observe that the mother has trouble controlling her children and may conclude that she lacks parenting skills. At the same time, batterers often can perform well under observation, and children may appear relaxed and comfortable with the batterer in the presence of the evaluator. Children often behave better while in the batterer's care, partly because of conscious or unconscious fear of him (Pickering et al., 1993; Johnston & Campbell, 1993b). Children also may side with the batterer because they perceive him as the more powerful parent (Jaffe & Geffner, 1998; Liss & Stahly, 1993; Walker & Edwall, 1987) or may request to live with him as a result of traumatic bonding (Doyne et al., 1999).

The Batterer's Ability to Manipulate or to Intimidate Children's Statements to the Custody Evaluator.   It is not uncommon for a batterer to succeed in persuading the children that he is the victim in the adult relationship or that the mother's behavior causes the abusive incidents (see also Roy, 1988). A batterer who was previously neglectful of the children may abruptly make his children a high priority as a result of his desire to seek custody, and we have observed that this change can have a powerful emotional effect on children who have been craving more attention from him. Children may have difficulty disclosing domestic violence because of their fear of repercussions for themselves or for their mothers (Jaffe & Geffner, 1998). For these reasons, children's statements to professionals sometimes may obscure the family history or their own present feelings and wishes. For example, in response to questions during a custody evaluation of ours, a teen boy primarily spoke positively about his mother and negatively about his father. At the same time, however, he requested to be placed in his father's home, repeatedly expressing concern that his father had been falsely accused of domestic violence and that the father did not have friends. In other cases, children may request to be in the batterer's custody because of ways in which he has shaped their perceptions of their mother and because of his history of currying favor with them.

We also have seen indications of batterers pressuring or rehearsing their children's statements to the evaluator. In one case, for example, a 3-year-old boy said to the evaluator, "Give my dad a chance," but further questioning revealed that he did not know the meaning of the expression. Finally, in some cases, children exhibit signs of being afraid to express a preference to live with their mother because of concern over the batterer's reaction.

The Batterer's Economic Advantage.   Our divorced and separated clients generally have more financial resources than do their former partners, especially in the period immediately following separation (see also review in Ellis & Stuckless, 1996; review and bibliography in Schafran, 1994; review in Gender Bias Study Committee, 1990). These financial advantages can make it possible not only to hire a more experienced and skilled attorney but also to spend money on discovery, depositions, hearings, and trials. We receive many reports from battered mothers of settling cases on terms that they consider detrimental to their children because they cannot amass the resources to pay for a trial. In addition, we have observed some cases in which the batterer's economic advantages appeared to sway the custody evaluator, who felt that the children would be happier in the more fortunate class circumstances of the father (see similar observation in Dutton, 1992). Finally, courts may grant custody to the father if the mother is homeless, even if her economic position is largely the result of his failure to pay child support or of other economically irresponsible behaviors on his part (Gender Bias Study Committee, 1990). Domestic violence is an important cause of homelessness for women and children (Zorza, 1991).

Psychological Testing and Evaluation.   We find that psychological evaluation is widely used to assist in custody determinations, but there are various reasons to question its validity for this purpose (Zibbell, 1994), especially where a history of domestic violence is alleged.

Because of the absence of serious psychopathology in most batterers (see Chapter 1) and because of the potent traumatic effects of domestic violence on victims, batterers often outperform their victims in psychological testing. Battered women have higher rates than do non-battered women of symptoms associated with a large range of personality disorders and mental illnesses (review in Stark & Flitcraft, 1988), which can lead to incorrect diagnoses by evaluators not familiar with domestic violence trauma (Herman, 1992; Rosewater, 1987). The MMPI-2, for example, includes many questions that, if answered accurately by a battered woman, will contribute to elevated scale scores, such as whether she believes that someone is following her, whether she has trouble sleeping at night, whether she worries frequently, or whether she believes another individual is responsible for most of her troubles (Pope, Butcher, & Seelen, 2000). In an earlier study of the MMPI, battered women tended to have quite elevated scores for anger, alienation, and confusion, somewhat elevated scores for paranoia and fearfulness, and low scores for intactness and ego strength, regardless of race (Rosewater, 1987). We have observed that such test results are sometimes used successfully by a batterer to discredit a woman's reports of abuse, even when independent evidence of his behavior exists.

No psychological test exists that can determine whether an individual is a batterer or which batterers are most likely to reoffend (Gondolf, 1998a), nor have we encountered any test that can establish whether a woman's abuse allegations are true. Nevertheless, some prominent evaluators believe that psychological testing should be used routinely any time that abuse allegations are raised (e.g., Stahl, 1999).

Psychological tests, including both standardized tests such as the MMPI-2 and projective tests such as the Thematic Apperception Test (TAT) and the Rorschach, are poor predictors of parenting capacity and are commonly given inappropriate weight by custody evaluators (Brodzinsky, 1994; Zibbell, 1994). Efforts to detect psychological traits associated with likelihood to abuse children have been unsuccessful (review in Wolfe, 1985). Some individuals with substantial psychopathology parent fairly well because of healthy value systems or because of concerted efforts to insulate the children from the effects of the mental illness (Herman, 1992). At the same time, some psychologically normal people parent badly, because of abusiveness, selfishness, or unhealthy value systems (see American Psychological Association, 1994, on the importance of assessing the impact of value systems on parenting). Finally, one study of normative MMPI-2 data for parents in custody litigation found that several elevations were typical, including hysteria, paranoia, psychopathic deviant, self-favorability, over-controlled hostility, and others (Bathurst, Gottfried, & Gottfried, 1997), suggesting that test results should be interpreted cautiously in this context.

Poor Quality of Some Custody Evaluations. Despite claims of rigorousness by some custody evaluators, we find the overall quality of custody evaluation to be of concern. Both authors have had occasion to review dozens of evaluations, and we find the following problems to be chronic.

(a) Evaluators often do not grasp the basic dynamics of domestic violence (Lawton & McAlister Groves, 2000; Dalton, 1999), fail to ask about domestic violence or its effects on the children (McMahon & Pence, 1995), do not keep abreast of professional literature regarding abuse (Caplan & Wilson, 1990), or do not consider domestic violence a major factor in custody determination (Ackerman & Ackerman, cited in Doyne et al., 1999). Graduate training programs for psychologists "have largely ignored abuse as a specific content area" (Pope & Feldman-Summers, 1992, p. 353). Many professionals continue to believe that battering behavior is produced by phases of elevated conflict in relationships and that the problem will be resolved as situational stresses dissipate (Jaffe & Geffner, 1998). Given that custody evaluators are often mental health providers by profession, the above observations are consistent with research indicating that a high rate (91%) of therapists fail to identify the seriousness of domestic violence when it is presented to them in a scenario, that 40% do not consider it important to address the violence of which they are aware (Harway & Hansen, 1993), and that therapists frequently fail to recognize domestic violence in evaluating and diagnosing battered women (Gondolf, 1998b).

(b) Evaluators can be heavily influenced by their personal experience of the alleged batterer, can allow themselves to be manipulated by him (Dalton, 1999; Walker & Edwall, 1987), and can allow their concern for the hurt feelings that he expresses to override concern regarding the available evidence of his abusiveness.

(c) Evaluators regularly fail to investigate allegations of abuse, dismissing them on the basis of their impressions of the parties or of psychological test results. A large percentage of custody evaluators fail to seek third-party sources of information or even to review the relevant court records (Caplan & Wilson, 1990). In one case that we researched in which a mother had fled to a battered women's shelter with her children, the Guardian ad Litem reported to the court that the alleged batterer was not dangerous enough to warrant such flight; he wrote further that the children should be placed in the father's custody immediately because of the mother's unnecessary flight to shelter. We carefully reviewed the custody evaluator's reports in the case and found that he had not conducted any investigation into the domestic violence history or level of risk.

In some cases, evaluators may fail to examine evidence that supports the abuse allegations yet recommend that custody be switched to the alleged abuser as a consequence to the mother for having brought a false allegation (Rosen & Etlin, 1996). Some judges change custody to the father on this basis (Myers, 1997b).

(d) Evaluators sometimes assume that most abuse allegations are exaggerated or fabricated, despite the lack of evidence to support this view (Jaffe & Geffner, 1998). For example, a 1986 guidebook to custody evaluation does not address battering except to caution professionals regarding women's tendency to exaggerate reports of violence (Parry, Broder, Schmitt, Saunders, & Hood, cited in Jaffe, Wolfe, & Wilson, 1990). Evaluators may be unaware of the overall prevalence of domestic violence in society (Straus & Gelles, 1990) or of the evidence that it is even more common in couples that are divorcing (review in Kalmuss & Seltzer, 1986) and still more common in divorced couples who have ongoing custody and visitation conflicts (Johnston & Campbell, 1988). Lacking this awareness, evaluators may be highly suspicious of the frequency with which domestic violence allegations appear in their cases, when in fact that frequency is statistically predictable.

(e) Evaluators are sometimes guilty of unethical and unprofessional conduct. Both our professional experience and our research suggest that ethical and professional problems on the part of custody evaluators may be widespread (Senate Committee on Post Audit and Oversight, 2001; Silverman, Andrews, Bancroft, Cuthbert, & Slote, 2001). The concerns that are raised most commonly involve false or deliberately misleading statements by custody evaluators in reports to the court, and other acts of severe bias in favor of the batterer. There appears to be an urgent need for the establishment of oversight and review of the performance of custody evaluators.

Gender and Racial Bias. There is important evidence that fathers may be favored over mothers in custody disputes. For example, the Gender Bias Study commissioned by the Supreme Judicial Court of Massachusetts studied over 2,100 disputed custody cases and found that fathers win sole custody more than three times as often as do mothers and win at least joint custody in more than 70% of contested cases (Gender Bias Study Committee, 1990). Courts may assume that a father who seeks custody is unusually caring and concerned (Gender Bias Study Committee, 1990) and may be unaware of the frequency with which batterers seek custody. Mothers and fathers sometimes appear to be judged by different standards (Gender Bias Study Committee, 1990; Walker & Edwall, 1987), with mothers evaluated on the basis of their actual history of performance as parents and fathers evaluated on the basis of their expressions of emotion and their stated intentions for the future. Mothers also appear to be judged more harshly than are fathers for any period of separation from the children, which can, for example, have negative implications for a battered woman who may have needed to flee without her children at some point (Gender Bias Study Committee, 1990).

We also observe the presence of societal ambivalence regarding a mother's appropriate role in protecting her children from their legal father. Prior to separation or divorce, professionals and other community members (including child protective services) may be harshly critical of a mother whom they perceive as guilty of "failure to protect" her children from exposure to a batterer (Magen, 1999; Whitney & Davis, 1999; Edleson, 1998). However, a societal reversal tends to take place once a mother and an abusive father are no longer together. At this stage, we have observed that professionals often become suspicious of a mother's motives for attempting to protect her children and may attribute children's symptoms to the mother's alleged anxiety, overprotectiveness, or vindictiveness against the alleged abuser. Thus, battered mothers sometimes can be caught in a societal contradiction that works to the advantage of batterers (see similar observations in Jaffe & Geffner, 1998; Faller, 1991).

Courts and custody evaluators sometimes appear to apply different standards of proof to allegations regarding inappropriate parenting by fathers and those regarding mothers. We observe, for example, that allegations of domestic violence or of incest perpetration tend to require a high measure of supporting evidence, whereas allegations that a mother is attempting to alienate the children from their father (e.g., by making false accusations of abuse) are sometimes accepted with little or no factual basis (see also Rosen & Etlin, 1996). We further note a discrepancy between the strong weight placed on children's statements when they request visitation with their battering fathers and the simultaneous tendency to discount their statements when they do not desire such visitation.

Courts and custody evaluators tend to look more favorably on stepmothers than on stepfathers (Zorza, 1995; Utah Task Force on Gender and Justice, 1990; Gender Bias Study Committee, 1990). This bias creates an ironic twist, in which an underlying societal assumption that women are more nurturing and less dangerous to children than are men may assist a batterer to win custody.

Finally, we receive numerous reports of bias against battered mothers of color and against immigrant battered women in custody litigation. We are unaware of current research on this problem.

"Friendly Parent" Custody Presumptions.   Many states have established presumptions that custody should go to the parent who is most likely to foster a relationship between the children and the other parent. Such presumptions can work against battered mothers, who may be striving appropriately to restrict their children's contact with the batterer (Zorza, 1996). Some courts and legislatures, however, have specifically recognized that "friendly parent" provisions are not applicable to domestic violence cases (Lemon, 1999; Family Violence Project of the NCJFCJ, 1995; American Bar Association [ABA] Center on Children and the Law, 1994).

Shortage of Properly Trained Attorneys.   Overall, training of family law attorneys on domestic violence is low, the quality of representation provided to battered mothers is often inadequate, and few jurisdictions are structured in a way that gives a fair opportunity to those parties who wish to represent themselves (Family Violence Project, 1995).

BATTERERS' TACTICS IN CUSTODY AND VISITATION DISPUTES

Family courts and child protective services often appear skeptical of domestic violence or child abuse allegations brought by women in custody and visitation litigation, believing that such reports are exaggerated for strategic purposes (Jaffe & Geffner, 1998; Walker & Edwall, 1987). Familiarity with common tactics used by batterers in custody and visitation conflicts is important for professionals who intervene with families after separation, in order to avoid being drawn away from careful consideration of the evidence.

Projecting a Nonabusive Image.   Batterers can use a calm speaking style, sensitive language, and dramatic expressions of love for their children to persuade evaluators and court personnel that they are unlikely to be physically dangerous or psychologically injurious. They may persuasively characterize the adult relationship as having been mutually destructive and may account for the mother's allegations of abuse through such tactics as saying that she is upset because he had an affair or because her father abused her as a child. A batterer sometimes will admit to less serious acts of violence such as shoving the woman or throwing objects, thereby increasing his credibility and creating the impression that the woman is vindictive. We repeatedly hear statements from batterers along the lines of "I want to put our relationship behind us and just cooperate as well as we can to raise these children, but she isn't willing to let go of the past." Batterers tend further to be skilled at characterizing their former partners as dishonest, cruel, substance abusing, immature, or mentally ill (see also Ayoub et al., 1991) or as having problems with men in general (Walker & Edwall, 1987).

Use of His New Partner as a Character Reference. Many of our clients quickly become involved with a new partner after their relationship with the victim ends, and initially, they often treat the new partner relatively well (see also Pence & Paymar, 1993). We have observed in dozens of cases that the new partner becomes an ally to the batterer in conflicts with his former victim. We find in custody evaluations, for example, that the batterer's new partner may state adamantly that her partner could not possibly be abusive and that his former partner is fabricating her allegations. (On a number of occasions, our investigation has revealed extensive evidence that the man is in fact a batterer and potentially a dangerous one, which has created ethical dilemmas: Is it our responsibility to inform the new partner of the potential risk to her? Does doing so conflict with our appropriate role as custody evaluator?)

Using the Mother's Anger or Mistrust to Discredit Her. The batterer may be able to influence court personnel and custody evaluators by drawing attention to the mother's anger or mistrust (Walker & Edwall, 1987), which is common in women who have suffered abuse (Dutton, 1992; Rosewater, 1987) but which may not fit with the expectation among some professionals that a battered woman would present only as victimized or helpless. One influential theorist claims that a mother's anger is an indicator of false allegation in incest cases (Gardner, 1991, 1987), thus overlooking normative parental reactions to learning that a child has been abused. In addition, a batterer may strive to persuade court personnel that the mother's concerns about the children are overreactions based on her own feelings about him, although battered mothers' ratings of their children's problems have, in fact, not been found to differ significantly from those of independent observers such as teachers (Sternberg et al., 1998; Gleason, 1995).

Defensive Accusations.   A batterer is sometimes able to create confusion or uncertainty by accusing the victim of the same violent or verbally abusive behaviors of which he expects to be accused. He may state that his former partner was violent toward him and the children, controlling, unfaithful, or unwilling to accept the end of their relationship. In a number of cases of ours, the batterer reported to the court that the mother was blocking his telephone access to the children; in two of those cases, we were able to obtain tapes of conversations that indicated that the battered mother was not interfering with contact with the other parent but that the batterer *was.*

As discussed in Chapter 1, it is common for our clients to be skillfully dishonest, and they sometimes turn this ability to their advantage in custody and visitation litigation. For example, we have had a number of clients make claims in family court that they were being denied visitation by the mothers of their children during periods when the client had told us that he was opting not to see his children because of his anger or frustration.

Presenting Himself as the Party Who Is Willing to Communicate. Our clients are sometimes able to take advantage of the belief among professionals that the parents should communicate with each other despite any history of abuse (e.g., Johnston & Roseby, 1997). The operating assumption is that the more the two parents speak to each other, the better things will be for the children. However, we find that the reality in domestic violence cases can be the opposite, as the batterer may use communication to intimidate or to verbally abuse his former partner or in some cases to pressure her for a reunion. In many cases, a battered mother who declines all contact with the abuser may be doing what is best for her own recovery and for that of her children.

Manipulating Mediation or Dispute Resolution.   Mediation in domestic violence cases generally does not serve the interests of battered women and their children (ABA Center on Children, 1994; Hart, 1990b), although there are some indications that it can be used productively if the battered woman is participating voluntarily and if strict guidelines are followed (Maxwell, 1999; Magaña & Taylor,

1993). Mediators may have little training in domestic violence and may make serious errors as a result (Maxwell, 1999). Batterers can manipulate the mediation process by beginning with an extreme set of demands and then offering compromises from those positions; this strategy can have the effect of causing the mother to appear inflexible, as she expresses reluctance to "meet him in the middle." Battered mothers report to us that they sometimes make agreements in such circumstances that they believe are unfair or potentially harmful to their children, out of fear of the batterer or out of concern that the mediator will report to the judge that the batterer is being more willing to negotiate than she is (see also Liss & Stahly, 1993). Compromises that a battered mother makes in such circumstances may be used against her later, as in one case of ours in which the custody evaluator reportedly said to the mother, "If he's so dangerous, why did you give him unsupervised visitation before?" At the same time, a battered mother who does insist early in the legal process on supervised or restricted visitation may be accused of having been invested from the start in cutting the father off from his children.

Finally, mediation sessions can be opportunities for a batterer to intimidate his former partner with hostile facial expressions, muttered threats, and degrading accusations. Lawyers representing batterers sometimes act as arms of this intimidation, laughing derisively at statements made by the battered woman, ridiculing her, or threatening her with future legal actions. Batterers may re-create prior power dynamics by dominating the discussion in the session.

Using Litigation as a Form of Abuse.   Our clients can cause severe stress for their former partners through the use of court actions. Repeated motions for increased visitation, decreased child support, or other demands can cause both emotional distress and financial hardship to the mother, including the potential for her to lose her job because of repeated absences from work for court dates. Batterers who visit little with the children or who are inconsistent about paying child support may nonetheless file motions to have the children with them on key holidays or on the children's birthdays; the threat of being apart from her children at these important life events can cause emotional anguish to a battered mother. Written statements for court, such as affidavits, can contain statements that are emotionally injurious to battered women (Ellis & Stuckless, 1996).

Using the Battered Woman's Sexual Orientation Against Her.   If a battered woman becomes involved in a relationship with another

woman after separating from the batterer, he may be able to use her
lesbianism to his advantage in court proceedings. In a case that we
were involved in, the batterer was able to secure a court order prohibiting the woman from allowing the children to have any contact
with her new partner, although he had no such restrictions. In a case
from Florida cited by Fray-Witzer (1999), a judge awarded custody of
an 11-year-old girl to her father, who was a convicted murderer, on
the grounds that the girl should not be raised by lesbians.

Using Actions in One Court to His Advantage in Another. We
observe, for example, that when a charge is filed by the mother in
criminal court, the batterer may use this fact in family court as evidence of her efforts to keep him away from his children at all costs. If
he is acquitted of the criminal matter, he may be able to persuade the
family court that the allegation was malicious, and because judges and
jurors in criminal cases "expect more corroboration of physical
injuries in domestic violence cases than in other serious crimes," the
chances of such an acquittal are high (Gender Bias Study Committee,
1989, p. 587). Similarly, the batterer may be able to escape accountability in the criminal court by claiming, for example, that the woman
is bringing the criminal charges to gain leverage in the custody battle.
Clients of ours have sometimes told explicit lies in criminal court
regarding actions or dispositions in a family court, or vice versa.

Involving His Own Parents. We receive an increasing number of
reports of cases where the parents of batterers seek grandparent
visitation, thus increasing the emotional and financial stress for the
battered mother, reducing her time with her children, and increasing
the father's access to the children.

Additional Tactics for Discrediting Reports of Abuse

We wish to examine briefly a few important additional tactics
used by some batterers to discredit the mother's concerns. We begin
with the increasing use of the claim of *parental alienation,* a term used
to account for some cases in which children disclose sexual abuse or
refuse to visit with a batterer. In some cases, mothers may be accused
of alienating their children because they have given them accurate
information regarding the history of domestic violence. We believe that
such accusations overlook the potential benefits to children's recovery
of access to basic facts about the abuse in the home; in the case that
opens this chapter, for example, the batterer's repeated statements to

the children that the mother had falsely accused him of violence were causing them to become mistrustful and resentful toward her. Therefor, correcting the batterer's dishonest statements was critical to preventing him from damaging the children's relationships with their mother.

Mothers are sometimes accused of parental alienation for reporting domestic violence, physical abuse, or sexual abuse of their children to the court, and they may lose custody in these cases (Jaffe & Geffner, 1998). No scientific basis exists for the application of parental alienation theories to such cases (APA Presidential Task Force, 1996). In a criticism of the inappropriate use of the parental alienation concept, Jaffe and Geffner (1998) wrote, "In our professional experience in over 20 years of completing custody and visitation assessments, the nonidentification of domestic violence in divorce cases is the source of the real problems that occur" (p. 381).

Some batterers claim that children's resistance to visitation is the product of the mother's anxiety, which may reverse cause and effect. Mothers often do have appropriate anxieties about sending their children on visits with the batterer, especially in cases in which the children have made worrisome reports to her about past visits or are exhibiting signs of distress. Similarly, claims that enmeshment (mutual overdependence) exists between the mother and the child may be used to account for a child's reluctance to leave the mother to attend visitation, without attending to the possibility that the child's difficulty in separating is related to previous distressing experiences during visitation or to the effects of witnessing incidents of violence. Children who are victims of sexual abuse also have been observed to cling to their mothers (Finkelhor & Browne, cited in de Young, 1986).

As another tactic for discrediting the mother's concerns in custody evaluations, batterers can create skepticism by stating that the mother's allegations of domestic violence or of child abuse did not arise until the couple separated. However, it is widely recognized that battered woman sometimes tell no one about the abuse prior to separation because of shame, fear, and many other factors (Dalton, 1999). There are important reasons why child abuse reports may first arise at separation or divorce, including the fact that the mother's growing awareness of the batterer's mistreatment of the children sometimes is the precipitator of the separation (Jaffe & Geffner, 1998). Children also may disclose long-standing abuse at this time (Faller, 1991; MacFarlane & Waterman, 1986) because of their fear of being placed in the abuser's custody or of spending increased time alone with him. Another possibility is that child abuse may begin or intensify after separation because of an abuser's desire to punish or to harass his former partner (Faller, 1991; MacFarlane & Waterman, 1986), and a number of battered mothers have reported to us that they have returned to the abuser because he was abusing, neglecting, or threatening the children during visitation (see also Liss & Stahly, 1993).

Less common but apparently increasing are accusations of Factitious Disorder by Proxy (or "Munchausen by Proxy"), a type of psychological abuse in which a parent leads a child to think of herself or himself as chronically ill. This is a rare and complex syndrome, but it has been concluded to be present in some cases on the basis of poor evidence or of an inadequate understanding of the nature of the disorder (Mart, 1999). Batterers sometimes raise an allegation of Factitious Disorder by Proxy to account for children's negative reactions to visitation.

Finally, batterers in our cases often attribute a mother's allegations of child maltreatment to interparental tensions. However, evaluators should examine the possibility of opposite causality, with the escalating conflict between the parents resulting from the mother's efforts to intercede on her children's behalf. As one study of battered mothers found,

> The mothers' empathy with their children's needs pushed them toward confrontation with their husbands when the children became targets of their fathers' overwhelming needs or anger. The mothers then decided to take action on behalf of their children that they had not taken for themselves. (Ayoub et al., 1991, p. 204)

EFFECTS ON CHILDREN OF CUSTODY LITIGATION

The negative effects on children of custody and visitation litigation are widely recognized (Wallerstein & Blakeslee, 1989; Johnston and Campbell, 1988). In the context of domestic violence, professionals should be particularly alert to the insecurity that litigation causes to children regarding where they will be living; the stress caused to the mother, which can affect her parenting; the heavy demands on the mother's time that litigation can cause; economic hardships that can result from legal expenses and missed work; profound internal conflicts for the children regarding what to say to custody evaluators; and pressure or manipulation from either or both parents, which tends particularly to be applied by batterers. Custody litigation gives the batterer and the court a great deal of power over the life of the battered woman, and trauma survivors can experience setbacks in their recovery when they are forced to enter situations in which they are once again experiencing disempowerment (Herman, 1992). Thus, a batterer who pursues custody can compound the destructive effects that his past conduct has had on the family.

The risk that custody will be awarded to a batterer has the further effect of causing many battered women to feel forced to stay with abusive partners (Crites & Coker, 1988). Liss and Stahly (1993) reported that 20% of battered mothers involved in custody litigation stated that they had returned to the batterer at least once in the past due to his threats to hurt or take the children, and numerous partners of our clients have told us that the fear of losing custody is a prime reason why they delay leaving. Thus, the systemic failure to protect battered mothers from losing custody may be a contributor to keeping children in situations that are traumatizing them.

SUMMARY

Separation or divorce between a batterer and a battered mother does not reliably increase the safety and well-being of children, especially in cases where the batterer is the children's legal father with the right to pursue visitation or custody. Systemic responses by family courts, child protective services, therapists, and other human service professionals play a critical role in determining whether the separation will ultimately contribute to the children's safety and healing or will instead create a context for children and their mother to be further victimized. Batterers are sometimes able to take advantage of societal ambivalence toward mothers who attempt to protect their children from abusive fathers. The process of custody and visitation litigation itself can become a form of continued abuse of the mother, with important secondary effects on the children. Court personnel and custody evaluators sometimes lack a sophisticated understanding of the dynamics of domestic violence and its effects on family functioning or of the dynamics of trauma in general. Thorough investigation of allegations of domestic violence or child abuse is sometimes lacking, with courts relying instead on psychological testing or on stereotypes regarding abusers and victims. The risk to children from batterers is often underestimated, especially in cases of "lower-level" violence. Improved policies and practices in various areas are necessary to strengthen the ability of battered mothers to protect their children from the effects of unsupervised exposure to their battering fathers.

6

The Mismeasure of Batterers as Parents

A Critique of Prevailing Theories of Assessment

Responses by courts, child protective services, and therapists to the parenting of batterers, particularly after separation, can be influenced in problematic directions by currently influential models of assessment. These models are largely a product of the misapplication of prevailing theories of divorce and separation to cases involving domestic violence. At the root of these theoretical problems appears to be a failure to recognize domestic violence as a highly specialized field to which models and theories from other disciplines cannot be readily applied.

We center our discussion on the theories and recommendations proposed by Janet Johnston, Linda Campbell, Vivienne Roseby, and Richard Gardner. We choose these as our focal points for a number of reasons. First, the theories of these four authors effectively capture many of the critical problems with which we are familiar in the professional misreading of postseparation dynamics. Second, these theories have a large and growing influence over practice in courts, supervised visitation services, and therapy clinics that work in the divorce field. For example, prior to our own work (see Chapter 7), the only published guide to assessing risk to children from batterers was based primarily on Janet Johnston's typology of batterers (Massachusetts Domestic Violence Visitation Task Force, 1994, distributed by the Association of Family and Conciliation Courts), and a prominent custody evaluator recommended that this same formulation be used in making custody determinations in domestic violence cases (Stahl, 1999). A recent issue of *Family Courts Review* was devoted to the theme of parental alienation, a concept that grows from the work of Richard Gardner; Gardner's work on parental alienation has also been cited by Stahl (1999, 1994) and other writers (e.g., Vestal, 1999; Garrity & Baris, 1994), shaping their recommendations for working with families after separation. Finally, three of these four authors have made concrete observations regarding family dynamics in domestic violence cases that are strikingly similar to our own, although they have reached conclusions that contrast sharply with ours.

INFLUENTIAL THEORIES OF DIVORCE

The Concept of "High-Conflict Divorce"

A critical theoretical underpinning to existing approaches to evaluating the parenting of batterers is the widely used concept of "high-conflict divorce," which is elucidated by Johnston and Campbell (1988) (see also Garrity & Baris, 1994). Johnston and Campbell propose various dynamics in couples involved in ongoing custody and visitation conflicts, with the following central elements: (a) Both parents are likely to have personality disorders or more severe psychopathology, largely as a result of unresolved childhood issues; (b) the parents' additional unresolved feelings regarding their failed relationship are being channeled into fighting over the children; (c) each parent has developed a distorted, exaggeratedly negative view of the other, leading to mistrust; (d) cycles of reaction and counterreaction have set in between the parents, leading to further erosion of trust; and (e) children are feeling under pressure to take sides and may attempt to relieve that pressure by choosing to please one parent.

However, Johnston and Campbell (1988) have also found that a history of domestic violence is present in approximately 75% of intractable custody conflicts. Thus, many of the characteristics that the authors consider to be inherent to "high-conflict divorce" may actually be the dynamics of domestic violence. Below, we will examine several of the cases presented by Johnston and Campbell that suggest that precisely this error is taking place. Because of the contamination of this and similar studies by the inclusion of a substantial percentage of domestic violence cases, we consider the phrase "high-conflict divorce" to lack rigor at this point. In addition, we find that in many cases of ongoing custody and visitation litigation, neither parent exhibits signs of psychopathology in testing or evaluation. Finally, we observe on a recurring basis that the more appropriately a battered mother seeks to further the needs and interests of her children, the greater the apparent likelihood that she will have a highly conflictual relationship with the father after separation. It is our belief that the above theoretical outlook does not take this dynamic into adequate account.

The Assumption of Mutual Causation of Ongoing Custody Litigation

Underpinning many theories of divorce is the assumption that intractable conflicts over children are the product of inappropriate behaviors by both parents. For example, even in cases identified by Johnston and Campbell (1988) as involving "violence and abuse," they attribute the difficulties to "dysfunctional families" rather than to the abuser's behavior (p. xv). The authors describe parents in such families as "severely limited in their capacity to cooperate" (p. xv), without discussion of the barriers to successful cooperation with a batterer. Even in the more recent work by Johnston and Roseby (1997), domestic violence is discussed only as a *result* of poor relationship dynamics and never as a *cause*.

The following case example used by Johnston and Campbell (1988) illustrates the practice errors that can follow from an assumption of mutual responsibility for conflicts.

> One man broke into a sweat and threatened to kill his wife when his contribution to their conflict was broached. "I have had it! Next time I am going to shoot her! I just want to live in peace and quiet. I've been talking, but no one has been listening!" Realizing the extreme gravity of this threat, given this man's rage, the counselors immediately responded by taking responsibility for the situation that he found intolerable. They agreed to call an emergency meeting of the attorneys, help him obtain a restraining order against her provocations, warn his former wife that he had reached his limit, and then persuaded him to rid himself of his gun. (p. 100)

The above description implies that the counselors participated in communicating the man's threat to his partner, which is of considerable concern to us, as are various other aspects of the intervention.

Similar examples of the pitfalls of assuming mutuality appear at other points in Johnston and Campbell (1988). For example, the authors' only discussion of restraining orders is to state that spouses with "paranoid tendencies" sometimes seek them (p. 17). In a case example, the authors state that a father named Martin had pointed a gun at his partner Judith and on two other occasions had physically assaulted her, yet they analyze the causes of these incidents as mutual. They state that Martin and Judith had constructed "somewhat irrational images" of each other (p. 22), implying that Martin's threatening of Judith with a gun is not an adequate basis for her to fear him.

In another case example, the father, Keith, tried to choke the mother, Mary, on their final night together, and he then "smashed every mirror in the house" before leaving. Following this incident, Keith would call Mary "twenty and thirty times a day" for weeks, alternating between asking her to reunify with him and leaving death threats on her answering machine (p. 217). The authors then criticize Mary's inability 18 months later to share the authors' belief that Keith had changed, although they also acknowledge that he was continuing to use "occasional physical abuse" (p. 218). The counselors went so far as to focus with Mary on her "inordinate and excessive fears" regarding her child's safety. The questionable judgment used by the counselors in taking the above approach is indicated further by their own assessment of the father, in which they state the following:

> We had considerable doubts as to this father's longer-term capacity to be responsive to his son. As the boy grew older and sought to separate and develop independent views, we predicted that this man would be very threatened and this child would be increasingly exposed to the father's erratic behavior. (p. 219)

It is thus unclear why the mother's concerns were considered unfounded.

Johnston and Campbell (1988) describe their findings that some parents with higher psychopathology handle shared parenting after separation better than do some of those with lower psychopathology, calling into question their fundamental thesis that psychopathology is the driving force behind intractable postseparation conflicts. Notably, the authors' observations in this regard are consistent with our own, as we have stated that many batterers who are low in psychopathology are among those whose high entitlement, irresponsibility, and other characteristics are causing the most serious postseparation problems.

Discrediting of Concerns
Raised by Mothers and Children Regarding Visitation

Existing theories of divorce and separation often carry the under-lying assumption that mothers and children are usually exaggerating or distorting their concerns about the father's parenting. Johnston and Campbell (1988), for example, offer various explanations for children's reluctance to visit with the noncustodial parent in "high-conflict" cases, none of which has to do with the father's abusiveness. The authors describe such factors as the child's loyalty or protective-ness toward one parent and the child's desire to relieve ambivalent feelings by casting one parent as all good and the other as all bad. The authors made no reference to other possible causes of reluctance to visit, such as appropriate self-protectiveness.

Johnston and Campbell (1988) take a similar critical outlook on mothers who attempt to restrict contact between their children and a batterer. Through dozens of case descriptions, they fail to offer even one in which a mother acts as an appropriate protective parent after separation. In one revealing case example, the authors describe a girl named Wendy who had witnessed "numerous occasions" on which her father had physically abused her mother. However, the father had become clean and sober and his violence was now "only sporadic," and the child recognized that the father was "much improved" (p. 148). The authors are critical of the mother for her inability to see how much better the father was doing. The authors fail to explain why "sporadic violence" is not adequate cause for the mother's continued concern.

"Parental Alienation"

Johnston and Roseby (1997) devote a full chapter to the subject of children who become alienated from one parent, focusing on the role of the custodial parent in causing that alienation and on the role of children's internal loyalty conflicts. They appear to underestimate the role that domestic violence or child abuse may play in children's alien-ation from an abusive parent. For example, the authors state,

> Most rejected parents are not only hurt but highly affronted, even outraged, by the child's challenge to their authority and the lack of respect accorded them. Some try to reassert their parental position by force, which can end in physical struggles with the child. (p. 199)

This last sentence appears to be a reference to physical abuse of the child, yet the father's physical abusiveness is apparently considered the result rather than the cause of the child's desire for distance.

Johnston and Roseby describe the alienated parent as focused on authoritarian control and unable to attend to the child's underlying feelings, yet they seem largely to ignore the role of these parenting weaknesses in causing the alienation. In a revealing analysis of how domestic violence is framed in theories of parental alienation, they argue that children exposed to battering relieve their internal conflicts by casting the father as entirely to blame for the violence and the mother as entirely innocent. Thus, Johnston and Roseby characterize as pathological what we would consider a healthy view; in fact, we believe that an important aspect of children's recovery from exposure to batterers is their overcoming of the blaming of their mother and of themselves.

Crucial elements of the "mutual causality" perspective are captured in Johnston and Roseby's description of the case of Julianne, in which the authors acknowledge that the father's abusiveness and controlling behavior toward the daughter were unrelenting after separation despite efforts at therapeutic intervention. The authors' ending summary of the case states incongruously that Julianne's case illustrates *the impact of interparental conflict on the child* rather than the impact of the father's abusiveness. This regrettable tendency to assign blame equally to the nonoffending parent has important implications for battered women and their children.

Finally, Johnston and Roseby (1997) state that alienation from one parent occurs in children who have had early developmental failures with respect to individuation. We have often observed the opposite to be true, where the strongest and most independent children are among those refusing to visit with their battering fathers. These are sometimes families in which the batterer has not succeeded in causing divisions between the siblings and between mothers and their children. Thus, allegations of parental alienation sometimes arise in cases involving families with the best prospects for collective recovery, and such allegations may be used by the batterer to interfere with that progress.

The concept of parental alienation as it is currently used was first proposed by psychiatrist Richard Gardner (1987). The influence of Gardner's theories has been widely noted (Dallam, 2000; Myers, 1997a, 1997b; Rotgers & Barrett, 1996; Faller, 1988). Gardner (1991) states that "parental alienation syndrome" (PAS) is found almost exclusively in mothers and is used to gain revenge against former husbands. Gardner is particularly focused on sexual abuse allegations as indications of mothers' attempts to alienate their children from the father. His outlook regarding sexual abuse allegations is illuminated by his assertion that "the vast majority of children who profess sexual abuse are fabricators" (1987, p. 274) and by his section titled "The Child as Initiator," in which he states that children sometimes falsely accuse an adult of sexual abuse to retaliate against the adult for refusing *the child's* sexual advances (1987).

In cases of alienation, Gardner (1987) recommends "immediate transfer [of the child] by the court to the home of the so-called hated parent. . . . Often I will recommend a month or so of absolutely no contact with the 'loved parent,' with the exception of short telephone calls a few times a week" (p. 257). It should be noted that in virtually all of the cases that Gardner discusses, the abrupt break in contact that he proposes involves removing a child from the primary caretaker, yet he did not express concern about the possible traumatic effects of such an abrupt rupture in the child's primary attachment.

Gardner's apparent gender bias is further indicated by his contrasting proposals for responding to sexually abusing fathers and to alienating mothers. With respect to sexually abusing fathers, he writes that "the sexual exploitation has to be put on the negative list, but positives as well must be appreciated," and he emphasizes the importance of continuing the child's contact with the sexually abusing father and building the father-child relationship (cited in Dallam, 2000, p. 83). However, discussing cases in which mothers are found to be alienators, Gardner does not express parallel concerns about possible positive aspects of her relationship with her children; rather, he recommends complete breaks in contact with the mother, or such punitive steps as juvenile detention for children who refuse to go on visits with their father.

Gardner states in his writings that his formulations are based entirely on clinical observations rather than on research (e.g., 1987). Although we agree that important theoretical advances can be made through clinical work, the underlying assumptions of the observer can have a large impact on what he or she concludes. We therefore find it crucial that professionals who rely on Gardner's work look closely at the perspective revealed by his statements, such as the ones reviewed above.

Professionals who handle domestic violence cases should be aware of the impact of Gardner's theories on the practice of courts and custody evaluators. A comprehensive and insightful overview and analysis of Gardner's work with respect to parental alienation and assessment of incest allegations, and its regrettable influence on court practice, is available in Dallam (2000).

It is interesting to note that Janet Johnston's long-time colleague Judith Wallerstein has specifically criticized the tendency to overlook children's intrinsic reasons for their outlook.

> In our experience, the courts and the legal profession in America have been overly committed to an implicit perspective of children as passive vessels of parental attitudes and interests. To the contrary, children bring their own responses and their own feelings, perceptions, and conclusions to the crises within their families. . . . [T]he courts are all too willing to see the child's responses as reflecting adults' manipulation. (Wallerstein & Tanke, 1996, pp. 307, 328)

Underestimating the Risk of Child Sexual Abuse

We find that a widespread belief exists among professionals that allegations of sexual abuse during separation or divorce have a low level of credibility. This outlook seems to be reflected in the work of Johnston, Campbell, and Roseby, who make numerous references to reasons to discount a child's sexualized behaviors or disclosures of sexual abuse, without offering suggestions for how to distinguish cases where sexual abuse may be a reality (see, for example, Johnston & Roseby, 1997, Chap. 5).

It should be noted that observations made by these authors appear to confirm the risk of incest perpetration by batterers, but such observations are expressed in language that partially attributes responsibility to the child. Regarding domestic violence cases, for example, Johnston and Campbell (1993b) write,

> [The girls younger than 7 or 8 years of age] had repressed or intrusive memories of violent incidents, which were the basis for their realistic fears and phobic avoidance of their fathers. At the same time, these little girls often had "princesslike" relationships with their fathers, many of whom intermittently lavished attention on their daughters, while at other times being preoccupied with their own needs. This resulted in a great deal of confusion for the child; many of these girls appeared to have a double image of the father, viewing him both as a loving suitor and as a scary, dangerous man. In general, there were poor boundaries between these men and their daughters, especially among the substance-abusing men, with mutual seductiveness and provocation of his aggression. These fathers needed validation of their masculinity and attractiveness; they pulled for this affirmation from their little daughters, who became watchful and oriented to managing the father's narcissistic equilibrium and anger. (p. 287)

Johnston and Roseby (1997) focus one section on cases involving fathers who maintain poor boundaries with their daughters, including a case example in which the father frequently exposed himself to the child and another in which the father used his daughter to meet his "needs for intimacy" (p. 122). The authors state that girls in these kinds of cases sometimes start refusing to go on visits with the father because of internal conflicts, including their fear of stimulating the mother's jealousy by becoming the "Oedipal victor" (p. 122), their absorption of the mother's negative views of the father, and their desire to appease the mother. The authors do not discuss the possibility that the father's sexualization of the father-daughter relationship could be a reason for the daughter's reluctance to visit with him, nor do they mention the possibility that the boundary violations may have been indicators of more serious violations that the child had not yet felt ready to disclose. Last, they disregard the possibility that a child's overattachment to her mother could be a symptom of sexual abuse that has in fact occurred (de Young, 1986) rather than the cause of a false allegation or overreaction.

This apparent tendency to underestimate the risk of sexual abuse and to disbelieve children's reports appears to have grown partly from an underlying outdated Freudian perspective (Myers, 1997b). Johnston and Roseby (1997) state, for example, that girls fantasize about having sex with their fathers. Johnston and Campbell (1988) endorse the theory of the Oedipus complex, stating that the sexuality of young girls and boys is directed toward the parent of the opposite sex and that children wish to be the exclusive love object of that parent and to triumph over the competition of the same-sex parent. It should be noted that the theory of the Oedipus complex was developed by Freud in order to account for and to discredit the high rate of incest victimization that his adult female clients were reporting to him (Myers, 1997a; Herman, 1992; Masson, 1984).

Johnston and Roseby (1997) devote a chapter to a discussion of how children's distress over "high-conflict" divorce can lead to sexualized behaviors, basing these conclusions partly on Oedipal theory. The authors do not explain how they have ruled out sexual abuse in these cases, which would be especially important given their own observations of the tendency of batterers (and other fathers in "high-conflict" divorce) to sexualize their relationships with children (see also Johnston & Campbell, 1993b, p. 287, quoted above). It is true that children sometimes do respond to periods of high stress in their lives by beginning or increasing masturbation, but several of the cases described by Johnston, Campbell, and Roseby involve more serious indicators of possible sexual abuse, as we have seen.

We have observed the apparent effects of these theories in two cases handled by an evaluator who has stated that she relies on Johnston and Roseby's work. In one case, in which the child reportedly inserted her finger in her vagina (not a typical masturbation behavior in young girls) and then disclosed sexual abuse by her battering father, the evaluator dismissed the child's behaviors as "self-soothing responses" to the stress caused by the postseparation tension between the parents. In the second case, the evaluator acknowledged that the battering father in fact had sexually abused his young son, but she stated that the child was no longer affected by the violations and was now suffering only from the effects of interparental conflict.

Two other concerns regarding incest risk call for examination. First, Johnston and Roseby (1997) state, "If [sexual] abuse has occurred, the perpetrator's concern that the child may now disclose the facts in treatment can limit further incident" (p. 139). However, little is actually known about how a perpetrator's behavior is affected by his knowledge that the child is attending therapy; indeed, what has been established is that children have tremendous difficulty disclosing sexual abuse to professionals (DeVoe & Faller, 1999). Furthermore, in cases when the children do disclose, unsupervised (or poorly supervised) contact between the child and the perpetrator can provide an opportunity for the perpetrator to manipulate the child into recanting. Children sometimes are burdened with guilt about the effects that their disclosures have already had on the father or on the family, and so they may be highly reluctant to make new ones. We have been involved in a number of cases in which unsupervised visitation was granted on the questionable grounds that the child would be likely to disclose to the therapist if new sexual offenses were to take place. Follow-up studies of sexual abuse prevention education show only limited benefits (Reppucci & Haugaard, 1993), underlining the risks involved in relying on children to be able to protect themselves from sexual abuse.

Second, Johnston and Roseby (1997) state that children's sexualized behaviors after divorce could be a product of exposure to sexual contact in their parents' relationships with new partners and that such new relationships are "often conducted in an erotically charged and exhibitionistic atmosphere" (p. 134). No basis was offered for this serious claim, despite the risks involved in providing evaluators with an additional reason to dismiss sexual abuse concerns.

The implied, and sometimes explicit, criticism by all four of the above authors of mothers who support their children's sexual abuse allegations is particularly unfortunate given evidence that victims of sexual abuse recover more quickly when their mothers believe them and take protective action (review in Kendell-Tackett, Williams, & Finkelhor, 1993). In addition, these theorists draw attention to purported psychopathology in many women bringing allegations of incest, failing to examine the possible trauma to the mother from learning of the sexual victimization of her child, the tendency of the mother's symptoms to abate if the sexual abuse of the child stops, and the possible trauma to the mother of failure by the legal system to protect the child adequately (Newberger et al., 1993).

Improved Communication as the Solution

Present throughout the work of Johnston, Roseby, and Campbell is the assumption that improved communication between the parents will reduce the child's postseparation distress and make it easier for the child to visit with the noncustodial parent. This insight, although useful in certain contexts, is erroneous if applied to cases involving abuse. For example, it is appropriate for a mother to use caution in deciding how much information to give a batterer regarding a child's statements or behaviors, as she needs to be concerned about the possibility that the child will be retaliated against, pressured, or shamed by the batterer. Increased communication with a batterer can lead to brief improvements for the child during a period when the batterer is behaving more positively, but over time it often has the effect of drawing the mother into exposure to his verbal abuse, manipulation, and coercion. As we have seen in Chapter 3, pressuring a battered mother to reinvolve herself in unhealthy patterns of interaction with the batterer is likely to be detrimental to her mental health and thus to have negative repercussions for her children over time. Furthermore, improved communication cannot solve a batterer's problems of self-centered, neglectful, or abusive parenting and his teaching of destructive values to the children. There is no substitute for addressing such issues through appropriate specialized batterer intervention services. Approaches that push battered women into increased communication with the batterer overlook the important role that the battered mother's recovery and long-term freedom from abuse play in the well-being of her children.

THE USE OF A DOMESTIC VIOLENCE TYPOLOGY
TO ASSESS RISK TO CHILDREN

Johnston, Campbell, and Roseby have proposed a typology of domestic violence cases that purports to possess predictive value for the long-term well-being of children (Johnston & Roseby, 1997; Johnston & Campbell, 1993a, 1993b). Johnston and Campbell (1993b) state that this typology can be used in determining which cases are appropriate for joint custody (or sole custody to the batterer) and which are not, an assertion that has been echoed by other evaluators (e.g., Stahl, 1999). Prior to examining this typology, we wish to draw attention to a fundamental underlying problem: The only postseparation risk to children from batterers identified by the authors is the risk of exposure to continued violence by the batterer toward the mother. In fact, however, postseparation risks are many, including the risk of physical, sexual, or psychological abuse of the children by the batterer and the risk that he will undermine the mother-child relationships that are so critical to children's recovery. Because of this fundamental oversight, the formulation below would be inadequate even without the multiple additional weaknesses that are present.

Johnston, Campbell, and Roseby have divided batterers into the following five categories: type A, "Ongoing or Episodic Male Battering"; type B, "Female-Initiated Violence"; type C, "Male Controlled Interactive Violence"; type D, "Separation and Postdivorce Violence"; and type E, "Psychotic and Paranoid Reactions" (Johnston & Roseby, 1997; Johnston & Campbell, 1993a, 1993b). These five types are followed closely in the risk assessment published by the Association of Family and Conciliation Courts (Massachusetts Domestic Violence Visitation Task Force, 1994), although the types are given modified names. Because type E represents only a tiny percentage of cases, we will not consider it in any detail here. We examine the most important problems in the first four types below.

Type A, "Ongoing or Episodic Male Battering"

The authors describe this first type of battering as involving violence at "life-threatening levels" and state that this type "most closely resembles the battering spouse/battered wife syndrome, which has been well described in the literature." They describe the battering problem as internal to the man in origin, stating that the women who are victims of this chronic battering "did not generally provoke, initiate, or escalate the physical abuse." However, "a subgroup of them did not tolerate the abuse. Instead, they left the marital relationship early, soon after the abuse was first manifest. These were assertive women with high self-esteem and good reality testing" (Johnston & Campbell, 1993a, pp. 193–194). No factors other than self-esteem and reality testing are mentioned as playing any role in affecting women's ability to leave batterers. This oversight suggests an ignorance of the bulk of literature on battered women, in which various critical obstacles to leaving a batterer have been identified, including economic constraints, the woman's level of fear for her life, her concern about losing custody of her children, the quality of law enforcement response in her community, cultural or religious obstacles, traumatic bonding, and many others (e.g., Davies et al., 1998; Ulrich, 1998; Rosen, 1996; Kirkwood, 1993). Attempting to leave a batterer raises a particularly difficult set of obstacles for battered women that have children (Schechter & Edleson, 1998).

According to Johnston, Campbell, and Roseby, type A batterers are dangerous for unsupervised visitation, which is a positive step. However, both our clinical experience and the available research indicate that a very small percentage of domestic violence cases fit the restrictive criteria defining this category, which requires near-lethal violence and a woman whose behavior is never "provoking"; we have rarely seen such a case among the approximately 2,000 batterers with whom we have worked. Only a small minority of batterers use such extreme violence. Many dangerous batterers, such as those who use an escalating pattern of lethal threats but do not frequently carry out actual attacks, would not fit this criteria; several domestic violence homicides of which we have been aware have followed such a pattern. Furthermore, few victims are completely free of incidents in which they fight back, yell, challenge the batterer's authority, or engage in other behaviors that batterers define as provocations; thus, under the authors' formulation, highly dangerous batterers can be excluded from this category because of the behavior of the *victim*. We discourage professionals from basing their assessment of a batterer's dangerousness to his partner (or former partner) or to his children on the victim's behavior to any degree.

Type B, "Female-Initiated Violence"

The second type of domestic violence described by Johnston, Campbell, and Roseby involves women who have initiated all of the physical assaults and whose outbursts have been repetitive during the marriage, although the man may have been violent as well.

> In some cases, the man lost control, especially during the separation period, and no longer sought to placate or prevent the outbursts, eventually responding in kind to the woman's attacks. The effects of these physical exchanges were not minor; the majority escalated to high or severe levels of violence. (Johnston & Campbell, 1993a, p. 195)

However, the authors also state, "Few of these women did much physical damage with their violence: broken cups, torn clothing, and scratched faces were common" (p. 195). The appearance of gender bias should be noted here, as men who have violent partners are not defined as provoking the woman's violence in contrast to how the authors view provocation by females, even in cases where the men become highly violent themselves.

According to the authors, type B women did not describe themselves as fearful, simplifying the assessment process somewhat. However, we more commonly find cases in which a woman admits to having been the first to hit on many or most occasions but continues to assert that she is physically afraid of her partner and that she has suffered a pattern of psychological abuse. In such a case, the evaluator needs to assess the power dynamics of the relationship carefully, including the history of threats, psychological abuse, and injuries sustained, which the authors seem to overlook.

Type C, "Male Controlled Interactive Violence"

The third category is the critical one, as the great majority of domestic violence cases would tend to be placed here by professionals who attempt to apply this typology. Johnston and Campbell (1993a) state that the violence in this type of relationship results from "mutual verbal provocation" (p. 195) in which both sides hurl insults and yell at each other, building toward a violent episode.

> It was common for the woman to end up by screaming or trying to leave the scene. If she started screaming, her spouse would typically slap her in a misguided effort to quell her "hysteria." In this sense, he tended to see her as a child who needed to be disciplined or controlled "for her own good." If she tried to leave or refused to communicate with him, this would trigger attempts by the man to control her by pinning her down or blocking the exit. By virtue of their superior strength, these men essentially coerced and dominated their mates and were more likely to inflict injury, whereupon the women became their victims. (p. 196)

It is not clear to us that the above incident can correctly be characterized as the product of "mutual verbal provocation," given that the man used violence to prevent the woman from leaving and given her prior efforts to stop participating in the argument. Later in their description of this type of batterer, the authors state that the women often "resisted their [partners'] efforts at control." By this definition, the great majority of batterers with whom we have worked would be placed in this category.

The distinction between this category and type A, "ongoing or episodic male battering" (what we might call the "true batterer"), is unclear. The authors suggest that the first type of batterer is seeking power and control, whereas the batterer in this third category is responding inappropriately to mutual conflict. However, this distinction is inconsistent with the description above, in which the man sees the woman "as a child who needed to be disciplined or controlled" and attempts "to control her" by pinning or knocking her down. The authors state further that men in this category use violence to gain "their goal of compliance" and that "the exercise of physical control was seen as legitimate by the male" (p. 195) and that these men believe that the "male's role as husband and father should be authoritarian and dictatorial, if necessary" (Johnston & Campbell, 1993b, p. 292). All of these characteristics would appear to make a man fit the type A kind of batterer but here are used to describe the type C batterer, whose violence is "mutually provoked." Construct validity with respect to the batterer thus seems to be lacking.

Furthermore, it should be noted that those battered mothers who have the greatest worries for their children and who thus may be the most forceful in attempting to challenge the batterer's abusive behavior may be among the ones most likely to be defined as "mutually abusive" through the use of this typology.

According to Johnston and Campbell (1993a), "Interestingly, in a subgroup of this [third] profile of violence there seemed to be a degree of sexual excitement generated by their mutual brawls," and they provide a case example in which both parties allegedly derive "erotic pleasure" from the verbal abuse (p. 196). The authors do not state how they have concluded that the woman found the verbal abuse sexually exciting, nor do they state what percentage of cases included this dynamic. The authors are perhaps unaware of the sexual coercion that often accompanies battering, with rape present in 20% to 45% of battering cases (Campbell, 1995b; review in Bowker, 1983). Our clinical experience indicates that sexual coercion below the level of rape is present in an even higher percentage. It is true that some batterers do find violence sexually exciting, but research has demonstrated that they are among the *most* dangerous (Campbell, Soeken, et al., 1998).

Many batterers insist on having sex after abuse, and a battered woman should not be thought of as free to decline sex at such a time, given her awareness of his capacity for violence and her trauma from the abuse that has just occurred.

The authors' conclusions about the implications of their research for children are perhaps the most unfounded of their claims, particularly with respect to the distinction between type A and type C battering. Johnston and Campbell (1993b) state that children who are exposed to type C battering may be appropriately placed in the sole or joint custody of the batterer, depending on the circumstances, offering no rationale for this conclusion. They also state (1993a) that type C batterers are less likely to perpetrate postseparation violence, with no supporting data.

Type D, "Separation and Postdivorce Violence"

In Johnston and Campbell's fourth category of domestic violence, the batterer becomes violent as a result of the stress of divorce: "In this category, the violence was not ongoing or repetitive. In fact, it was limited to one, two, or several incidents, albeit sometimes very serious ones, around the time of the separation or divorce" (1993a, p. 197). The authors state further that in this type of case, there is a "good prognosis" for healthy parent-child relationships after the divorce (1993b, p. 294), thereby suggesting that a batterer in this category is not likely to be dangerous to his children.

Several problems are present in this construct. First, in some cases a woman leaves a relationship because a pattern of mounting intimidation by the abuser has finally escalated to violence. In such a case, the separation is the *result* of the violence, not the cause. Second, the fact of separation can make many batterers highly volatile, because of their entitlement and possessiveness (see Chapters 1 and 5). Violence in response to separation is not correctly seen as a sign of lower dangerousness in the long term; in fact, the literature on lethality assessment of batterers uniformly indicates that those abusers whose violence escalates in response to the ending of a relationship are particularly dangerous in the ensuing period (Websdale, 1999; Daly & Wilson, 1988) and that there is a high risk that children will be exposed to the batterer's violence or become direct targets of it (Langford et al., 1999).

Additional Problems Present in This Typology

Analysis of Johnston, Campbell, and Roseby's findings regarding their five categories of domestic violence is made difficult by the sparseness of the data that they provide. The earlier publication (Johnston & Campbell, 1993a) includes no data tables and offers no numbers of cases for each category. The second publication (Johnston & Campbell, 1993b) provides one data table regarding outcomes for children among the different types but does not label which differences are statistically significant. The authors state, "Although not all of the findings reached statistically significant levels of difference, the children's adjustment was fairly consistent with theoretical predictions" (p. 296). However, examination of the data table reveals that girls actually fared better if they came from type A homes than from type C homes, further limiting the usefulness of this model.

Our clinical experience indicates that the great majority of domestic violence cases do not properly meet any of the definitions provided for in these five categories. Although most batterers do exercise "chronic pervasive control," as the type A batterer is presented as doing, their physical violence usually does not rise to "life-threatening" levels. For their part, most victims periodically fight back physically, yell or swear in arguments, or in other ways attempt to redress the power imbalance that abuse engenders, and they do so even with those batterers who are highly violent. On this typology, however, these women can be defined as mutually provocative and thus regarded as type C victims—that is, as sharing responsibility for their own abuse.

Finally, the small sample size and lack of statistical significance of some of the findings, combined with data presented by the authors that actually contradict their own interpretations, suggest strongly that clinical practice and court response should not be based on this formulation. Interestingly, Johnston and Campbell (1993b) write that their findings are "preliminary and exploratory" (p. 296), but they contradict this stance by making specific recommendations regarding custody, visitation, and therapeutic intervention based on their formulation (1993a, 1993b). To use these findings to predict future violence in batterers is inconsistent with a view of the data as preliminary and exploratory. Furthermore, Johnston (1994a) states that "the potential for future violence and the conditions under which it is likely to recur also vary among these different types or patterns" (p. 9). Unfortunately, the above typology has been used to formulate concrete proposals regarding custody and visitation policy and has sometimes been cited as a valid formulation by other writers on custody practice (e.g., Maxwell, 1999; Stahl, 1999; for a related critique of the above typology, see Dalton, 1999).

THE OVERLOOKED IMPLICATIONS OF JOHNSTON, CAMPBELL, AND ROSEBY'S OWN OBSERVATIONS

Johnston, Campbell, and Roseby's observations of the effects of domestic violence on family functioning are strikingly similar to our own, despite the contrasting conclusions that they reach. Johnston and Campbell (1993b) describe a number of the dynamics that we too have identified elsewhere in this book: (a) the tendency of young boys exposed to domestic violence to be aggressive and defiant and sometimes to be "manipulative and controlling, especially with their mothers" while simultaneously being confused and worried for her safety; (b) the tendency of early adolescent sons of battered women to explode in "rageful attacks on the mother," which are described as "reminiscent of those they had witnessed by the father," and the mothers' inability to control these boys; (c) the fact that these adolescent boys actually wished for a close relationship with their mother but were afraid of becoming "passive, weak, and victimized" as they perceived her to be; (d) the tendency both of younger and of older boys to be afraid of the batterer and "constricted and obedient" in his presence while simultaneously "attracted to him because of his power"; (e) the father's tendency to be "preoccupied with his own needs and inconsistently available to his son"; and (f) the father's tendency to give contradictory messages to his son regarding aggressiveness (all quotations from p. 290).

Further similarities between their work and ours exist, including their observations that (a) families with battering tended to have "a great many splits and alignments among the family members and . . . children's alliances kept shifting from one parent to the other," with physical fights among siblings being common; (b) the fathers tended to have "peer-like" relationships with their sons, and the boys "enjoyed a kind of 'we're men together' camaraderie that increased their self-esteem but also gave them permission to use aggression and coercion to get what they wanted, especially from their mothers and sisters"; (c) the older boys tended to have little respect for authority, particularly from their mother; and (d) the fathers tended to be more "controlling and punitive" with their daughters than with their sons (all quotations from p. 293).

These observations are divided roughly evenly between type A batterers (the first paragraph in this section) and type C batterers (the second paragraph). Johnston and Campbell are thus describing very serious parenting problems in both categories of batterers, giving further indication of the limited practical significance of these categories for identifying which batterers will be more or less harmful to children, which is the purpose for which Johnston has proposed that they be used.

In another parallel to our findings, Johnston and Roseby (1997) observed that "young boys who witness their father's powerful, aggressive posturing tend to manage their fears of him by merging with him and incorporating his disparaging view of the mother (and of women in general)" (pp. 200–201). They provided a case example that describes in detail how the witnessing of domestic violence drove a teenage boy named Robert away from his mother and how a therapeutic process that allowed him to work through the effects of the violence he had witnessed not only led to the re-formation of a close bond between mother and son but actually led the boy to decide to move back to his mother's home.

Finally, we have discussed above the observations of these authors that support our conclusions regarding the risk of sexual abuse by batterers.

Thus, Johnston, Campbell, and Roseby's own observations support most of our central conclusions regarding the parenting of batterers and the dynamics of their families (see Chapters 1 through 3 above). These authors occasionally concur with us on issues of practice as well. For example, Johnston and Roseby (1997) state, "The danger lies in the court's failure to ensure that appropriate investigations are made into allegations of abuse, neglect, and domestic violence, and in not acting to protect the child and the victim parent in situations where it is warranted" (p. 243). Johnston (1992) further recommends that the parenting of a battered woman not be judged in the immediate aftermath of separation, acknowledging the ways in which her victimization may have diminished her parenting capacity, and suggests that "friendly parent" provisions (see Chapter 5) not be applied to a parent who is trying to protect a child from witnessing violence.

Furthermore, Johnston and Roseby (1997) make useful recommendations for the creation of multidisciplinary evaluation teams for custody and visitation cases involving histories of domestic violence. However, they do not include battered women's specialists or batterers' specialists on their proposed teams, thus leaving out the professionals with the greatest expertise in the area in question.

SUMMARY

Numerous problems present in existing theories of divorce and approaches to evaluating the parenting of batterers have the potential to contribute to practice errors. Some of these problems involve the misapplication of prevailing models of divorce and separation, which were not designed for application to cases involving domestic violence and the family dynamics that it engenders. Such misapplication is reflected in the work of Janet Johnston, Linda Campbell, and Vivienne Roseby, which has developed wide influence on the practice of courts, supervised visitation centers, and mental health centers. The work of Richard Gardner also has had a marked impact on court practice, despite its failure to consider the impact of violence and abuse on women and children and its overt gender bias. We believe that it is critical to examine the impact of these models when applied to domestic violence cases and to develop new models and approaches to risk assessment that can incorporate a sophisticated understanding of the family dynamics engendered by the parenting of batterers. We now turn to examining one such model for assessing and responding to the risk to children from batterers.

7

Supporting Recovery
Assessing Risk to Children From Batterers and Structuring Visitation

The growing awareness of the risk posed to children by domestic violence has raised a complex and at times overwhelming set of questions for family and juvenile courts and for child protective services. The interest in maintaining the strongest possible connections between children and both parents sometimes collides with concerns about protecting children from exposure to abuse and assisting them to recover from traumatic experiences that they may have endured. The need therefore arises for a sophisticated approach to assessing risk to children from unsupervised contact with batterers, one that incorporates current knowledge of the attitudinal and behavioral profile of batterers and its implications for parenting. Furthermore, the approach needs to recognize the wide range of types of risk to children that batterers pose; level of physical violence alone is not an adequate basis on which to assess which batterers are dangerous to children, as some "lower-level" batterers are among the most psychologically destructive. Finally, risk assessment must be undertaken in light of the long-term goal of creating a context in which children can heal emotionally.

Our discussion here focuses primarily on assessing risk to children from batterers after separation. Many of the issues that we cover are also applicable to assessing risk to children while families are still together. However, risk assessment when a batterer and a battered woman are still living together involves a number of additional factors, including the mother's ability to protect her children, the level of access that the mother and her children have to community resources and supports, the mother's past history of help-seeking behavior (whether successful or not), and the ability of child protective services to gain enough access to the family to adequately monitor safety (Whitney & Davis, 1999). After separation, on the other hand, a battered mother loses whatever ability she may have had previously to directly monitor the batterer's conduct with the children, and thus her ability to ameliorate his risk becomes even more limited.

SOURCES OF RISK TO CHILDREN
FROM UNSUPERVISED CONTACT WITH BATTERERS

The use of the risk assessment guide provided later in this chapter requires a familiarity with the central concerns that are in need of evaluation. As discussed earlier, the risks posed to children by batterers go well beyond the possibility of the traumatic witnessing of acts of violence. We have identified the following concerns to be of the greatest practical significance.

Risk of Continued or Intensified Undermining of the Mother's Authority and of Mother-Child Relationships. The emotional recovery of children who have been exposed to batterers appears to depend more on the quality of their relationship with the nonbattering parent than on any other single factor (see Chapter 5). The quality of the parent-child relationship is critical in the recovery of divorced children in general, even in the absence of violence or abuse (Johnston et al., 1989). Battering behavior can undermine mother-child relationships in a wide array of ways, and this interference tends to continue or to increase after separation (see Chapter 3) and in this respect represents one of the most serious developmental risks to children over the long term.

Risk of Rigid, Authoritarian Parenting. Recovery in traumatized children is best facilitated by a nurturing, loving environment that also includes appropriate structure, limits, and predictability. The authoritarian parenting style common to many batterers is not conducive to emotional healing, particularly for children whose trauma is related to exposure to domestic violence. Rigid or harsh parenting can intimidate children who have been exposed to violence, making it difficult for them to develop the sense of safety necessary for emotional recovery. Current incidents of the batterer's verbal aggression or physical intimidation toward the children can act as traumatic reminders of earlier violence. In addition, it is difficult for children to make progress in the recovery of their own voices and self-esteem and in the overcoming of destructive values that they may have learned (see Chapter 2) if they are simultaneously being exposed regularly to a batterer's dictatorial and overpowering approach.

Risk of Neglectful or Irresponsible Parenting.   Because of their self-focus, batterers tend not to be able to focus on their children's needs for extended periods of time or to exhibit long-term consistency (Johnston & Campbell, 1993b; Ayoub et al., 1991). After separation, this problem can be exacerbated by the tendency of many batterers to become preoccupied with their grievances toward the former partner. Moreover, in our experience, postseparation custody or visitation plans typically put batterers in the position of caring for their children for longer uninterrupted periods of time than they have previously done. Finally, we find that many batterers are deliberately neglectful as a result of their desire to curry favor with their children, failing to impose appropriate safety or eating guidelines, bedtimes, or other structure. For these and perhaps other reasons, the structure and predictability necessary for children's recovery is not typically provided. This absence can have the further effect of interfering with the mother's ability to provide such a structure in *her* home, as children may become increasingly unwilling to tolerate her authority if they are enjoying inappropriate freedoms while in the batterer's care.

The neglectful parenting of some batterers reaches a level that raises safety concerns, with children being left unattended or with inappropriate caretakers. Our separated or divorced clients also tend to use poor judgment in exposing their children to movies and video games that involve material that is frightening, violent, or inappropriately sexual; partners of our clients report that children sometimes remain afraid or upset because of such exposure for days or weeks following a visit. Children who have been exposed to domestic violence may be unusually disturbed by violence in media (Eron et al., cited in Graham-Bermann, 1998), at the same time as they appear to be particularly subject to its influences on their value systems.

Risk of Exposure to New Threats or Acts of Violence Toward Their Mother.   A large percentage of serious domestic violence assaults occur after separation (Tjaden & Thoennes, 2000), and children witness these incidents at a high rate (Hester & Radford, cited in Peled, 2000). A battered mother who seeks a restraining order has nearly four times the risk of reabuse than does a restraining order plaintiff who does not have children with the abuser (Carlson, Harris, & Holden, 1999). There are also indications that risk of sexual assault of the woman by the batterer increases during and after separation (review in Mahoney & Williams, 1998), and a substantial number of sexual assaults of battered women are witnessed by children (Campbell & Alford, cited in Wolak & Finkelhor, 1998). In addition, children are sometimes injured directly during these assaults, either intentionally or by accident, including sometimes becoming victims of homicide (Langford et al., 1999). Nearly half of the perpetrators of domestic violence homicides have no criminal record involving violence, and in a large portion of cases, children witness either the killing or its immediate aftermath (Langford et al., 1999). Nearly half of domestic violence homicides occur a month or more after the couple has separated, and some take place years later (Langford et al., 1999). The existence of visitation can provide the batterer with access to information about the mother's and children's movements and activities, which can contribute to their risk. In several cases of ours, for example, the batterer has learned from the children that the mother has begun a new relationship, leading to a dangerous escalation in his behavior. In two recent cases of ours involving mothers who were in battered women's shelters with their children, custody evaluators appointed by the court have disclosed the woman's whereabouts to the batterer. Some batterers take advantage of times when they call to speak to the children by telephone to threaten or to verbally abuse the mother.

The retraumatizing effects of exposure to new acts of physical or verbal violence can be important impediments to children's recovery. For example, a partner of one of our clients reported that her son's nightmares regarding violence, which had stopped for over a year, began to occur regularly again following a frightening verbal assault by the batterer during a visitation exchange.

Risk of Psychological Abuse and Manipulation.   Batterers have been observed to have verbally abusive parenting styles (see Chapter 2) and to have a tendency to involve the children as weapons in the abuse of the mother (see Chapter 3). This risk appears to increase distinctly after separation, as many batterers use the children as weapons in ongoing efforts to control or to intimidate the mother in the absence of other strategies for doing so (McMahon & Pence, 1995; Walker & Edwall, 1987).

Partners of our clients frequently report emotionally abusive acts to their children during visitation. In one case, the batterer told a

3-year-old girl that he was seeking custody of her, and for the next 2 years she suffered chronic nightmares in which she was being taken away from her mother by her father, by monsters, or by strangers. In another case, the batterer made frequent references to his daughter to the effect that she was getting fat, ridiculed her about her eating habits, and told her, "You're going to turn into a cow like your mother." The mother reported that the child would come home and intermittently refuse to eat for 2 to 3 days after each visit, preoccupied with the belief that she was overweight.

Finally, further parentification of the children is a risk. We have had numerous cases in which batterers have caused children to become burdened with concern for their fathers' suffering and for injustices that he claimed to have suffered at the hands of their mothers and the family courts. Visitation can become an important opportunity for the batterer to manipulate the children (Erickson & Henderson, 1998).

Risk of Physical or Sexual Abuse of the Child by the Batterer. Multiple studies have demonstrated the dramatically elevated rate of physical and sexual abuse of children by batterers (see Chapters 2 and 4). There is no evidence currently available that this risk decreases after separation, and there are many sound reasons to believe that it actually *increases* as a result of the mother's inability to monitor or to intervene in the batterer's parenting and of the retaliatory style common to many batterers after separation.

The apparent absence of child abuse by a batterer while a family is together does not preclude its onset after separation. For example, one study found that roughly 10% of incest perpetrators attribute their actions to a desire to retaliate against the mother (Williams-Meyer & Finkelhor, cited in McCloskey et al., 1995), and clinicians have made similar observations of the motives of some perpetrators (MacFarlane & Waterman, 1986). We have observed that children who are recovering successfully from exposure to domestic violence may become increasingly defiant with their father or may even challenge him about incidents that they witnessed, which can put them in increased danger of physical assault. (This risk is also described in Johnston & Roseby, 1997.)

Risk of Inconsistency. Our clients sometimes drop in and out of their children's lives repeatedly. We observe, for example, the recurring phenomenon of batterers who do not visit their children for a period of months and then appear at a family court requesting to have the children on holidays or birthdays or seeking 48-hour visitation every other weekend. This behavior can be disruptive to the custodial home and manipulative of the children's emotions, and it may continue patterns of emotional injury from the batterer's neglect prior to separation. When a court grants such a request, the batterer experiences reinforcement of his entitled view that his status and privilege as a father need not be tied to the sacrifices or consistency demanded of other parents. This value system may be absorbed by children who observe the court's response.

Risk of Child Learning Attitudes That Lead to Domestic Violence. Sons of batterers have dramatically elevated rates of domestic violence perpetration when they reach adulthood (Silverman & Williamson, 1997; Straus, 1990; review in Hotaling & Sugarman, 1986), and there are indications that daughters of batterers are at increased risk of domestic violence victimization (review in Hotaling & Sugarman, 1986). Thus, a batterer's negative influence on his children's belief system needs to be taken into account (see Chapter 2). In addition, professionals should consider the messages that children may take from systemic responses; for example, a court decision to place a teen boy in the custody of his battering father may be read by the teen as an endorsement of his father's behavior and as a confirmation that his mother was to blame. We have observed the development of key attitudes underpinning domestic violence in children as young as 8 or 9 and occasionally younger. Therefore, the goal of fostering a relationship between children and their battering father needs to be balanced with the need to restrict his level of influence as a role model.

Risk of Abduction. A majority of parental abductions take place in the context of domestic violence, and most of these are carried out by batterers or by their agents, often with short- or long-term traumatizing effects on the children (Greif & Hegar, 1993). Parental abductions are in general carried out primarily by fathers or by people acting on the father's behalf, typically not occurring in the immediate aftermath of divorce but rather either before the couple separates or two or more years subsequent to the separation. About half of paternal abductions are carried out by failing to return the child from an authorized visit. There is little variation by class or race in the risk of abduction, except for a somewhat lower than average rate among Hispanics. Finally, family abductions are roughly 90 times as common as are stranger abductions (Finkelhor et al., 1990). In abductions related to domestic violence, 90% are carried out by the violent partner, and in half of these cases, the abduction had been threatened before it occurred (Greif & Hegar, 1993).

Risk of Exposure to Violence in Their Father's New Relationships. Both researchers and counselors of batterers have observed the likelihood that a batterer will repeat his violent behavior in a series of relationships (Dutton, 1995; Woffordt et al., 1994; Kalmuss & Seltzer, 1986). We do not observe that a batterer's level of past physical violence alone is an effective way to distinguish those batterers most likely to reoffend with a new partner, and we thus recommend that evaluators assess the extent to which a batterer has addressed the underlying causes of his battering behavior (see Chapter 8). A new partner who is being abused is not likely to disclose the battering to custody evaluators or to child protective services because of her own belief that he will change, his success in influencing her view of his former partner, or her fear of retaliation by him should she disclose, especially given the high emotional stakes when litigation is involved.

A GUIDE TO ASSESSING RISK
TO CHILDREN FROM BATTERERS

Because of the wide range of potential sources of psychological and physical injury to children from batterers, risk assessment is of necessity a process requiring careful investigation and evaluation. In our experience, children generally fare better if they have some degree of contact with the batterer, with the exception of cases in which the batterer is too dangerous even for a supervised setting or when seeing the batterer is too frightening or upsetting to the children. The challenge, however, is how to structure contact in a way that is safe for children and that supports their overall recovery needs (see Chapter 5), that minimizes the risk that the batterer will undermine mother-child relationships, and that restricts his influence over the development of the children's value system.

We describe in detail below the factors that we have found to be critical in making such an assessment. Information about these factors cannot be gathered from the batterer alone, as his descriptions of his conduct and even of his own attitudes are unreliable (Adams, 1991; Follingstad et al., 1990). Information therefore needs to be sought also from the partner or former partner, the children, friends and relatives, court and police records, child protective records, school personnel, and other relevant sources. At the same time, the absence of a documentary record cannot be assumed to prove that allegations of domestic violence are false; only about one fifth of intimate partner rapes, one quarter of intimate physical assaults, and one half of stalking incidents involving female victims are ever reported to police (Tjaden & Thoennes, 2000).

1. The Abuser's History of Physical Abuse Toward the Children

Batterers have an increased statistical risk to physically abuse their children (Straus, 1990; Suh & Abel, 1990; Bowker et al., 1988), and there are reasons to believe that this risk may continue or even increase after separation (see Chapters 2 and 5). Mothers, children, and other witnesses should be asked what the father's approach to discipline has been, how he reacts when he is angry at the children, and what punishments or consequences he uses. Child protective records should be reviewed carefully. Additional questions include the following: Does he spank the children? Has he ever left marks? Does he ever grab the children roughly? Has he been involved in fights (including any that appeared mutual) with his older children? Does he minimize or justify physically abusive behaviors that he has used?

With respect to this form of abuse as well as various other concerns discussed below, evaluators should be alert to indications of the batterer pressuring or manipulating children to *keep secrets* about his behavior toward them or their mother, which we believe substantially increases risk to the children.

Case Example. A batterer who petitioned the court to expand his visitation reported to the custody evaluator that he periodically slapped his 12-year-old boy in the head, stating that this was the only way to gain his cooperation. The father also described an incident from three years earlier in which he had punished the boy (9 years old at the time) by holding his head low over a rain barrel and splashing handfuls of water up into his face, causing the boy to sputter and to gasp for air. When he described this incident to the custody evaluator, the father laughed about it and stated that his wife's concerns about it were a typical example of how she blew things out of proportion. Based on the father's continued justification and minimization of both past and present abuse, the evaluator concluded that the risk of continued physical abuse of this child was high. (The batterer had engaged in very few assaults on the mother over the course of the relationship, although one of them had caused serious injury.)

2. The Abuser's History of Neglectful or Underinvolved Parenting

In cases in which a history of neglect, endangerment, or very low involvement is present in the batterer's parenting, a number of concerns about unsupervised contact should arise. These concerns include whether the batterer will protect the children's safety and health adequately, whether he will attend to their emotional needs, and what his motives are for pursuing custody or visitation. Also, several studies show that a father's low rate of involvement in caring for his children during their early years increases his statistical risk of perpetrating incest (review in Milner, 1998).

Some questions to explore include the following: Does the batterer have any history of disappearing for hours, days, or weeks at a time? Has he ever refused to attend to children's medical needs, such as by refusing to drive the mother to the hospital? Has he ever threatened to abandon the family without support? Has he chronically ignored the children or failed to take caretaking responsibility?

In our experience, the great majority of batterers involved with family court litigation assert that they have been highly involved parents. These reports can be tested by asking detailed questions that elicit the depth of his knowledge and compassion regarding his children: Can you tell me the names of your children's current teachers? Can you tell me the names of as many past teachers as possible? Could you please describe each child's first year of life? How did their toilet training go? What are each child's current strengths and weaknesses? What skills is each child currently attempting to develop? Witnesses as well can be asked about what specific caretaking behaviors the batterer has exhibited.

We have found in a few cases that batterers who were seeking custody or expanded visitation had abandoned children from past relationships, which should raise concerns about the man's capacity for commitment to the children and his current motives for attempting to increase his influence over them. Finally, we observe that batterers sometimes seek custody or increased visitation despite the fact that they are not currently using all of the visitation time that they are allotted.

Case Example.   A father who was an alleged batterer sought custody of his 18-month-old son. The custody evaluator asked him what the child's sleep habits had been immediately after birth, and he reported that the child slept between 10 and 12 hours per night without interruption from the first day home from the hospital. The mother stated that the child awoke roughly every 2 to 4 hours to take a bottle. (She further stated that the father was involved with another woman during the child's infancy and was not spending nights at the home, which would appear to account for his unrealistic ideas about a newborn's sleep patterns.) In addition, the father was currently visiting with the son for approximately 4 hours a week, by his own account, although he was permitted a 24-hour overnight. He stated that he kept the visits short in order not to anger his former wife. During an observation of the father with his son, the evaluator asked the father to change the boy's diaper as a way to assess his competence. The father responded with visible discomfort that he did not have diapers in the house.

3. The Abuser's History of Sexual Abuse or Boundary Violations With the Children

We would expect as a matter of course that any substantiated history of sexual abuse of the children by a batterer be treated with great seriousness. However, we find that some professionals believe that sexual abuse is not likely to recur once it has been disclosed (because of the perpetrator's fear of further disclosure) or that the perpetrator can change even in the absence of any admission of his past acts. These beliefs are inconsistent with the literature on child sexual abuse perpetrators (e.g., Leberg, 1997; Salter, 1988).

Allegations of boundary violations that do not rise to the level of sexual abuse nonetheless need careful examination as well, partly because of the increased risk of incest perpetration by batterers (McCloskey et al., 1995; Sirles & Franke, 1989; Paveza, 1988). Poor boundaries can be psychologically destructive in themselves, can lay groundwork for sexual abuse in the future, or can be warning signs of undisclosed sexual abuse that may already be taking place (Salter, 1995). Questions to explore include the following: Does the batterer respect his children's right to privacy? Does he maintain proper privacy himself? Does he expose the children to pornography or allow the children access to it? Does he maintain relationships with any of his children that have a romantic or sexualized quality? Does he pressure the children to give him physical affection against their wishes? Does he engage the children in inappropriate sexual conversation? Are there indications of pressure to keep secrets?

Case Example. Following the separation between an alleged batterer and his partner, a teenage daughter of the mother (by a different father) made a detailed and highly credible disclosure of a history of serious boundary violations on the alleged batterer's part, approaching the legal definition of sexual abuse. These disclosures were supported by another credible adolescent. The couple's 5-year-old son, who was the subject of custody litigation, was showing a number of sexualized behaviors and was heard making peculiar comments about his genitals. Although the boy denied sexual abuse in a specialized evaluation, the Guardian ad Litem nonetheless recommended a number of safeguards surrounding the father's visitation with the son, including short visits without overnights, the child's participation in therapy, and the father's participation in batterer intervention. (The mother alleged two incidents of physical violence, which the father denied. However, the father's own accounts included examples of psychological abuse on his part that involved a high degree of mental cruelty.)

4. The Batterer's Level of Physical Danger to the Partner or Former Partner

The batterer's level of physical violence both during the relationship and after separation is an important indicator of risk to the children. The higher his level of violence toward the mother, for example, the greater the risk that he will physically abuse the children (Straus, 1990). Level of previous violence is one predictor of future violence toward the children's mother (Weisz, Tolman, & Saunders, 2000), to which the children may be exposed; furthermore, level of violence is one indicator of likelihood to attempt to kill the mother, which can involve homicide of children (Websdale, 1999; Langford et al., 1999). Sexual assaults of the mother are also correlated to overall frequency of violence by batterers (Bowker, 1983) and to likelihood of the batterer to physically abuse children (Bowker et al., 1988). The mother's own assessment of the likelihood of repeat assaults should be considered carefully, as a recent study found it to be the single strongest predictor of future violence by a batterer (Weisz et al., 2000). Threats of abuse are also highly correlated with future physical violence (Follingstad et al., 1990), including postseparation violence (Fleury, Sullivan, & Bybee, 2000), and both threatened and actual homicide attempts may take place in cases in which the previous history of violence had primarily involved lower levels of violence (McCloskey et al., 1995). Violence during pregnancy is a further indicator of overall risk to commit frequent or severe violence to the mother, with only minor variations by race or economic class (Campbell, Soeken, et al., 1998; Fagan, Stewart, & Hansen, 1983).

Questions to examine include the following: How severe and frequent have physical assaults been? Has he ever choked her? What types of injuries has the mother received? Has she felt the need to obtain a restraining order? Has the batterer violated that order? Has he ever threatened to kill her or the children? Has he ever killed or attacked pets or used other terrorizing tactics? Is he extremely jealous or possessive? Has he owned weapons before, and does he currently have access to them? Has he been sexually violent to the mother? Is he severely depressed or despondent? Is he paranoid? Does he engage in stalking behavior? Has his violence escalated over time? Has he ever assaulted her during pregnancy? Has violence escalated during or after separation? What is his criminal record? Does he chronically abuse substances? Does he have generalized problems with violence? Has he been violent toward the children? Are there indications of antisocial personality disorder? Does he use pornography? (The above indicators are based on Weisz et al., 2000; Campbell, Soeken, et al., 1998; Holtzworth-Munroe & Stuart, 1994; Fagan et al., 1983. For studies of pornography and sexual aggression, see review in Koss et al., 1994; Demare, Briere, & Lips, 1988; Malamuth & Check, 1985.)

Case Example.   A father who was recently released from jail (where he was sent after a conviction for domestic violence) was seeking visitation with three children ranging in age from 4 to 9. His criminal record included over 40 arrests and over 20 convictions, one of which involved a weapons charge and a number of which occurred during his teenage years. The custody evaluator contacted three previous partners, all of whom reported suffering physical assaults. A review of the father's employment history revealed a history of jobs lost due to lying or stealing at work. Based on these and additional findings, the custody evaluator recommended a full psychological evaluation for possible Antisocial Personality Disorder, concluding that even supervised visitation could not take place safely until the batterer had received both intensive mental health assistance and specialized batterer intervention services.

5. The Batterer's Level of Psychological Cruelty
Toward the Partner or Former Partner and Toward the Children

We find that a batterer's capacity for cruelty toward his adult victim or toward the children is an important predictor of how safe children will be in his care and of how great his determination may be to gain revenge against the mother. Evaluators should ask questions such as the following: What have been his most emotionally hurtful acts toward the mother? Does he continue to justify those acts, and if so, how? What have been his most emotionally hurtful acts toward the children? What past behaviors of his have appeared to cause them the greatest distress? Has he ever engaged in acts that appeared to be deliberately designed to harm the children emotionally?

Case Examples. One client of ours whose physical violence was relatively low had gone into his partner's belongings and destroyed all of her childhood photographs, diaries, and mementos. He also once had thrown his partner out of the house naked and locked the door, humiliating her publicly. In another case, after separation, the batterer had betrayed a confidence that the woman had shared with him early in the relationship, spreading widely details of her experiences of childhood sexual victimization. In both cases, the women reported that these acts were far more cruel than were any of the man's physical assaults. In the second case, the parents divorced, and the battered woman reported to us various ongoing acts of psychological cruelty to the child by the batterer after separation, with marked emotional effects.

6. The Batterer's History of Using the Children as Weapons and of Undermining Mother-Child Relationships

In our experience, a batterer's history of using the children as weapons or of undermining the mother's parenting is a good predictor of postseparation parenting behavior. In fact, we have yet to encounter a case in which a batterer who engaged in such behaviors chronically while the family was together improved substantially in this regard after separation.

Examples of questions to ask include the following: Has the batterer tended to change his treatment of the children when angry at the mother? Has he encouraged them to have negative beliefs about their mother? Has he ever prevented or discouraged her from attending to a child? Has he chronically undermined her authority with the children? Has he made threats to her involving the children, such as threats to hurt them, kidnap them, or take custody of them? When she has objected to his behavior regarding the children in the past, has he responded by intensifying the behaviors about which she was complaining? Has he used favoritism or engaged in other behaviors that cause divisions within the family? Has he used the children to frighten her, such as by driving recklessly with children in the car when angry at her? Has he threatened to quit his job in order to not have to pay child support? During visitation, does he involve the children in activities that he knows they are not permitted at home?

Case Examples.   We have had several cases in which separated batterers have specifically instructed their children to create problems at home, including one in which a young child was encouraged to physically assault her mother. In a well-publicized case, a state appellate court found that a batterer had instructed the child to stab his mother with a plastic knife. Numerous other case examples involving use of the children as weapons and undermining of mother-child relationships are provided in Chapter 3.

7. The Batterer's Level of Willingness to Risk Physically or Emotionally Hurting the Children Incidental to His Abuse of Their Mother

We have observed that behavior by the batterer that may not be deliberately intended to harm or to endanger the children, but that nevertheless has that effect, is an important indicator of his likelihood to use similarly poor judgment in the future. Such acts may demonstrate that his desire to abuse his victim tends to override his concern for the children; much of the harm to children from batterers appears to result from the batterer's reckless focus on retribution toward the mother, which is likely to increase after separation.

Some questions to ask include the following: Was he violent or psychologically abusive during any of the mother's pregnancies? Has he been violent in the presence of the children, and what has been their proximity to those acts of violence? Has he ever assaulted her while she was holding a child? Has he ever thrown objects at or around the victim in ways that put a child at risk? Has he ever pushed a child out of his way in order to get to her? Has he called the mother degrading names or humiliated her in front of the children? Has he tended to abandon his child care responsibilities when angry at her?

Case Example.   One separated batterer, upon hearing that his former wife had a new man living at her house, went to her home and began yelling statements such as "If I find out he's living here, someone is going to get hurt" while the mother stood holding their 2-year-old son. The mother reported that following the father's departure, the child curled up in a fetal position and would not talk or move for 20 minutes. While the couple was together, this batterer had an extensive history of putting the child at risk with thrown objects, reckless driving, and other behaviors targeting the mother.

8. The Level of Coercive or Manipulative Control That the Abuser Has Exercised Over His Partner During the Relationship

We find that the more severely controlling our clients are toward their partners, the more likely they are to involve the children in the pattern of abuse and the more likely they are to be authoritarian in their parenting style. In addition, a dictatorial level of control toward children has been associated with increased risk both of physical abuse (review in Milner & Chilamkurti, 1991) and of sexual abuse (Leberg, 1997; Maltz & Holman, 1987; Herman, 1981). Assessment thus should address the following questions: Has he impeded his partner from having social or professional contacts, such as by forbidding her to see certain friends or relatives, to attend school, or to have guests at the house? Does he control family finances in a coercive way or exclude her from important financial decisions? Has he tended to silence his partner's voice in arguments and in decision making? Has he chronically shown contempt or disregard for her opinions? Does he monitor her movements, such as by requiring her to account for her whereabouts at all times? Is he arrogant? Is he dictatorial or minutely controlling toward the children?

Control is not always exercised in an overtly coercive way; as we have seen, it is common for batterers to be highly manipulative. We observe that our most manipulative clients are sometimes the ones who cause the greatest psychological harm because of their effectiveness at persuading children to blame their mother and themselves for the abuse. Questions to examine in this regard include the following: Is he successful at convincing people that he has been the victim in the relationship? Has he tended to twist his partner's statements or actions? Does he make extreme swings between kindness and abusiveness? Has he succeeded at times in sowing divisions within the family? Is there evidence that he is frequently dishonest and is comfortable and convincing when lying? Is he described by his partner, children, or other witnesses as "crazy-making"?

In some cases, careful investigation by the custody evaluator may reveal that the batterer has a severe and chronic problem with lying. We have observed children to fare poorly in unsupervised visitation in these cases, as the batterer may lie frequently to conceal his parenting behavior and may lie chronically to the children directly in ways that cause confusion for them or that create tensions in their maternal relationships.

9. The Abuser's Level of Entitlement, Self-Centeredness, or Selfishness

As discussed in Chapter 1, "entitlement" refers to the nearly universal tendency among batterers to perceive themselves as deserving special rights and privileges that do not apply to other family members, which is a driving attitudinal force behind abuse (see also Silverman & Williamson, 1997; Pence & Paymar, 1993; Edleson & Tolman, 1992; Adams, 1991). Entitlement manifests itself through such dynamics as the batterer's selfish focus on his own needs, his enforcement of double standards, and his tendency to see family members as personal possessions. Specific attitudes of entitlement are better predictors of which men will batter than are the presence or absence of traditional sex-role attitudes (Adams, 1991). Our clinical experience is that the most highly entitled batterers are the most resistant to change and in addition tend to exercise chronically poor judgment regarding their children. High entitlement tends to lead to role reversal, wherein a batterer expects his children to take care of his needs (see Chapter 1). In a small percentage of our cases, these problems are further exacerbated by characterological narcissism that predates the emergence of battering behavior and that exhibits itself both within the family context and in other spheres of life. Narcissism has been identified as one factor increasing the chance of reoffending in batterers (Hamberger & Hastings, cited in Tolman & Bennett, 1990).

The highly entitled batterer may be reluctant to put the children's needs ahead of his own and may feel justified in using the children as weapons. Sharing decision making with him may be impossible because his entitlement leads him to expect his needs to be catered to by the mother or the children and makes it difficult to persuade him to take the needs of others into account. Therefore, shared legal or physical custody with a highly entitled batterer exposes the children to the likelihood of long-term ongoing tension between the parents. We also observe that the highly entitled batterer can be grandiosely persuaded that the well-being of his children depends primarily on their relationship with him, underestimating the importance of their mother.

Finally, high expectations of catering and caretaking by family members have been linked to propensity for incest perpetration (see Chapter 4). For example, Groth (1982) has written that for many perpetrators, "Sexual access to his daughter is experienced as part of his narcissistic entitlement as the head of the family" (p. 222).

Questions to examine in this area include the following: Is the batterer frequently and unreasonably demanding? To what extent does he become enraged or punishing when he is not catered to or when he feels inconvenienced? Has he, for example, become irate when pregnancy or the presence of an infant caused his partner to be less attentive to him? Is he furious if she will not sacrifice her needs or the children's needs in order to accommodate him? Does he define the victim's attempts to defend herself as abuse of him? Does he have pronounced double standards regarding his conduct? Does he make the children responsible for his needs or feelings? Does he show signs of viewing the children as owned objects?

Case Example.   An alleged batterer who had custody of his children was failing to comply with the court's order to have them participate regularly in therapy. School personnel reported to the custody evalua-tor that the children (ages 7 and 9) were making references to physical abuse at home and were reporting that they were expected to do the food shopping, meal preparation, and house cleaning. The father was discouraging the children from bringing friends to the home and was running a dictatorial home. The children's therapist stated to the eval-uator that they were highly guarded at the few sessions that they had attended and had reported that their father questions them intrusively after each session. When the evaluator raised the therapist's concerns with the father, he stated belligerently, "Those are my children, and I have a right to know what is being said in their therapy sessions." The evaluator thus was left with concerns about the levels both of control and of entitlement and about respect for the children's boundaries. (The mother's home was unfortunately not an appropriate custodial choice in this case, so the evaluator recommended increased vigilance by child protective services and possible placement of the children with relatives.)

10. The Batterer's Substance Abuse History

Although substance abuse problems do not cause battering and 75% or more of physically abusive incidents occur without the pres-ence of alcohol (Kaufman Kantor & Straus, 1990), substance abuse does appear at higher rates in batterers (review in Bennett, 1995) and can contribute to a batterer's volatility and resistance to change. Marijuana, for example, has been found to decrease the chance that a batterer will stop his violence over time (Woffordt et al., 1994). Batterers who abuse substances have higher rates of physically abusing children than do other batterers (Suh & Abel, 1990). Substance abuse also has been linked to lethality in batterers (Websdale, 1999; Campbell, 1995a) and to increased risk of sexual abuse (Becker & Quinsey, 1993; Herman, 1981). Batterers who abuse alcohol have substantially higher rates than do other batterers of reoffending following participation in batterer programs (Gondolf, 1998a). When an evaluator learns of a substance abuse problem that is now allegedly resolved, he or she should carefully examine what the batterer's process of recovery has been, what level of insight he exhibits into the addiction, and what his current plan of treatment or self-help is.

Case Example.   A batterer who admitted an extensive history of alcohol abuse (though he continued to deny the battering in the face of substantial evidence) stated that he was fully in recovery through AA and a hospital-based treatment group, with nearly a year of sobriety. However, when the evaluator asked him to describe the insights that he had gained through his recovery programs, he stated that his former wife had caused his drinking problem by denying him visitation with their daughter. He acknowledged ten drunk driving arrests during recent years, including three convictions, beginning when the couple was still together. (His drunk driving arrests after separation were in fact the main reason why he had been denied visitation; he was reversing cause and effect.) The evaluator concluded that the batterer had not accepted responsibility for his drinking and was minimizing its effects. It was recommended to the court that unsupervised visitation be conditioned on increased participation in his hospital-based treatment group and on participation in a batterer program.

*11. The Batterer's Refusal to Accept the End
of the Relationship or to Accept His Former Partner's Decision
to Begin a New Relationship*

A batterer who is unwilling to accept the end of the relationship is more dangerous to his partner (Adams, 1989) and, in our experience, can be an increased risk to involve his children as weapons of control or of abuse. Batterers who are particularly jealous and possessive and who refuse to accept the end of a relationship are at high risk for further violence (Weisz et al., 2000), including potential lethal violence (Websdale, 1999; Daly & Wilson, 1988). In such circumstances, children are at increased risk for exposure to new acts of violence toward the mother; for example, a majority of killings related to domestic violence take place when the victim is attempting to end the relationship or has already done so (Websdale, 1999; APA Presidential Task Force, 1996).

Evaluators should examine the batterer's level of investment in retaliating against his victim for perceived wrongs from the past. Perceptual distortions that are typical to batterers can lead a man to define his victim's history of efforts to protect herself or her children as abuse of him, for which he wishes to exact retribution. This can be true even in cases in which the separation was initiated by the batterer.

The batterer's level of willingness to accept his former partner's right to begin a new relationship can influence his parenting. Our clients who perceive their children as owned objects, for example, tend to become enraged at the prospect of their children developing an attachment to another man. Evaluators should ask questions such as the following: Did he abruptly request custody or expanded visitation upon learning that his partner had decided definitively not to return to him or upon learning that she had a new partner? Is he depressed or despondent regarding the breakup? Has he warned his former partner not to start a new relationship? Has he threatened or assaulted anyone that she has dated? If she has a new partner, has the batterer attempted to frighten the children about him? Does he attempt to make the children feel guilty about their attachment to the mother's new partner?

Case Example.   A client of ours who was fairly accepting of the end of his relationship nonetheless insisted in sessions, "No other man is going to be around my children." His former partner did in fact start a new relationship, of which the batterer learned through the children. She reported to us that the children came home from a visit with the batterer and told her that they didn't want the new man to be there. When she asked them why not, they responded, "Because Daddy doesn't want him here, and it is making Daddy feel bad." Our client was arrested shortly afterward for a restraining order violation when he was apprehended looking in the windows of the family home.

12. The Batterer's Level of Risk to Abduct the Children

Domestic violence is involved in half or more of cases in which a parent abducts a child (Greif & Hegar, 1993) and most of these abductions are carried out by fathers or by their agents (Finkelhor et al., 1990). Even in cases in which there is no history of explicit threats, evaluators should be alert to indications of possible abduction such as abrupt passport renewal, efforts to get the children's passports away from the mother, suspicious maneuvering, or unexplained travel plans.

Case Example. School personnel reported to the custody evaluator that the batterer had appeared at school one day saying that he needed to take his girls home with him. The bus monitor refused to take the girls off of the bus, saying that she had not received any notice from the mother authorizing him to take them home. He stated, "I have joint custody, you don't need authorization from her, I pick them up often, the principal knows about it." The bus monitor then assented, but she asked the father first to accompany her to the school office quickly to get authorization from the principal. As she began walking toward the office, the father abruptly ran in the other direction and drove away rapidly in his car. Based on this report, the evaluator then sought, and found, other evidence that the batterer had planned to remove the children from the state that day.

13. The Abuser's Level of Refusal to Accept Responsibility for Past Violent or Abusive Actions

In some cases, a batterer may admit to substantial portions of the alleged abuse but assert that he has changed. He may simultaneously portray his partner's or former partner's behavior as highly provocative, in an effort to persuade the evaluator that she shares responsibility for his actions. Some batterers claim to have changed through overcoming a substance abuse problem or participating in therapy to address childhood issues; however, it is rare for abusers to change by working on any issue other than the abusiveness itself (see Chapter 8). Certain signs can be useful in identifying a batterer who has *not* changed, including continuing to blame his victim for his behavior toward her, denial or minimizing of documented abuse, blaming his behavior on alcohol or on childhood issues, or lack of ability to accept responsibility for the effects of his actions on his partner or children.

14. The Batterer's Mental Health History

Although not generally causal in domestic violence, a mental illness can contribute to the volatility and intractability of a battering problem (Websdale, 1999; Edleson & Tolman, 1992). Therefore, a mentally ill batterer may require a long period of supervised visitation while the multiple problems are addressed (or even may need permanent supervision). If a psychotherapist and a batterer program are involved simultaneously, it is important for the two providers to be in close communication and collaboration.

In the absence of serious mental illness, we find that a batterer's participation in psychotherapy can be counterproductive, as it may distract him from working on his abusive attitudes or even equip him with additional excuses. Therefore, batterers without a substantial history of mental illness should participate in a batterer program alone, or in conjunction with substance abuse treatment where indicated.

Evaluators also should be aware that psychological testing and evaluation are in general poor predictors of parenting capacity (Brodzinsky, 1994; Zibbell, 1994), even without the additional complexities involved in assessing a batterer's parenting. Mental health testing is also inadequate to identify which batterers are the most dangerous (APA Presidential Task Force, 1996), to identify the risk of incest perpetration (Milner, 1998; Myers, 1997a; Hall, 1988), or to distinguish between batterers and nonbatterers (O'Leary, 1993). Thus, psychological testing and evaluation with alleged or established batterers should be used only for the purpose of ruling out psychiatric concerns.

Assessment of physical, sexual, and psychological risk to children based on the above factors is a complex process, but we have found that it can nonetheless be performed in a reasonable length of time. (We typically are given 20 to 30 hours in which to complete a custody and visitation investigation, over roughly 7 weeks.) As the reader can no doubt discern, no formula exists for weighing the above factors; the severity in each area as well as the overall pattern has to be evaluated in each particular case. In all cases, however, the battered mother's perceptions of the batterer's risk to the children should be considered carefully; we find that the mother can be a critical source of insights into what kinds of parenting problems the batterer has had in the past and is most likely to manifest in the future.

There are a few additional evaluation issues that we wish to review briefly. (a) Children who have called the police themselves, have disclosed the domestic violence to outsiders, or have disclosed abuse of themselves by the batterer may be at particular risk for retaliation or for manipulation. (b) Observation of batterers or alleged batterers with their children is of limited value, because most batterers can perform well under observation and because children can have strong attachment to a batterer as a result of intermittent reinforcement and traumatic bonding (see Chapter 2). (c) Batterers are more likely than are nonbatterers to seek custody of children (APA Presidential Task

Force, 1996; Liss & Stahly, 1993; Walker & Edwall, 1987), and so a batterer's motives for seeking custody or increased visitation should be examined (APA Presidential Task Force, 1996). (d) Professionals sometimes hope that granting increased visitation or joint custody to a batterer will placate him and thus reduce his tendency to involve the children in future conflicts, but we have not found this approach to be successful. (e) Although some professionals believe that all parents in acrimonious divorces use the children as weapons, we find that batterers do so considerably more than do battered women.

Finally, evaluators should cautiously avoid making assumptions about risk to the children that are based on the class or race of the batterer. We are particularly aware of recurring cases in which evaluators underestimate the risk to children from well-educated, professionally successful, white batterers.

STRUCTURING CUSTODY AND VISITATION

The central goal in structuring custody and visitation in domestic violence cases should be the safety and security of the child's primary residence and support for the healthy flourishing of the child's relationships with his or her siblings and with the nonbattering parent. Creating a strong relationship with the battering father is also valuable but should never be permitted to eclipse the primary goal. As Wallerstein and Tanke (1996) state regarding divorce in general,

> All of our work shows the centrality of the well-functioning custodial parent-child relationship as the protective factor during the post-divorce years. When courts intervene in ways that disrupt the child's relationship with the custodial parent, serious psychological harm may occur to the child as well as to the parent. (p. 311)

These concerns are accentuated in battering cases.

With rare exceptions, it is not in children's best interests to be placed in the custody of a battering father (APA Presidential Task Force, 1996; ABA Center on Children, 1994; National Council of Juvenile and Family Court Judges [NCJFCJ], 1994), and nearly all states in the United States have some statutory restriction on the making of such awards (Lemon, 2000). Joint custody and frequent visitation exchanges have been demonstrated not to further children's postdivorce adjustment except in cases in which both parents support such a plan, and in fact they may lead to markedly worse outcomes in cases in which tensions between the parents remain high (Johnston, 1994b; Wallerstein & Blakeslee, 1989; Johnston et al., 1989), as is typically true in domestic violence cases.

Because there are strong indications that children's sense of security is a critical factor in their potential for resilience following exposure to domestic violence (Cummings, 1998), custody and visitation planning should treat security for children as a top guiding principle. Even in the absence of domestic violence, "children of divorced families are more likely to be anxious about being lost, about being separated, and about unpredictable disasters that might occur, than are children raised in well-functioning intact families" (Wallerstein & Tanke, 1996, pp. 331–332). Supervised visitation should perhaps be considered the norm for domestic violence cases (ABA Center on Children, 1994), especially for the first 1 to 2 years following a separation. For example, a presumption exists in Louisiana that a batterer's visits with his children should be supervised until a number of conditions are met (cited in Sheeran & Hampton, 1999).

In most cases, supervised visitation can adequately meet the children's need for a relationship with their battering father while not incurring many of the risks described above. The exceptions to this guideline should be cases in which the batterer was the children's primary caretaker prior to separation or in other ways had an unusually high level of involvement in their care. Even in such cases as these, unsupervised visitation should not begin prior to a careful evaluation, unless it is already occurring and there is no significant cause for immediate concern. Supervision of visits by a batterer should be the norm until after the batterer has completed a specialized batterer program (APA Presidential Task Force, 1996), and that program should address both the batterer's behavior and his attitudes (Jaffe & Geffner, 1998). Although batterer programs vary in quality, there is evidence that many programs succeed both in reducing recidivism and in increasing victims' feelings of safety (Gondolf, 1998a).

In cases in which the risk of physical violence by the batterer toward the mother or children or of abduction of the children is found to be low, visits may not need to be supervised in a visitation center but can take place in other settings in the presence of a professional supervisor. It is essential that such a supervisor be trained in the dynamics of domestic violence, its impact on family functioning, and the range of concerns regarding the parenting of batterers, including subtle manipulations and boundary violations that can take place.

A small portion of batterers are so dangerous that even a supervised visitation center cannot ensure safety, in which case contact with the children should be suspended (Straus, 1995). In cases in which the danger level is lower, it still may be helpful to some children to have a period without visitation with the abusive parent in order to gain relief from the attendant stress (Kelly, 1993). We find in a majority of cases that following such a hiatus, children can benefit from some kind of contact with their battering fathers (see also Straus, 1995). We do not recommend that visitation with a battering father be imposed over a child's objections, however, for reasons that we discuss below.

We encourage the use of a tiered approach to visitation, so that a batterer who conducts himself appropriately and is participating seriously in a specialized batterer program is gradually moved toward more normal contact with his children. The tiers that we use in shaping recommendations are the following:

a. Visitation supervised at a visitation center

b. Visitation supervised in the community by a trained supervisor

c. Visitation supervised by friends or relatives (for flight risk only)

d. Visits of 2 to 4 hours without supervision

e. Daylong visits without supervision

f. Overnight visitation (not recommended in most battering cases)

Supervision by friends or family members (tier C) is recommended only to prevent abduction, as it is not adequate to address other concerns (ABA Center on Children, 1994).

We generally discourage overnight visitation with batterers for a number of reasons (see also NCJFCJ, 1994; ABA Center on Children, 1994). First, it is likely to be difficult for children who have been exposed to a batterer's violence to feel safe in his care at bedtime and through the night. Second, overnight visits have a substantially longer total duration and thus increase opportunities for problems to be revealed in the batterer's parenting. Longer visits also increase a batterer's influence over the children's perceptions, thus increasing his opportunity to undermine their relationships with their mother and to shape their value systems. Third, resilience in children exposed to domestic violence has been shown to be affected by their access to supports outside the family (review in Jaffe, Wolfe, & Wilson, 1990); overnight visitation takes away significantly from the time that children have access to their normal extrafamilial resources. We find in general that overnight visitation with batterers usually is imposed to meet the needs of the father rather than those of the children.

We recommend overnight visitation only when all of the following conditions are present: (a) The separation has occurred more than 2 years previously; (b) the children are 10 years or older; (c) the batterer is found by evaluation not to be a serious risk to undermine the mother's parenting or to abuse the children; (d) the batterer has completed or is completing a full year in a batterer program with good participation; and (e) the children desire overnight visitation. We would consider exceptions to the first two conditions in cases in which geographical distance makes day visits impractical or where the batterer had been the children's primary caretaker.

Visitation with a batterer, especially overnight, should in no case be imposed over a child's objections. Children who have been exposed to domestic violence need to be empowered to question the batterer's behavior and authority and not to unthinkingly follow his model or instructions. Requiring children to visit with a batterer against their will, may encourage children to take a passive stance toward the batterer and to see his power as not subject to challenge. It also may unintentionally imply societal approval of his behavior. Perhaps even more important, forced visitation can drive wedges between mothers and their children, as children may then blame the mother for the emotional injuries that they suffer during visitation and may feel abandoned by her for requiring them to go; the legal risks that she runs if she does not comply with the court order are not comprehensible to them.

A batterer's progress down through the visitation tiers suggested above should be conditioned on his serious participation in a specialized batterer program (ABA Center on Children, 1994) and on his exhibiting other signs that he is giving up the use of abusive, controlling, or entitled behaviors. It should not be based exclusively on *his conduct in the supervised visits*, because the majority of batterers behave themselves fairly appropriately in supervised settings.

Because of the manipulation and intimidation that can take place through telephone contact, we also recommend that during any period of supervised visitation, the batterer's telephone contact with children be monitored either through tape recording (with notice to the father) or through the mother listening to the phone call (see also Walker & Edwall, 1987).

The progress of children's recovery from exposure to abuse (and from the parental separation) should be monitored as the batterer moves down the visitation tiers. Any setbacks in their well-being should be evaluated for possible connection to the visitation plan, and adjustments should be made accordingly. If children are highly distressed by visits, the structure of visitation should change or visits should be suspended (see also Straus, 1995). Moving between two homes is often stressful for children even when no history of violence exists between the parents, and these stresses can be accentuated in the context of domestic violence (Straus, 1995).

Evaluation of visitation arrangements should address the following questions: Are the children strengthening their connection to their mother? At the same time, are they becoming less worried about her and overattached to her (in cases in which this is an issue)? How are their other trauma-related symptoms progressing, such as problems falling asleep, nightmares, attention deficits, or hypervigilance? Are they developing some critical thinking skills with respect to the abuse that they witnessed or of which they were targets? Is their overall psychological strength growing? Have they increased their ability to challenge or to disagree with their father? Are they becoming less preoccupied with avoiding his displeasure? Is he supporting their therapy (if relevant) and supporting their recovery in other ways? Is he supporting their relationships with their mother?

The central goals for children should be kept in view at all times: their emotional recovery, their development of skills that will make them less likely to tolerate (or to keep secrets about) abuse in the future, and their development of analytical abilities that will allow them to avoid the batterer's negative influence on their perceptions and values. Toward this end, we recommend that children participate in groups for children who have been exposed to domestic violence, as these groups have been shown to be particularly effective contributors to recovery (Peled & Edleson, 1992). When such groups are not available or when children's behavioral or emotional difficulties are too severe for them to be able to participate in a group, therapy with a provider specially trained in the effects of domestic violence on family dynamics is an option (see Chapter 9). In order that both children and parents see the court as holding the batterer accountable for his actions, costs of children's therapy should be borne by him to the fullest extent possible (ABA Center on Children, 1994).

When a batterer is awarded unsupervised visits, even ones short in duration, we recommend that explicit conditions be placed on his conduct. Depending on his particular history of parenting behaviors, these restrictions can involve such items as prohibiting him from speaking badly about the mother (or about her new partner), requiring him to provide appropriate structure regarding food, safety, and bedtimes, or requiring him to take the children home at any point should they request that he do so. In our experience, batterers respond best when behavioral expectations are explicit and when the consequences of failure to cooperate are clear. For example, we recommend that visitation move back one or more tiers each time a batterer fails to comply with the stated restrictions. Minor transgressions should not be overlooked, as our clients tend to push limits until they encounter a negative consequence, beginning with such actions as failing to follow the schedule for dropoffs and pickups (see also Walker & Edwall, 1987).

We also recommend that batterers be required to permit unrestricted phone contact between the children and their mother during visits. Such phone contact can contribute to the children's sense of safety and security and can increase the batterer's sense that his conduct with the children is being monitored. We recognize that frequent phone contact during visitation sometimes can cause the children to miss their mother more rather than less, but this drawback is outweighed by the benefits in most cases.

Restrictions on alcohol use also can be helpful when relevant, but only if the batterer is enjoined from drinking *at all times*. Visitation orders sometimes state that a visiting parent is not to drink while the children are in his or her care. This is not an effective restriction, as the parent can be under the influence of alcohol consumption that took place prior to the visit. In addition, alcoholics cannot manage their drinking, and thus permitting alcohol consumption outside of visits invites alcohol abuse during visits as well. In cases in which there are concerns about a parent's substance abuse, the parent should be required to address the addiction, which most substance abuse specialists agree is unlikely to take place while even occasional use continues.

Parent training can be a helpful condition of visitation in cases in which there are concerns about the batterer's skill level. However, our experience indicates that such training is of limited value unless participation in a batterer program is required simultaneously, because a batterer's parenting issues cannot be separated well from his underlying abusive profile.

Children's sense of safety after separation can be enhanced when they perceive their mother to be safe as well. Visitation plans should therefore take the mother's safety needs into account. Exchanges for visitation are danger points both for mothers and for children (Sheeran & Hampton, 1999), and provisions for monitored exchanges or exchanges in well-lit locations close to the public eye are important. Supervised visitation centers and police stations are sometimes available as safe exchange sites. However, ongoing concerns about the safety of exchanges should be taken as a sign that unsupervised visitation may not yet be appropriate.

Finally, in preparing reports for the court, custody evaluators should be aware of the risks of retaliation against children by a parent (particularly an abusive one) for statements by the child to which the evaluator refers (Lawton & McAlister Groves, 2000).

SUMMARY

Batterers present numerous risks to their children, with the children's exposure to acts of domestic violence being only one such risk. Some batterers are considerably more dangerous to children than are others, and the level of dangerousness cannot be discerned by examining the batterer's history of physical violence alone. After separation, risk to children from batterers appears to increase in several ways rather than to decrease as is sometimes believed. Assessing the emotional, physical, and sexual safety of children in unsupervised contact with a batterer is therefore a complex process involving the examination of many factors. Evaluators need to be familiar with the range of sources of trauma to children from batterers and with the particular dynamics that may be present in a batterer's postseparation parenting. An extensive set of factors should be examined in assessing risk. The structuring of visitation plans that are safe and that best facilitate children's emotional progress and recovery requires the use of various levels of supervision and lengths of visitation and the engagement of the batterer and the children in relevant services.

8 🖋

Is It Real?

Assessing and Fostering Change in Batterers as Parents

Professionals in various capacities may find themselves called upon to assess change in a batterer's capacity to be a safe and responsible parent. Improvement in the parenting of a batterer is inseparable from his progress in overcoming his abuse toward partners, as his problematic behaviors toward children spring primarily from the same source (see Chapter 1). Although assessing change in a batterer's parenting also involves attention to important additional areas (as we will see below), the first step usually if not always involves addressing the underlying behaviors and attitudes of his pattern of abuse.

A batterer may tell a custody evaluator, "I used to have a bad temper, but that was a long time ago and I've grown up a lot since then." A mother may say to a child protective worker, "He used to hit me, but he's really calmed down in the last couple of years, and he's not like that anymore." A batterer intervention counselor may hear from a client, "This program has opened my eyes, and I would never do what I did again." Claims of change made by our clients often have little underlying substance, however, and professionals need to assess carefully whether or not a batterer has made meaningful progress.

Change cannot be correctly judged to have taken place just because of a recent period without physical violence. For example, Feld and Straus (1990) found that it was common even among severely violent batterers for 12 months or more to pass without violent incident, and Dunford (cited in Woffordt et al., 1994) found violence recurring after violence-free periods of more than 2 years. Gelles and Straus (1988) found that the average batterer assaults his partner three times per year, giving further indication of the likelihood of domestic assaults to be separated by extended periods. Further, batterers tend to carry their abusive behavior from relationship to relationship (Dutton, 1995; Woffordt et al., 1994; Kalmuss & Seltzer, 1986).

A batterer's motivation for stopping his abuse (or for creating the appearance of having done so) can come from various sources, including hoping for a reunion with his partner, trying to persuade child protective services to close his case, or attempting to win custody of his children. Regardless of the original source of motivation, we find that batterers do not continue to participate in batterer intervention or to make other serious efforts to change in the absence of outside pressure (see also Adams, 1989).

Assessment of change may be complicated by the awareness among many batterers of the types of language most likely to impress human service professionals. Our clients may seek to gain trust and sympathy by speaking analytically of their childhoods, describing painful processes of denial and self-confrontation, or using the language of feelings to open up about their guilt, insecurities, or fears.

Our clients typically find abusive behavior rewarding, as they are able to use it to enforce a high degree of catering to their selfish needs, to impose double standards, and to exercise control. The attachment that many batterers feel to continuing to abuse is evidenced, for example, by the fact that many batterers compensate for periods of using less physical violence by increasing their use of threats (Edleson & Brygger, 1986). Batterers are observed to increase their verbal and emotional abuse while participating in batterer programs (Gondolf, 1988). Meaningful change in batterers is thus an extended and difficult process. Our clients who claim to have changed sometimes speak in romantic or vague terms about how they overcame their abusiveness, sometimes referring to religious conversions or to other rapid transformations in outlook. However, those batterers who have made deep and lasting changes invariably attribute their progress to hard work, painful self-examination, and a willingness to make a lifelong commitment to reform.

STEPS TO CHANGE IN BATTERERS

Based on our work with batterers, we have identified 12 steps that are indispensable for a batterer to be able to become a responsible and safe parent. These steps are not intended to be a chronological sequence (although they do form a logical sequence to some extent), and we do not necessarily find that our clients progress through these steps in any particular order. The fact that we have identified 12 steps is coincidental and should not be interpreted as drawing any parallel to programs for recovery from addiction; although battering and addiction have some common characteristics, their differences outweigh their similarities (for further discussion, see Bancroft, 2002).

1. *The batterer must disclose fully the history of physical and psychological abuse toward his partner and children.* The client has to overcome the denial and minimization that accompany a battering problem. A batterer does not stop his abuse if he continues to deny or to "forget" significant portions of what he has done. (Similar observations have been made about the indispensable role of full disclosure in treating child sexual abusers; see Leberg, 1997.) Disclosure and acceptance of responsibility are interwoven processes, so that a batterer who is making serious progress on owning his problem will also tend to make increasing disclosures over time.

2. *The batterer must recognize that the behavior is unacceptable.* The client has to agree that what he did was wrong and cannot be repeated (see also Sonkin, Martin, & Walker, 1985). This step involves above all relinquishing excuses that blame the victim, including the claim that she provoked him, and letting go of any other justifications. This process involves recognizing not only that physical violence is wrong but also that other forms of abuse and manipulative behavior toward his partner and children are not justifiable.

3. *The batterer must recognize that the behavior was chosen.* The client has to accept responsibility for his actions (see also Sonkin et al., 1985). This means he has to stop using excuses such as that he was out of control, that he was drunk, that he was abused as a child, or that he was under stress. He needs to accept that his behavior was intentional and goal-oriented (Pence & Paymar, 1993).

4. *The batterer must recognize and show empathy for the effects of his actions on his partner and children.* Moving beyond such vague phrases as "I hurt her" or "I made her afraid," the client should be able to identify in detail the destructive impact that his behavior has had on his partner and children (Pence & Paymar, 1993). He also has to develop an *emotional connection* to these effects, so that he

experiences empathy for his partner and children (Mathews, 1995; Edleson & Tolman, 1992). (The similarity with sexual offender treatment arises again; see Pithers, 1999.) This step needs to include accepting the *long-term* effects on mothers and children, including how long their mistrust of him may last (Pence & Paymar, 1993; Sonkin et al., 1985). He needs to be able to discuss his history of abusiveness without reverting to a focus on his own emotional injuries, grievances, or excuses.

5. *The batterer must identify his pattern of controlling behaviors and entitled attitudes.* The client has to recognize that his violence was made possible by a larger context of behaviors and attitudes on his part (Pence & Paymar, 1993). He needs to be able to identify what his specific forms of day-to-day abuse and control have been (Edleson & Tolman, 1992) as well as the underlying outlook and excuses that drove those behaviors. He needs further to identify how he involved the children in this behavior pattern as witnesses, targets, or pawns and what attitudes he used to justify those actions. Batterers who continue emotional abuse tend to return eventually to violence, because they have failed to address the attitudes that cause abuse. Even if a batterer does not use violence again, the negative impact on his family of continued emotional abuse can be serious (Jacobson & Gottman, 1998), especially given the traumatic effects of violence from which family members may already be suffering.

6. *The batterer must develop respectful behaviors and attitudes.* The client needs to develop the ability to respond respectfully to his partner's grievances, to meet consistently his financial and parenting responsibilities, and to treat his partner as an equal. He has to be willing to give up his selfish focus on his own needs and to be able to consistently put the children's needs first, moving beyond his habits of entitled expectations for service. Finally, he has to develop ways of thinking that are consistent with nonabusive behavior in relationships, including accepting his partner's right to be angry (Sonkin et al., 1985) and developing a respectful outlook on his partner and children. Batterers who make attitudinal changes in batterer programs make more substantial behavioral improvements (Gondolf, 2000), and changing the batterer's belief system has been described as the central element in his process of overcoming abusiveness (e.g., Russell & Frohberg, 1995). We find that clients who stop abuse for a period but who fail to develop alternative attitudes and behaviors leave a void that is gradually refilled with their previous conduct.

7. *The batterer must reevaluate his distorted image of his partner.* The client has to recognize that he has developed an exaggeratedly negative view of his partner (or former partner), based largely on her resistance to his abuse and control. We find that clients who fail to reevaluate their internal construction of their victims return to abusing, even if they appear to be making good progress on other steps. Many of our clients, particularly those who abuse their children physically, sexually, or psychologically, have a similar problem with developing distorted views of their children, which needs equally to be addressed.

8. *The batterer must make amends both in the short and in the long term.* In our experience, batterers who make substantial progress in recognizing the damage that they have done develop a sense of *indebtedness,* as does anyone who accepts responsibility for a wrongful act. Such an awareness properly leads to steps to make up for the negative effects that his abuse has had both on his partner and on his children. The process of making amends includes the responsibility after separation to be a responsible parent who supports the children's relationships with their mother.

9. *The batterer must accept the consequences of his actions for him.* Part of how a client demonstrates that he is looking seriously at his abuse is by accepting that his behavior has, and should have, consequences for him (see also Sonkin et al., 1985). A client who continues to blame his partner for the money that he is spending on the abuser program or who insists that his former partner owes him "another chance" is probably failing to take this step, as is a client who insists that his history of battering should not be affecting his access to unsupervised and overnight visits with his children.

10. *The batterer must commit to not repeating abusive behavior.* Long-term change in our clients appears to require an unconditional commitment not to repeat the use of physical intimidation, psychological cruelty, or coercion toward his partner or children. Unfortunately, we observe that batterers sometimes take the attitude that a period of nonabusive behavior is a sort of credit that can be spent for an occasional act of violence or cruelty, "because I have done well for so long." In the same vein, comments such as "She can't expect me to change overnight" may be warning signs of imminent regression.

11. *The batterer must accept change as a long-term (probably lifelong) process.* In keeping with their entitled attitudes, batterers typically

want the process of overcoming abusiveness to involve limited effort and time. Those clients whom we have seen make lasting changes have accepted that they will always have to be working on their abuse issues and monitoring themselves closely, similar to an addiction recovery process. They have remained in the batterer program for 2 years or more, and upon leaving the program, they have recognized that their work was not over.

12. *The batterer must be willing to be accountable.* Those batterers who change accept the need to be answerable for their past and future actions and agree to the creation of structures that will make accountability possible (Pence & Paymar, 1993). They accept that their partner or former partner and their children may continue to challenge them regarding past or current behaviors. Should they behave abusively in the future, they consider it their responsibility to report those behaviors honestly to their friends and relatives, to their probation officer, and to others who will hold them accountable.

MISCONCEPTIONS REGARDING CHANGE IN BATTERERS

In contrast to the essential steps outlined above, certain other changes that are sometimes considered to be necessary in overcoming a battering problem are in fact not so. These include the development of emotional insight, the development of a softer or "gentle man" type of personal style, or the ability to be supportive toward other men in a batterer intervention group. We find these criteria to be biased toward certain cultural and class styles of what is desirable male behavior (specifically, those of upper- and middle-class whites) and to have little relationship to a man's capacity to be in a respectful, nonviolent relationship and to be a responsible parent. "Progress" in these areas can create a misleading impression of change in batterers who are in fact not dealing with the critical issues.

Furthermore, *anger management programs are not appropriate for men who batter.* These programs generally will not address any of the above 12 steps and therefore cannot assess the batterer's progress. As we addressed in Chapter 1, anger is a relatively minor issue in battering behavior. Anger management programs are not designed to address violence toward intimate partners, which has markedly different dynamics from violence that takes place in other contexts. Moreover, anger management programs typically do not address parenting issues, do not contact victims, and do not address the batterer's surrounding pattern of verbal, psychological, economic, and sexual abuse (see also Massachusetts Department of Public Health, n.d.).

EVALUATING CHANGE IN BATTERERS AS PARENTS

Evaluating change in a batterer's parenting begins with a detailed examination of the 12 steps delineated above. In our experience, the preponderance of batterers who claim to have changed return to battering, and those who have involved their children in the abuse tend to do so again, so evaluators need to exercise caution in concluding that a batterer has overcome his abusiveness and is ready to parent responsibly. Again, superficially positive statements such as "I know I'm responsible for my own actions" or "I have done some things I'm not proud of" reveal little in themselves about the depth of a man's progress.

Assessment of a batterer's progress on these steps needs to start with an examination of the batterer's current behavior toward his partner or former partner and toward his children. Has he in fact given up the use of insults and name-calling, stopped becoming irate when he is inconvenienced or is asked to meet his responsibilities, and begun to show empathy for the mother's needs and feelings? Is he developing the ability to focus on his children well, to put their needs ahead of his own, and to show understanding for their feelings? Most important, is he *consistent* in showing respectful and responsible behavior? (Brief, erratic periods of improvement are common in batterers and do not reflect change.)

Critically, the batterer's behavior during periods of anger, upset, or stress needs to be examined. Most of our clients can remain calm and reasonable during periods that do not involve major challenges, thereby creating a false impression of progress. Can the batterer now, for example, listen to his partner's (or former partner's) side of an argument and respond respectfully even when he is angry, or does he revert to shouting her down and dominating the conversation? When he is enraged, does he nonetheless parent appropriately, or does he use his feelings as an excuse to revert to manipulating the children against their mother or involving them in his conflicts with her? Evaluators sometimes make the mistake of dismissing evidence of backsliding in an abuser on the grounds that the regression happened under unusual stress or frustration; however, it is precisely under such conditions that the greatest distinctions may appear between abusers who are genuinely changing and those who are not.

In our experience, most batterers can change their behavior toward their partners or children dramatically during a period in which they have motivation to do so. Our clients often take on a new personal style when awaiting a court date, when pursuing litigation for custody or visitation, or when child protective services become involved with their family. Their parenting can shift sharply at such a time to showing interest, involvement, and patience. These improvements should not be expected to endure beyond the immediate crisis, however, unless accompanied by an extensive collection of other indicators of change.

Specific indicators that evaluators can use in monitoring fundamental change in the batterer's orientation toward his children include the following: (a) Has the batterer exhibited a number of years (as opposed to weeks or months) of consistently improved parenting behavior? (b) Are there no indications that the apparent improvements in his parenting behavior are actually motivated by a desire to control or to punish his former partner, such as by turning the children against her? (c) Has he participated well in parent education classes and taken other steps to make himself a more informed parent? and (d) Has he accepted complete responsibility for the previous problems in his parenting of the children, identified the attitudes that were driving those problems, and developed the ability to empathically discuss the effects that he has had on his children?

Evaluation should rely on multiple sources of information (including reports from the batterer's partner or former partner), not on his own statements alone. Reports from batterer intervention programs can be helpful but should be examined carefully to make sure that the relevant indicators of change have been thoroughly reviewed.

We fairly commonly encounter examples of *nonbattering* fathers whose parenting improves after separation, as the need to care independently for their children leads them to break previous patterns of passivity or preoccupation. However, we have not encountered this type of spontaneous parenting improvement in batterers, whose parenting deficits are considerably more complex and generally require outside intervention to overcome.

CREATING A CONTEXT FOR CHANGE

We observe that batterers are most likely to make progress in their parenting and underlying abuse issues when a proper context is created. The low rate of change that is observed in batterers may be largely a product of the widespread social misunderstanding of the circumstances necessary to lead batterers to work on their problem seriously. Professionals can contribute to creating a context that fosters change in batterers, drawing from the following elements:

(a) Express in the clearest terms possible the behaviors that are expected of the batterer, the behaviors that are not acceptable, and the consequences of behaving in unacceptable ways (see also Jacobson & Gottman, 1998).

(b) Impose consequences each time that inappropriate behavior takes place, without warnings and without overlooking minor transgressions. The consequences generally need not be harsh; what is important is that they be predictable and that no excuses or promises from the batterer keep them from being imposed. Impose a set of clearly increasing consequences for each violation of expected behaviors (like the "staircasing" approach to sentences for drunk driving offenses). This approach is particularly important for courts, both in criminal and in family matters.

(c) Monitor the batterer's behavior as closely as possible, so that he understands that he will be held accountable for his actions (Jacobson & Gottman, 1998). Avoid relying on his own reporting of his conduct regardless of how earnest he may sound.

(d) Offer a mixture of education and confrontation. We find that because their belief systems are complex and long established, our clients have trouble integrating confrontation that lacks adequate education. On the other hand, clients offered education without confrontation tend to apply the concepts to other abusers but not to themselves. Styles of counseling need to take the batterer's racial and cultural experience into account (Carrillo & Tello, 1998). (Working with adolescent batterers also requires some modification in approach; see Sousa & Cooper, 1997.)

(e) Communicate and demonstrate to the batterer that you are not swayed by his excuses, that you do not unquestioningly accept his version of what has taken place, and that you are not manipulable. These messages can be given to the client without creating an atmosphere of hostility, through a style that is firm but friendly.

(f) Make culturally and linguistically appropriate services available to batterers of color and to immigrant batterers, including making the option of homogeneous groups available whenever possible (West, 1998).

(g) Offer unconditional support and resources to the batterer's partner (or former partner) and children. A batterer's change depends largely on his perceptions of whether he can get away with continuing to abuse. We have observed that those women who receive the strongest services and the most solid support from friends, relatives, and the legal system are in the best position to demand that the batterer deal seriously with his issues. Research shows that unified community responses can decrease recidivism much more than can isolated responses (Murphy, Musser, & Maton, cited in Hamby, 1998). (For a more detailed discussion of the process of change in batterers, see Bancroft, 2002.)

The development of parenting programs specifically designed for battering men is an important development in fostering change, and such programs are resources to draw upon when they are available (see, e.g., Mathews, 1995).

SUMMARY

Positive change in the parenting of a batterer is closely interwoven with his progress in overcoming his underlying abuse issues. For this reason, it is unusual for a batterer to make major parenting improvements without participation in specialized batterer intervention, combined with experiences of structure, monitoring, and consequences. We have identified 12 steps that are indispensable to assessing the depth of a batterer's progress in overcoming his problems as a partner and as a parent, and we suggest that certain additional markers be examined to explore further the specific changes that he has made with respect to parenting attitudes and conduct. Batterers are more likely to make substantial changes when a context for that change is created in their community through systems of education, confrontation, consequences, and accountability, focusing on his role both as partner and as parent.

9

Improving Community Responses to the Parenting of Batterers

The understandings about the parenting of batterers that have been reviewed in the preceding chapters have far-reaching implications for professional practice. Improved intervention with battering fathers has the potential to contribute to emotional and physical safety for battered women and their children and in the long term to improve the quality of life for batterers themselves. This chapter offers specific suggestions for professionals in a range of areas, including therapists, child protective personnel, family and juvenile courts, domestic violence programs, custody evaluators, and supervised visitation centers. These recommendations may need to be adapted to fit the needs of various cultural or immigrant groups or may not be appropriate for some groups (e.g., Carrillo & Tello, 1998).

Certain guiding principles apply to the full range of professionals intervening in families affected by domestic violence. The first and most critical is the need to be aware of the effects of domestic violence on family interaction patterns, including the dynamics of the relationships between mothers and children, the relationships among siblings, and the interactions between family members and the outside world (see Chapter 3). Statements made to professionals by batterers *or by their family members* should not be accepted at face value, and dynamics within the family sometimes are revealed to contrast sharply with original appearances. In some families affected by domestic violence, children may see the batterer as likeable and entertaining and perceive their mother as distant, mistrustful, and depressed; the siblings in such a family may have bitter tensions and divisions among themselves. Another family affected by similar abuse may present with the children unified with each other and with their mother, with little apparent internalization of the batterer's abuse. A superficial reading of the contrasting dynamics of these families can lead professionals to overlook the underlying similarities.

As part of augmenting sophistication in the analysis of family dynamics, we recommend that a broad range of professionals familiarize themselves with literature on abuse-related trauma (e.g., van der Kolk & McFarlane, 1996; Herman, 1992) and on traumatic bonding (Dutton, 1995; Dutton & Painter, 1983, 1993; Herman, 1992). Many of the practice errors that we encounter result from inadequate preparation in these critical concepts.

The second general principle is that a batterer's behavior toward his adult partner *in itself* reveals important information about his parenting. The battering of a mother, even if the children never see or hear the violence, affects children's relationship with her and her ability to care for them (see Chapter 3). Battering of a mother thus needs to be understood as a *parenting decision* on the abuser's part, a decision that sheds important light on his ability to think well about the children's safety and well-being and therefore is reflective of decisions he is likely to make in the future (see also Jaffe & Geffner, 1998).

Along with these two fundamental points are a number of others that we think call for the attention of professionals across all disciplines. To begin with, some batterers are more physically dangerous or psychologically injurious to their children than are others. These two kinds of risk are not collapsible; some of the less violent or terrifying batterers with whom we have worked have been among the most psychologically injurious to children. Risk to children from a batterer should therefore be carefully evaluated following the guidelines in Chapter 7.

Professionals involved in domestic violence cases sometimes underutilize the battered woman's own knowledge about her specific batterer and his risk to children. A battered mother is often able to predict accurately what types of parenting problems the batterer is likely to exhibit, based on her knowledge of his past behaviors toward the children. We also find that battered women often develop a strong overall ability to predict a batterer's future behavior (see also Weisz et al., 2000), a skill that appears to be developed for its survival value.

Risk to children from a batterer cannot be assumed to decrease when the parents' relationship ends, and in fact it may intensify (see Chapter 7). Psychological and physical danger to children from a batterer can continue for years following a divorce or separation. We therefore recommend that professionals in all categories seek ways to contribute to the safety of battered mothers and their children and to create a context for emotional healing after the batterer is no longer in the home. In part, this goal involves examining strategies for preventing batterers from winning custody of their children and for reducing the granting to batterers of unsupervised contact.

Gender bias continues to be an issue contributing to practice errors in domestic violence cases. We observe, for example, (a) the application of different criteria to evaluating the parenting of fathers and mothers, (b) the assumption that mothers' concerns for their children are exaggerated, (c) a double standard that blames a mother for failing to protect her children while living with the batterer but then criticizes her harshly after separation (such as by accusing her of "parental alienation") if she does take proper protective steps, and (d) making greater allowances for anger in fathers than in mothers.

A useful guiding concept that has emerged from collaborations between child protective services and battered women's programs is that the best way to contribute to the safety of the children of a battered woman is to further the safety of their mother (Whitney & Davis, 1999). This contribution involves assisting the mother with her own recovery from the effects of abuse, guiding her in becoming a more effective advocate for her children, and including her as part of the team that seeks strategies for safety for her family. The success of these efforts depends in part on the ability of professionals to develop respect for battered women, avoiding the condescension and impatience that we sometimes encounter in professional responses. Similarly, professionals from various disciplines can explore ways to provide supportive parenting groups for battered mothers, the value of which is confirmed by research (Jouriles et al., 1998). Collaboration between battered women's programs and child protective services increases the effectiveness of response to children exposed to batterers but also requires the overcoming of certain historical tensions between mother-focused and child-focused providers (Beeman, Hagemeister, & Edleson, 1999). We also recommend highly the model of joint group work for mothers and children described by Rubenstein and Lehmann (2000).

Finally, we propose that all professionals adopt the phrase "children exposed to batterers" rather than "children exposed to domestic violence," as a way to encapsulate our understanding that the traumatic effects on children of growing up with an abused mother have their roots in a wide range of behaviors exhibited by the batterer, not just in his physical violence. This phrase has the additional advantage of making clear that the batterer, and not the battered mother, is visually the *agent* of the children's primary difficulties.

The recommendations below are not exhaustive, as full guidebooks could be written for each professional field on the handling of domestic violence cases. These points should be understood as salient ones that we wish to emphasize.

CHILD THERAPISTS, FAMILY THERAPISTS, AND PROGRAMS FOR CHILDREN EXPOSED TO DOMESTIC VIOLENCE

Direct work with children exposed to batterers should include (a) advocating for their immediate and long-term safety, (b) assisting them to heal from the traumatic effects of witnessing domestic violence, (c) assisting them to heal damaged relationships with their mothers and siblings, and (d) providing education to clarify and replace destructive values that have been absorbed (Peled & Davis, 1995) and especially to help them to attribute responsibility for abuse to the abuser and not the victim or the children (Wagar & Rodway, 1995). For most children, these goals can be met best through participation in a psychoeducational group (Peled & Davis, 1995; ABA Center on Children, 1994), in certain cases in conjunction with individual or family therapy. Psychoeducational groups have been demonstrated to be successful in helping children to recover emotionally, to reduce their self-blame, and to increase their ability to identify abusive behaviors (Sudermann, Marshall, & Loosely, 2000; Peled & Edleson, 1992), although the effect on reducing their blaming of their mothers has not been studied to our knowledge. Individual therapy is necessary for children who are too distressed or disruptive to participate in a group and in areas where groups are not available.

Our specific recommendations to therapists and program directors include the following:

1. Children exposed to domestic violence need to feel safe to express the range of emotions that they feel toward the batterer, including their fear, anger, sadness, and love (Peled, 2000; Peled & Davis, 1995). Providers need to be careful to use language that criticizes the batterer's *behavior* (e.g., "It was wrong for him to frighten your mother like that") but that does not attack him as a *person* (e.g., "Your father is a bad man"). It is important that children not feel pressure to renounce their affection for the batterer. At the same time, they need help in understanding that they are not betraying him when

they reveal the violence or speak openly about how it has affected them.

2.   Children of battered women need information about the history of the violence and other forms of abuse that their mother has endured. This information needs to be conveyed in limited and age-appropriate amounts and needs to avoid particularly frightening or painful details. Providers (and battered mothers themselves) have to strike a delicate balance in determining how much to tell children: Too little information can leave children confused and self-blaming and can contribute to ruptures between mothers and children if children blame the mother for circumstances that were largely beyond her control; too much information, on the other hand, can increase children's fear and can add to their burden of responsibility for their mother's safety or emotional distress.

It is also important to elicit carefully from children the knowledge of the batterer's abuse that they already have (which is sometimes greater than either parent realizes), in order to relieve the children of any burden of solitary knowledge and to make it clear to them that they are free to talk about it.

3.   Children need assistance in exploring ways that the batterer may have interfered with their relationships with their mother through such tactics as conditioning their view of her, misleading them about the history of abuse, making them feel ashamed to be close to her or reliant upon her, or encouraging them to disrespect her authority.

4.   Conjoint work with mothers and children or with siblings should be included as a part of work with children of battered women whenever possible. Restoring damaged family relationships and re-establishing the mother's parental authority (Rubenstein & Lehmann, 2000) are key to the future emotional health of children. Children's relationship to their nonbattering parent needs to be recognized as the single most important factor in their long-term thriving. This work should include some attention to how the batterer has introduced tension into the relationships between family members.

5.   Effective work with children of a battered woman depends in part on effective outreach to the mother. This goal is served best by approaching the mother with respect and compassion and by treating her as the expert on her own children. Providers need to seek extensive training for themselves on the dynamics of domestic violence, in order

to understand the mother's trauma and the complex obstacles that she faces in bringing safety to herself and her children (see, e.g., Davies et al., 1998).

6.   The maintenance of confidentiality is crucial in working with children exposed to batterers, because a child can be in danger from a batterer should he find out that the child has disclosed the presence of domestic violence. This need sometimes collides with a professional's duty to make a child abuse report in cases in which the child has been endangered or injured by the battering. Decisions of whether and how to make child abuse reports need to be informed by an awareness of the risk to the child of the reporting process itself.

7.   Psychoeducational group counseling is a particularly valuable resource for children exposed to domestic violence. Group work lends itself well to the mixture of emotional and cognitive processing that children need. Guides exist for running such groups (e.g., Peled & Davis, 1995; Wilson, Cameron, Jaffe, & Wolfe, 1986); where such guides do not address some specific issues raised in this book, providers are encouraged to develop their own curriculum elements based on information given here and in other sources.

8.   Those children who are not appropriate for participation in groups because of severe emotional or behavioral problems (see assessment guidelines in Peled & Davis, 1995) can benefit from the integration of educational components into their individual therapeutic work.

9.   Problems in children's attitudes and belief systems need to be addressed. As reviewed in Chapter 2, children exposed to battering commonly absorb incorrect beliefs such as that (a) victims are to blame for "provoking" violence or for causing the violence in other ways, (b) perpetrators of violence are not responsible for their actions, (c) taking power over others is the route to safety and self-esteem, (d) it is appropriate for males to be aggressive and demanding and females should cater to males, (e) females are passive and victimized, (f) people who complain of mistreatment should be ridiculed, and other distorted values and perceptions. Psychotherapy with children that does not directly address these issues will not adequately contribute to overcoming the negative socializing impact of exposure to batterers.

The children's process of reevaluating their understanding of past abuse and learning to correctly attribute responsibility to the abuser rather than to their mothers or to themselves is an important but emotionally charged one, and children will need assistance with the complicated feelings that may emerge for them (Peled & Edleson, 1992).

10.   The effectiveness of group work with children can be enhanced by the provision of simultaneous groups for mothers that follow a parallel curriculum (Peled & Davis, 1995) or by working with mothers and children in conjoint groups (Rubenstein & Lehmann, 2000). Some programs using this model include joint activities for the children and mothers to do during the week following group sessions, based on the similar themes addressed in both groups.

11.   One particularly effective model of leadership for psycho-educational groups is to pair an experienced domestic violence advocate with a mental health practitioner who is trained in domestic violence issues, ideally in a male-female team.

12.   Therapists working with children exposed to battering need to be prepared to provide *advocacy,* which is sometimes an unfamiliar practice. The provider may in particular need to advocate with child protective services, family courts, schools, and the mother herself to address the child's needs for ongoing safety from the batterer and for strengthening of the mother-child relationship.

13.   Working with children of battered women while the batterer is still in the home or when children have unsupervised contact with him may be dangerous for the child, as the child may confront the father with concepts or information learned in the therapy and then experience retaliation by him. (Children's tendency to confront parents with material learned in the groups is discussed in Peled & Edleson, 1992.) Programs thus need to institute policies that take this risk into account, such as substituting individual therapy in dangerous cases.

14.   Work with children exposed to battering needs to include attention to traumatic bonding (see Chapter 2) and to the child's identification with the aggressor both as a traumatic effect and as a survival skill.

15.   Because of the tendency of batterers to cause ongoing conflict within the family, we sometimes find that both mothers and children are exhausted from years of tension in their relationships. Given

this context, conjoint work with battered mothers and their children can benefit from discussions and exercises that foster sharing compliments, reviewing memories of positive times together, and learning more about each other as people. Attempting to air and to resolve conflicts can be counterproductive unless balanced with these more positive types of activities.

16.   Both battered mothers and their children tend to have histories of distorting their own goals and personalities in order to orient themselves toward pleasing the batterer and thereby to avoid his abuse as much as possible (Roy, 1988). It is therefore productive for therapists to guide clients in exploring their own desires and identities with the goal of rediscovering who they are.

17.   It may be frightening for family members of a batterer to accept how limited their control over his behavior actually is. The illusion that they can manage the batterer, an illusion that can be reinforced by periods of time during which they seem to succeed in doing so, can be a source of comfort for traumatized women and children. However, this illusion can simultaneously increase their danger because a batterer cannot, in fact, be reliably managed. It also increases the tendency of family members to blame one another; each time the batterer has an abusive incident, family members may seek a scapegoat on the assumption that someone must have failed to manage him properly. Therefore, the restoration of relationships within the family involves coming to terms with the fact that family members cannot control the batterer's behavior and are not responsible for doing so.

18.   Many children of battered women need assistance with processing the effects of the batterer's intermittent attention. His self-involvement or physical absence can alternate with periods in which he gives the children highly focused and entertaining attention (this pattern is similar to how some narcissistic parents operate with children). Although children can accumulate resentments regarding this dynamic, we observe that those feelings may remain largely unconscious or be channeled toward their mother or siblings. Children's conscious orientation toward the batterer in these cases tends to be one of idealizing him, working hard to earn his attention and approval, and feeling grateful for whatever positive attention they do attain.

19.   Therapists should not take neutral stands with children regarding a batterer's violence or cruelty. Children are typically

already confused about whether or not these behaviors are acceptable, and a therapist's neutrality can further that confusion. Inappropriate behavior should be named as such, and this naming should be followed with exploration of the child's emotional experience of these acts.

Similarly, a stand of strict neutrality between the parents may not be appropriate for therapists working with children of battered women. For example, it may make sense for the therapist to assist the battered mother in locating services for herself (including legal representation) or to advocate for her in other ways.

20.   Like survivors of other kinds of abuse or trauma, children exposed to the battering of their mother can be resilient (Jaffe & Geffner, 1998). Some sources of resilience include the child's skills or interests, positive peer relationships, the stronger aspects of the child's relationship with the mother, relationships with other trusted adults including relatives, and internal coping mechanisms. Therapists should explore these sources of resilience and foster the child's ability to draw strength and clarity from them.

21.   Symptoms of posttraumatic stress disorder in children differ in some ways from those in adults (Rossman & Ho, 2000). Children exposed to domestic violence have significantly higher rates of attention and hyperactivity problems (Gleason, 1995) and of depression, which can lead to misdiagnoses (Rossman & Ho, 2000). Therefore, a diagnosis of such symptoms should not be assigned without exploring possible traumatic causes.

22.   We highly recommend *Groupwork With Children of Battered Women* (Peled & Davis, 1995) as a guide to running programs for children exposed to domestic violence. However, we also recommend that this curriculum be expanded to include important themes raised in this book, especially the healing of mother-child relationships and the overcoming of blaming the mother.

23.   Mentoring programs can be a helpful resource for children exposed to battering. We have seen that boys in particular tend to crave positive male role models and gravitate toward them if they are available.

24.   Children who have witnessed domestic violence may be afraid to express, or even to allow themselves to feel, certain emotions,

which can interfere with their recovery. They may associate anger with violence, for example, or may have been humiliated by the batterer for crying (especially common for boys). Therefore, education and permission regarding expression of emotions is important (Peled & Edleson, 1992).

25. Because of the high overlap between exposure to domestic violence and sexual victimization both inside and outside of the home (McCloskey et al., 1995), all children of battered women should receive sexual abuse prevention education.

CUSTODY EVALUATORS

In the context of allegations of domestic violence or of a pattern of coercive control that includes elements of physical intimidation, custody evaluation needs to be carried out with particular care by an evaluator familiar with the dynamics of domestic violence and of the parenting of batterers. Our specific practice recommendations include the following:

1. The top priority of a custody evaluator should be the conducting of a thorough *investigation*. Such an investigation cannot be performed through clinical evaluation alone (American Psychological Association, 1994). The evaluator needs to pursue a wide range of sources of evidence, including (a) interviews with the parties and with the children when appropriate; (b) interviews with friends, relatives, school personnel, and other witnesses; (c) records from police, child protective services, courts, and medical providers; (d) interviews with previous partners of the parents, particularly of the alleged batterer; (e) examination of criminal records of the parents; (f) tape recordings, correspondence, diaries, and other documents; and (g) other potential sources of evidence that may come to the evaluator's attention during the course of the investigation.

2. Examination of the credibility of the parties through the review of the above sources of evidence is critical. Statements made to custody evaluators vary widely in their honesty and accuracy. Careful investigation sometimes reveals a marked difference in the level of honesty of the parties. In cases in which the alleged batterer is found to be dishonest in important or chronic ways, the allegations may be strengthened.

3. The absence of police or medical records does not in itself indicate that domestic violence allegations have been fabricated or exaggerated. Thorough investigation typically reveals other important sources of evidence.

4. The evaluator's personal impressions of which party appears to be more truthful can lead to erroneous conclusions in cases involving domestic violence allegations. We find that when a thorough investigation is conducted, the evaluator rarely needs to base recommendations on such impressions (see Chapter 5).

5. Psychological testing and evaluation cannot establish which parent is telling the truth regarding domestic violence allegations, nor can it establish whether a particular man is a batterer or a particular woman has been battered. Psychological evaluation should be used only for treatment planning in cases in which serious mental health concerns are present. Psychological evaluations should be interpreted cautiously (American Psychological Association, 1994) and are inappropriate for predicting dangerousness or parenting ability in batterers (see Chapters 5 and 7).

6. Children's statements to evaluators need to be interpreted cautiously, and the evaluator should test carefully for signs of coercion, manipulation, or rehearsal by either parent. We find it common for children to deny domestic violence even in cases where extensive independent evidence is present; furthermore, as a result of the mother's trauma and other factors, it is not uncommon for children to speak more positively of the batterer than of the battered woman. Children's statements need to be interpreted with an understanding of the typical dynamics of families where domestic violence is present (see Chapter 3) and of traumatic bonding (see Chapter 2). At the same time, children's statements need to be weighed carefully and not assumed to be simple reflections of parental opinions (see Chapter 6).

7. Observations by the evaluator of the children's interactions with each parent call for similar circumspection in their interpretation. An hour-long observation reveals little about the dynamics of either household, and most batterers perform well under observation. Evaluators should have specific goals for what they wish to learn from the interaction, avoid drawing conclusions that are overly broad, and consider the impact that a batterer can have on family interaction patterns, including traumatic bonding.

8. If the evaluator becomes persuaded that the allegations of domestic violence are substantially accurate, risk to the children from unsupervised contact with the batterer should be assessed with caution (see Chapter 7). Such an assessment should not be based solely on the batterer's level of physical dangerousness, nor on his statements to the evaluator.

9. Many influential theories of divorce and separation are not applicable to cases involving batterers. Evaluators should not proceed on the assumption that ongoing tensions between the parents are mutually caused. Similarly, it should not be assumed that the battered woman could improve her children's experience by being more forgiving or trusting toward the batterer, improving her communication with him, or being more supportive of her children's relationships with him (see Chapter 6). We observe that the more appropriately a battered mother seeks to further the needs and interests of her children, the greater the likelihood that she will have a highly conflictual relationship with the father after separation.

10. A battered mother should not be criticized for her concern that the batterer will abuse the children in ways similar to his abuse of her. As we have discussed, both research and clinical experience indicate strongly that a high proportion of batterers recreate key aspects of the abusive style that they use with the adult partner in their relationships with their children.

11. Careful assessment should be made of the ability of an alleged batterer to focus on his children's needs and to put those needs ahead of his own, as this is an area in which a high proportion of batterers are weak as parents. Assessment should include both his past and his current behavior in this regard.

12. A batterer's presentation to a professional of himself and of his beliefs can be misleading (Adams, 1989). Observations that an alleged batterer presents as calm, articulate, insightful, or emotionally wounded by the divorce or by denial of visitation should not be weighed heavily in assessing the presence or severity of domestic violence perpetration. Similar caution should be used in weighing the fact that the alleged batterer may espouse philosophies of mutual kindness, egalitarianism, or the importance of putting the children's needs ahead of other concerns, especially if these are not consistent with his past and current behavior.

13.   Recommendations about custody and visitation need to be made with attention to the physical and emotional safety of the children and of their mother and to the children's need for a life context that supports recovery from trauma (see Chapter 5). A battered mother's knowledge and beliefs about what kind of contact with the batterer will work best for her children should be weighed heavily in the process of planning visitation. We encourage the use of the guidelines provided in Chapter 7 for determining the length, frequency, and structure of postseparation contact between batterers and their children, including the degree of supervision required. The paramount goal in domestic violence cases is to promote the strongest relationship possible between children and the nonbattering parent.

14.   Prior to submitting a report in a domestic violence case, the evaluator should consider the potential impact of each recommendation on mother-child relationships and on relationships among siblings.

15.   A custody evaluator who does not have a professional background working in domestic violence programs should seek consultation from a domestic violence professional on all custody evaluations that involve allegations of battering (American Psychological Association, 1994).

16.   Assessment of parenting capacity should include evaluation of the parents' *values* with respect to parenting (American Psychological Association, 1994). The examination of values is of increased importance in domestic violence cases, for reasons reviewed in Chapters 1 through 3.

17.   Joint custody and frequent exchanges for visitation lead to markedly worse outcomes for children when imposed in cases in which tensions between the parents remain high (Johnston, 1994b), as is consistently true in custody disputes involving domestic violence. In such cases, it is preferable to award sole custody to the nonbattering parent and to create visitation schedules that do not involve frequent exchanges (see Chapter 7).

FAMILY COURTS

Most of the recommendations for custody evaluators given above apply generally to the decision-making process within family courts and to the concepts that should underlie that process. We include the following additional recommendations for court personnel:

1. Specific training and credentialing programs should be offered for custody evaluators. Custody evaluators need to have extensive knowledge in the following areas: (a) thorough and effective investigation, (b) assessment of parenting skills, (c) assessment of parent-child relationships and level of bonding (including traumatic bonding), (d) assessment of allegations of child abuse and neglect, (e) assessment of allegations of domestic violence and their relevance to custody and visitation plans, (f) assessment of allegations of substance abuse, (g) assessment of mental health, (h) dynamics of divorce in battering and nonbattering cases, and (i) laws and legal procedures applicable to custody and visitation litigation. No professional discipline covers this range of areas, and most professional training programs offer attention to few or none of these; some courts have a preference for using licensed mental health practitioners as custody evaluators, who might typically have preparation in only two or three of the above areas, whereas a professional with a background in child protection (for example) might typically be trained in as many as five or six. Custody evaluators should be recruited from a range of professions including domestic violence, mental health, substance abuse, parent education, and probation and should be required to complete a training program that is designed specifically for custody evaluators. Such requirements already exist in certain states and provinces.

As part of their specific training on this issue, custody evaluators handling cases involving allegations of domestic violence need to understand the family dynamics that can result from domestic violence (see Chapter 3) as well as the multiple risks to children from unsupervised contact with batterers, proper risk assessment procedures, and appropriate structuring of visitation in domestic violence cases (see Chapter 7).

2. Shared legal or physical custody is not advisable in domestic violence cases except when supported by both parents, because of the tendency of most batterers to cause ongoing conflicts that affect the children.

3. Allegations of domestic violence should not be treated as fabricated or exaggerated in the absence of a thorough and sophisticated investigation.

4.   Unsupervised contact between children and a batterer is generally not advisable (ABA Center on Children, 1994) until an extended period of time (a year or more) has passed since the parental separation occurred. Even then, such contact should be granted only when all of the following circumstances are present: (a) The batterer has completed a specialized batterer intervention program; (b) the batterer is not a present danger to the children physically or sexually; (c) the batterer does not have a severe history of undermining mother-child relationships; and (d) the children wish to visit with the batterer. Unsupervised contact may need to be introduced somewhat more quickly if the batterer was previously the children's primary caretaker or if the parents live far apart, but this should be done only if the risk to the children is not found to be high.

5.   We discourage the granting of overnight visitation in most domestic violence cases, for reasons discussed at length in Chapter 7 (see also NCJFCJ, 1994; ABA Center on Children, 1994).

6.   Visitation should not be imposed over a child's objections in domestic violence cases, with the possible exception of a limited number of professionally supervised visits in cases in which children can tolerate such visits without traumatic after-effects. The long-term risks involved in disempowering children with respect to their relationship with a battering father generally outweigh the potential benefits.

7.   Custody of children should not be awarded to batterers except in the rare cases in which the mother is incapable of caring for the children safely, no alternate appropriate placement is available, and the batterer is not found to be dangerous to his children. In such cases, the custody determination should be revisited if the mother is able within a reasonable length of time to make the necessary changes to be an appropriate parent or if the children are found to be endangered in the batterer's home.

8.   We believe that children of battered women benefit when their mothers are treated with patience, courtesy, and respect by court personnel, including judges. This respect becomes even more important when making rulings that are not consistent with the mother's wishes.

9.   Conflicts over custody, visitation, or child support should not be mediated between a battered mother and a batterer unless she

chooses voluntarily to participate in mediation (ABA Center on Children, 1994; Hart, 1990b). Batterers often succeed in manipulating mediation, and battered mothers may for various reasons consent to terms that they do not believe to be good for their children (see Chapter 5). When chosen by the mother, voluntary mediation should follow specific and restrictive guidelines (Magaña & Taylor, 1993), and judges should review any stipulated agreement carefully with the parties to make sure that it has been arrived at freely and that it is in the best interests of the children. In any case, court-based mediators, including probation officers, should not mediate issues in domestic violence cases but should act only as fact gatherers to assist the judge (Gender Bias Study Committee, 1989).

10. The setting of child support levels needs to include more gathering of evidence by court personnel regarding the parents' income and other resources, because of the high level of dishonesty shown by some batterers during child support hearings and on related documents. We receive widespread reports from battered mothers of misrepresentation by the batterer of his resources, with resultant large financial losses to mothers and children. Consequences should be imposed for false statements on financial forms and should be applied also to attorneys who are aware of the false statements (Gender Bias Study Committee, 1990). Domestic violence court proceedings do not always address child support adequately (Menard & Turetsky, 1999), yet financial issues can be critical to the battered woman's safety and ability to avoid reinvolvement with the batterer.

11. Courts should expand the practice of referring children of battered women to specialized psychoeducational groups when available, as such services appear to be unique contributors to children's healing. Courts should not permit batterers to block children's participation in such programs.

12. Child abuse reports that are determined by child protective services not to have adequate supporting evidence should not be treated as false allegations (Finkelhor, 1994). The court should consider the following possibilities: (a) The allegation was accurate but the child was not prepared to disclose to professionals; (b) the allegation was accurate but the child protective service deemed it not to be serious enough to warrant intervention; or (c) the allegation may not have been accurate but was the result of an honest misunderstanding on the part of the parent who made the allegation or was an

appropriate response to worrisome behaviors that turned out to have other (nonabuse) causes. Deliberately false allegations occur at lower rates than is commonly believed, even during custody and visitation litigation (see Chapter 4).

13.   In domestic violence cases, the best interests of the children are not separable from the best interests of the battered mother (Whitney & Davis, 1999). Therefore, the safety and well-being of the mother need to be taken into account in making custody and visitation determinations.

14.   To the fullest extent possible, batterers should be held responsible for the costs both of supervised visitation (NCJFCJ, 1994) and of therapy for the children (ABA Center on Children, 1994). Furthermore, courts should expand the practice of assigning some portion of the battered mother's legal fees to the batterer, once a finding of domestic violence has been made in custody and visitation litigation (Gender Bias Study Committee, 1990).

15.   Requests by battered mothers to relocate are commonly in the best interests of their children, and a rebuttable presumption should exist that such requests be granted (NCJFCJ, 1994). Relocation in divorce cases in general is often in the children's best interests, especially if it allows the custodial parent to make important life progress (Wallerstein & Tanke, 1996).

16.   Couples counseling (or other kinds of conjoint therapy or mediation sessions) should generally not be ordered in domestic violence cases (Schechter & Edleson, 1998).

17.   Anger management programs should not be used in place of specialized batterer intervention programs, as they focus on a wholly different set of issues from those necessary for addressing batterers' problems as partners and as parents (see Chapter 8).

18.   We recommend that court personnel be familiar with the *Model Code on Domestic and Family Violence* (NCJFCJ, 1994) and with the detailed domestic violence visitation recommendations in Appendix A of Sheeran and Hampton (1999).

19.   Family courts should set standards for custody evaluation in cases in which allegations of domestic violence are present. These

standards should specify the types of evidence that the evaluator must seek and consider and should elucidate all of the steps of a proper investigation/evaluation in such a case. Furthermore, the standards should discourage the routine use of psychological testing in such cases and should specify the uses to which the results of such testing may and may not be put.

AGENCIES AND COURTS WITH
CHILD PROTECTIVE JURISDICTION

Domestic violence is present in 60% or more of child protective cases (Whitney & Davis, 1999). Evaluation of the mother's parenting, including her potential for improvement, needs to take into account the batterer's impact on her abilities to care for her children and to establish parental authority (see Chapter 3). The risk to children from the batterer requires examination of multiple factors (see Chapter 7). Finally, children vary tremendously in the degree to which they are negatively affected by exposure to domestic violence (Jaffe, Wolfe, & Wilson, 1990), depending on several factors, some of which include the severity of the violence, the level of manipulativeness of the batterer, the mother's level of success in supporting them and in shielding them from negative effects, and the children's access to resources in the community that support resilience (see Chapter 3).

In addition to the application of the above principles, we make the following specific recommendations:

1. In cases in which a mother cannot be an appropriate caretaker or the child's behavior has become unmanageable for her, alternatives to placement with the battering father should be sought. We have observed that younger children may be especially vulnerable to traumatization as a result of fear of the batterer, and older children may be especially vulnerable to the batterer's influence over their value systems, including the development of attitudes that support domestic violence (see Chapter 2).

2. Child abuse reports occurring during custody and visitation litigation should be treated with the same degree of care as those arising at other times and should be properly investigated.

3. Assisting battered women to regain authority over their children involves a complex mix of factors, including legal steps to

increase her safety, holding the abuser accountable for his actions, involving the children in specialized domestic violence services, and involving the mother in battered women's services (Whitney & Davis, 1999). Child protective services and juvenile courts need to address each of these steps. Such assistance must be tailored to the particular situation; a parent whose authority has been chronically undermined, for example, may require different assistance from one who has intrinsic limit-setting difficulties or skill deficits.

4. A battered mother's fear of losing custody of her children (either to the state or to the batterer) presents a significant obstacle to the ability of child protective services to gain accurate information from her regarding the history of domestic violence. Therefore, providers should make efforts to use a supportive and noncoercive approach to battered mothers in order to build trust, toward the goal of effective teamwork in protecting the children's interests.

5. In cases in which child protective services have successfully persuaded a battered mother to leave the batterer, we have found that it is not uncommon for the batterer to seek (and sometimes to obtain) custody of his children in a family court. Child protective services therefore need to be prepared to keep cases open and to advocate for the woman in the family court process in order to protect the children's safety.

6. Child welfare investigators need to explore the power dynamics in every family that is investigated. For example, if a house is found to have an empty refrigerator or if children have unmet needs for medical attention, investigators need to establish whether one parent controls access to money or to use of the vehicle and whether the imposition of fear is being used to control the mother's actions.

7. In domestic violence cases in which out-of-home placement of the children is necessary because of such factors as the batterer's high level of dangerousness, the mother's substance abuse, or physical abuse of the children by either parent, child protective services should ensure that the battered mother is offered a range of appropriate services. These should include battered women's services, substance abuse treatment, and mental health counseling by providers trained in trauma. Long-term placement or permanent termination of the mother's parental rights can often be avoided through the provision of such services.

8.   Determinations that a batterer has overcome his problem should be made with caution (see Chapter 8).

9.   We recommend *Effective Intervention in Domestic Violence and Child Maltreatment Cases: Guidelines for Policy and Practice* (Schechter & Edleson, 1998) as a critical guidebook for child protective and court personnel in responding to child protective concerns in families affected by battering.

10.   Specialized batterer intervention programs can be an important resource for batterers, particularly when they include attention to the batterer's parenting (Schechter & Edleson, 1998).

11.   Couples counseling should generally not be ordered in domestic violence cases (Schechter & Edleson, 1998).

PARENT TRAINERS

Approaches to parent education need to be informed by an understanding of domestic violence (Schechter & Edleson, 1998). Specialized parent education courses are needed for battered mothers and for batterers, as using standard parenting curricula in domestic violence cases can have unintended results. Issues that should be addressed include the impact of battering on family functioning and the obstacles faced by a battered mother in maintaining parental authority. All curriculum themes should be examined for their possible impact on battered mothers or batterers participating in the course. Parent educators should be aware of the tendency of batterers to distort concepts from parent education courses for their own purposes; we have observed, for example, that our clients often use insights from parent education to criticize the mother's parenting rather than to examine their own.
Additional recommendations include the following:

1.   Battered mothers should not be taught that they can improve conditions for their children by increasing or improving communication with the batterer, as this can have results opposite to the intended ones and can interfere with her own recovery from abuse-related trauma, with resultant implications for her children.

2.   Parent trainers should consider the possibility that batterers not be permitted to participate in parent education unless they are simultaneously engaged in specialized batterer intervention. We raise this possibility because of the tendency that we have observed in batterers to use their learning in unintended ways to harm children, partners, or former partners and their tendency to use certificates of completion from parent education courses in their efforts to win custody or expanded visitation.

3.   Parent educators are often in the position of attempting to persuade a batterer of the same principles of sound parenting of which the battered mother has tried for many years to convince him. In such cases, the batterer will be reluctant to admit to himself that his partner was correct, because of the attitude of superiority toward her that is central to his profile. Thus, educators should be aware that batterers may have deep resistance to accepting the concepts being presented, even while superficially pretending to agree.

4.   Because battered mothers and batterers are likely to be present in any parent training course (even if they do not identify as such), *all* parent education should include attention to the following concepts related to domestic violence: (a) Effective parenting in a two-parent family depends largely on how one parent treats the other parent. Mistreating a partner, including any form of violence or abuse, is not responsible parenting; (b) children need their parents to model mutual respect, equal responsibility for domestic work and child care, and non-violence; (c) children need their parents to model accepting responsibility for one's own actions and not to model blaming one's behavior on others; (d) children need their parents to model listening well to each other even when angry and not using anger as an excuse for insulting, demeaning, or intimidating; and (e) exposing the children to violence is psychologically harmful to them and is the responsibility of the parent who uses the violence and not of the victim.

5.   Parenting classes that are designed for batterers need to clearly address the issue of violence and responsibility for that violence, the impact of violence on children, the inappropriateness of using provocation as an excuse for violence, and the roots of battering in issues of power and control (Mathews, 1995), in addition to the points mentioned above. Furthermore, they need to address minimization and denial about the effects of violence and the need for the batterer to support mother-child relationships.

6.   In our experience, adolescent batterers are often more open than are adult batterers to sincerely applying concepts from parent training to develop a more compassionate and effective parenting style. Parent trainers therefore should make particular efforts to reach out to younger fathers.

7.   Parent trainers could cooperate productively with batterer intervention specialists on designing approaches to working with batterers on their parenting, combining parenting education with constructive confrontation of underlying abusive attitudes.

PSYCHOLOGICAL EVALUATORS

1.   Psychological evaluators should not form conclusions regarding whether or not a man being evaluated is a batterer, whether or not a woman being evaluated is a battered woman, or what level of risk to children is posed by a specific batterer or alleged batterer. There is no reliable way to base such conclusions on psychological testing or evaluation.

2.   Psychological evaluators should strive to make clear in their reports the correct uses of their observations and conclusions (e.g., diagnosis of mental illness, treatment planning) and the incorrect uses (e.g., evaluation of parenting capacity, determination of whether an individual is an abuser or is a victim of abuse, determination of which parent should have custody of children). The evaluator should explain in his or her report the limited ability of psychological tests to distinguish symptoms related to trauma from other kinds of symptoms, and should be familiar with the literature on expected test results for battered women and for individuals involved in disputes over custody and visitation (see Chapter 5).

BATTERER PROGRAMS

Batterer intervention programs need to expand their level of attention to children's issues (particularly with respect to the parenting of batterers) and to weave that awareness into all of their counseling, collateral work, and policies (Schechter & Edleson, 1998). Our specific recommendations include the following:

1.   The curriculum of each batterer program should include (a) education on appropriate parenting, including the distinctions between permissive, authoritative, and authoritarian parenting styles; (b) education on the effects on children of exposure to domestic violence; (c) identification and confrontation of behaviors that undermine the mother's parenting authority or that damage her relationship with her children; (d) identification and confrontation of behaviors that involve using the children as weapons against the mother; and (e) education on the effects of child sexual abuse and the proper respecting of children's boundaries.

2.   Batterer programs should contact any current or past partners of the batterer with whom he has children to inquire about his conduct as a parent and to find out whether he is involved in ongoing litigation regarding custody or visitation (Pence & Paymar, 1993). The program should inform the battered mother of any arrests that the batterer has had for domestic violence offenses of which she may not be aware. The program should provide the battered mother with any information that she requests regarding the batterer's participation in the program and his history of offenses against other women (with the exception of confidential information collected from other current or past partners of his).

3.   Batterer programs need to develop linkages to programs for children exposed to domestic violence, to therapists who work with children, and to other individuals and agencies providing group, individual, or advocacy services to children.

4.   Batterer programs should be prepared to advocate for the protective needs of children with child protective services and family courts, including custody evaluators.

BATTERED WOMEN'S PROGRAMS

Battered women's programs are increasingly addressing the needs of children, including hiring child advocates within program staffs. We make the following recommendations in support of this positive trend:

1.   Curricula for battered women's support groups should include education on the batterer as parent and the effects of battering on mother-child relationships. We observe that batterers are often able

to manipulate the battered woman along with her children into believing that he is a good parent and that the mother's difficulties in her relationships with her children are entirely of her own making.

2.   Battered women's programs could productively collaborate with parent trainers on designing approaches to parent education with battered women. Valuable approaches to working with battered mothers on their parenting are already available to draw from (see p. 194).

3.   Battered women's programs should seek to influence the types of therapy, education, and advocacy that are made available to children in their communities and to form alliances with concerned mental health professionals when possible. Therapists, programs for children exposed to domestic violence, police and school departments, family and juvenile courts, child protective services, and other community agencies intervening with children should be encouraged to accept training from the battered women's program on the dynamics of domestic violence (including a mother's obstacles to leaving a batterer), the effects on children of exposure to batterers, and the family dynamics that can result.

4.   Specialized services are needed for battered mothers who are involved in custody and visitation disputes, to enhance their ability to successfully protect their children and to contend with the retraumatizing effects of litigation on the mother (Taylor, Barnsley, & Goldsmith, 1996). Services should include specific support groups, legal advocacy, and written materials related to postseparation issues.

SUPERVISED VISITATION CENTERS

1.   Reports to courts by supervised visitation centers should emphasize that a batterer's level of risk to children (and any possible lessening of that risk) cannot be measured by his behavior during supervised visitation.

2.   Visitation centers should develop protocols to prevent manipulation of staff by batterers (Children's Visitation Program, 1998).

3.   Visitation center staff need extensive training on batterers as parents, including risks to children from subtle behaviors.

4.   Batterers visiting with their children in a visitation center should never be out of the visual range and earshot of center staff. All materials brought into the center by the batterer, such as gifts for the children or books to read, should be examined by staff for appropriateness, safety, and any possible written messages. Whispering or passing notes should not be permitted, so that all communications can be monitored (YWCA of Western Massachusetts, n.d.).

5.   Batterers should be permitted to give gifts only on holidays and birthdays, in order to discourage manipulation of the child through purchases (Children's Visitation Program, 1998).

6.   Toys that involve or depict violence should not be used with children who have been exposed to domestic violence, and batterers should not be permitted to give such toys as gifts (Children's Visitation Program, 1998).

7.   Visitation centers should limit their role to supervising visits and documenting events and should not involve themselves in making recommendations to the court regarding future contact, as the blending of roles can compromise their effectiveness (Straus, 1995).

8.   Supervised visitation centers should have a policy that the battering parent is to pay the full cost of supervision unless the court requires otherwise. This policy is important to avoid adding financial stress to the custodial home and to send clear messages to all parties regarding whose behavior has caused the need for supervision (see also NCJFCJ, 1994).

FAMILY LAWYERS AND BAR ASSOCIATIONS

1.   More training needs to be made available to family law attorneys on the dynamics of domestic violence and on the risks posed to children by exposure to batterers. Attorneys need to receive particular training on proper strong representation of battered women in custody, visitation, and child support litigation.

2.   Bar associations should seek to expand the availability of pro bono and low-cost legal services for battered women who are involved in custody or visitation litigation.

3. Standards should be created for the legal representation of alleged batterers in custody and visitation disputes, permitting attorneys to provide proper legal services but discouraging them from acting as a batterer's agent in the abuse of a battered woman.

SUMMARY

A sophisticated understanding of the batterer as parent can improve interventions by professionals in a wide range of fields and assist in the avoidance of practice errors. Written policies for approaching domestic violence can further guide providers in navigating the complexities and risks of these cases. The potential for children and their battered mothers to benefit from improved professional practice is great. The example set by positive changes in the professional response to children exposed to batterers can also play a wider educational role in communities, assisting to reform the underlying problematic social and cultural concepts that allow domestic violence to continue.

References

Adams, D. (1989, July/August). Identifying the abusive husband in court: You be the judge. *Boston Bar Journal, 23–25.*

Adams, D. (1991). *Empathy and entitlement: A comparison of battering and non-battering husbands.* Unpublished doctoral dissertation, Northeastern University, Boston, MA. (Available from Emerge, 2380 Massachusetts Ave., Cambridge, MA, 02140.)

Adamson, J., & Thompson, R. (1998). Coping with interparental verbal conflict by children exposed to spouse abuse and children from nonviolent homes. *Journal of Family Violence, 13*(3), 213–232.

American Bar Association Center on Children and the Law. (1994). *The impact of domestic violence on children: A report to the president of the American Bar Association.* Washington, DC: American Bar Association.

American Psychiatric Association. (1994). *Diagnostic and statistical manual of mental disorders* (4th ed.). Washington, DC: Author.

American Psychological Association. (1994). Guidelines for child custody evaluations in divorce proceedings. *American Psychologist, 49*(7), 677–680.

American Psychological Association Presidential Task Force on Violence and the Family. (1996). *Violence and the family.* Washington, DC: American Psychological Association.

Arroyo, W., & Eth, S. (1995). Assessment following violence-witnessing trauma. In E. Peled, P. Jaffe, & J. Edleson (Eds.), *Ending the cycle of violence: Community responses to children of battered women* (pp. 27–42). Thousand Oaks, CA: Sage.

Augustyn, M., Parker, S., McAlister Groves, B., & Zuckerman, B. (1995). Silent victims: Children who witness violence. *Contemporary Pediatrics, 12*(8), 35–57.

Ayoub, C., Grace, P., Paradise, J., & Newberger, E. (1991). Alleging psychological impairment of the accuser to defend oneself against a child abuse allegation: A manifestation of wife battering and false accusation. In M. Robin (Ed.), *Assessing child maltreatment reports: The problem of false allegations* (pp. 191–207). New York: Haworth Press.

Bachman, R. (2000). A comparison of annual incidence rates and contextual characteristics of intimate-partner violence against women from the National Crime

Victimization Survey (NCVS) and the National Violence Against Women Survey (NVAWS). *Violence Against Women, 6*(8), 839– 867.

Bancroft, L. (forthcoming, Sept. 2002). *Why does he do that? Inside the minds of angry and controlling men.* New York: Putnam.

Bandura, A. (1978, Summer). Social learning theory of aggression. *Journal of Communication,* 12–29.

Banyard, V. (2000). Trauma and memory. *PTSD Research Quarterly, 11*(4), 1–7.

Barbaree, H. E., & Marshall, W. L. (1989). Erectile responses among heterosexual child molesters, father-daughter incest offenders, and matched non-offenders: Five distinct age preference profiles. *Canadian Journal of Behavioral Science, 21*(1), 70–82.

Bathurst, K., Gottfried, A. W., & Gottfried, A. E. (1997). Normative date for the MMPI-2 in child custody litigation. *Psychological Assessment, 9*(3), 205–211.

Becker, J., & Quinsey, V. (1993). Assessing suspected child molesters. *Child Abuse and Neglect, 17,* 169–174.

Beeman, S., Hagemeister, A., & Edleson, J. (1999). Child protection and battered women's services: From conflict to collaboration. *Child Maltreatment, 4*(2), 116–126.

Bennett, L. (1995). Substance abuse and the domestic assault of women. *Social Work, 40*(6), 760–771.

Bennett, L., Goodman, L., & Dutton, M. A. (2000). Risk assessment among batterers arrested for domestic assault: The salience of psychological abuse. *Violence Against Women, 6*(11), 1190–1203.

Bergen, R. K. (1996). *Wife rape: Understanding the response of survivors and service providers.* Thousand Oaks, CA: Sage.

Berk, R., Fernstermaker Berk, S., Loseke, D., & Rauma, D. (1983). Mutual combat and other family violence myths. In D. Finkelhor, R. Gelles, G. Hotaling, & M. Straus (Eds.), *The dark side of families: Current family violence research* (pp. 197–212). Beverly Hills, CA: Sage.

Berlin, P., & Vondra, J. (1999). Psychological maltreatment of children. In R. Ammerman & M. Herson (Eds.), *Assessment of family violence: A clinical and legal sourcebook* (pp. 287–321). New York: Wiley.

Bilinkoff, J. (1995). Empowering battered women as mothers. In E. Peled, P. Jaffe, & J. Edleson (Eds.), *Ending the cycle of violence: Community responses to children of battered women* (pp. 97–105). Thousand Oaks, CA: Sage.

Bonilla-Santiago, G. (1996). Latina battered women: Barriers to service delivery and cultural considerations. In A. R. Roberts (Ed.), *Helping battered women: New perspectives and remedies* (pp. 229–234). New York: Oxford University Press.

Bowker, L. (1983, June). Marital rape: A distinct syndrome. *Social Casework: The Journal of Contemporary Social Work,* 347–352.

Bowker, L., Arbitell, M., & McFerron, R. (1988). On the relationship between wife beating and child abuse. In K. Yllo & M. Bograd (Eds.), *Feminist perspectives on wife abuse* (pp. 159–174). Newbury Park, CA: Sage.

Bresee, P., Stearns, G., Bess, B., & Packer, L. (1986). Allegations of child sexual abuse in child custody disputes: A therapeutic assessment model. *American Journal of Orthopsychiatry, 56*(4), 560–569.

Brodzinsky, D. (1994). On the use and misuse of psychological testing in child custody evaluations. *Professional Psychology: Research and Practice, 24*(2), 213–219.

Bukatko, D., & Daehler, M. (2001). *Child development: A thematic approach* (4th ed.). Boston: Houghton Mifflin.

Bureau of Justice Statistics. (1996). *Female victims of violent crime* (Report No. NCJ-162602). Washington, DC: U.S. Department of Justice.

Campbell, J. (1995a). Prediction of homicide of and by battered women. In J. Campbell (Ed.), *Assessing dangerousness* (pp. 96–113). Thousand Oaks, CA: Sage.

Campbell, J. (1995b). Addressing battering during pregnancy: Reducing low birth weight and ongoing abuse. *Seminars in Perinatology, 19*(4), 301–306.

Campbell, J., Oliver, C., & Bullock, L. (1998). The dynamics of battering during pregnancy. In J. Campbell (Ed.), *Empowering survivors of abuse: Health care for battered women and their children* (pp. 81–89). Thousand Oaks, CA: Sage.

Campbell, J., Soeken, K., McFarlane, J., & Parker, B. (1998). Risk factors for femicide among pregnant and non-pregnant battered women. In J. Campbell (Ed.), *Empowering survivors of abuse: Health care for battered women and their children* (pp. 90–97). Thousand Oaks, CA: Sage.

Caplan, P., & Wilson, J. (1990). Assessing the child custody assessors. *Reports of Family Law, 27*(2), 121–134.

Carlson, B. (1984). Children's observations of interparental violence. In A. R. Roberts (Ed.), *Battered women and their families* (pp. 147–167). New York: Springer.

Carlson, B. (1990). Adolescent observers of marital violence. *Journal of Family Violence, 5*(4), 285–299.

Carlson, M., Harris, S., & Holden, G. (1999). Protective orders and domestic violence: Risk factors for re-abuse. *Journal of Family Violence, 14*(2), 205–226.

Carnes, C. N., Nelson-Gardell, D., Wilson, C., & Orgassa, U. C. (2001). Extended forensic evaluation when sexual abuse is suspected: A multisite field study. *Child Maltreatment, 6*(3), 230–242.

Carrillo, R., & Tello, J. (Eds.). (1998). *Family violence and men of color: Healing the wounded male spirit.* New York: Springer.

Cayouette, S. (1999). Running batterers groups for lesbians. In B. Leventhal & S. Lundy (Eds.), *Same-sex domestic violence: Strategies for change* (pp. 233–242). Thousand Oaks, CA: Sage.

Children's Visitation Program. (1998). *Program criteria and intake packet.* Greenfield, MA: Author.

Choice, P., Lamke, L., & Pittman, J. (1995). Conflict resolution strategies and marital distress as mediating factors in the link between witnessing interparental violence and wife battering. *Violence and Victims, 10*(2), 107–119.

Clark, A., & Foy, D. (2000). Trauma exposure and alcohol use in battered women. *Violence Against Women, 6*(1), 37–48.

Courtois, C. (1999). *Recollections of sexual abuse: Treatment principles and guidelines.* New York: Norton.

Crites, L., & Coker, D. (1988, Spring). What therapists see that judges may miss. *The Judges' Journal,* 40–42.

Cummings, E. M. (1998). Children exposed to marital conflict and violence: Conceptual and theoretical directions. In G. Holden, R. Geffner, & E. Jouriles (Eds.), *Children exposed to marital violence: Theory, research, and applied issues* (pp. 55–93). Washington, DC: American Psychological Association.

Cummings, J., Peplar, D., & Moore, T. (1999). Behavior problems in children exposed to wife abuse: Gender differences. *Journal of Family Violence, 14*(2), 133–156.

Curry, M. A., & Harvey, S. M. (1998). Stress related to domestic violence during pregnancy and infant birth weight. In J. Campbell (Ed.), *Empowering survivors of abuse: Health care for battered women and their children* (pp. 98–108). Thousand Oaks, CA: Sage.

Dallam, S. (2000). The Parental Alienation Syndrome: Is it scientific? In E. St. Charles & L. Crook (Eds.), *Exposé: The failure of family courts to protect children from abuse in custody disputes* (pp. 67–93). Los Gatos, CA: Our Children Our Future Charitable Foundation. (Available from OCOFCF, P.O. Box 1111, Los Gatos, CA 95031-1111.)

Dalton, C. (1999). When paradigms collide: Protecting battered parents and their children in the family court system. *Family and Conciliation Courts Review, 37*(3), 273–296.

Daly, M., & Wilson, M. (1988). *Homicide.* New York: Aldene de Gruyter.

Davidson, T. (1978). *Conjugal crime: Understanding and changing the wife-beating pattern*. New York: Hawthorn Books.

Davies, J., Lyon, E., & Monti-Catania, D. (1998). *Safety planning with battered women: Complex lives/difficult choices*. Thousand Oaks, CA: Sage.

Demare, D., Briere, J., & Lips, H. (1988). Violent pornography and self-reported likelihood of sexual aggression. *Journal of Research in Personality, 22*, 140–153.

DeVoe, E., & Faller, K. (1999). The characteristics of disclosure among children who may have been sexually abused. *Child Maltreatment, 4*(3), 217–227.

de Young, M. (1986). A conceptual model for judging the truthfulness of a young child's allegation of sexual abuse. *American Journal of Orthopsychiatry, 56*(4), 550–559.

Dobash, E., & Dobash, R. (1983). Patterns of violence in Scotland. In R. Gelles & C. P. Cornell (Eds.), *International perspectives on family violence* (pp. 147–162). Lexington, MA: Lexington Books.

Doris, J. (Ed.). (1991). *The suggestibility of children's recollections*. Washington, DC: American Psychological Association.

Douglas, M. A. (1987). The battered woman syndrome. In D. J. Sonkin (Ed.), *Domestic violence on trial: Psychological and legal dimensions of family violence* (pp. 39–54). New York: Springer.

Doyne, S., Bowermaster, J., Meloy, R., Dutton, D., Jaffe, P., Temko, S., & Mones, P. (1999). Custody disputes involving domestic violence: Making children's needs a priority. *Juvenile and Family Court Journal, 50*(2), 1–12.

Dutton, D. (1995). *The domestic assault of women: Psychological and criminal justice perspectives*. Vancouver, British Columbia: UBC Press.

Dutton, D., & Painter, S. (1983). Traumatic bonding: The development of emotional attachments in battered women and other relationships of intermittent abuse. *Victimology: An International Journal, 6*(1–4), 139–155.

Dutton, D., & Painter, S. (1993). The battered woman syndrome: Effects of severity and intermittency of abuse. *American Journal of Orthopsychiatry, 63*(4), 614–622.

Dutton, M. A. (1992). *Empowering and healing the battered woman*. New York: Springer.

Echlin, C., & Marshall, L. (1995). Child protection services for children of battered women: Practice and controversy. In E. Peled, P. Jaffe, & J. Edleson (Eds.), *Ending the cycle of violence: Community responses to children of battered women* (pp. 170–185). Thousand Oaks, CA: Sage.

Edleson, J. (1998). Responsible mothers and invisible men: Child protection in the case of adult domestic violence. *Journal of Interpersonal Violence, 13*(2), 294–298.

Edleson, J., & Brygger, M. P. (1986). Gender differences in reporting of battering incidences. *Family Relations, 35*, 377–382.

Edleson, J., & Tolman, R. (1992). *Intervention for men who batter: An ecological approach*. Newbury Park, CA: Sage.

Eisenstat, S., & Bancroft, L. (1999). Domestic violence. *New England Journal of Medicine, 341*(12), 886–892.

Elbow, M. (1982, October). Children of violent marriages: The forgotten victims. *Social Casework: The Journal of Contemporary Social Work*, 465–471.

Ellis, D., & Stuckless, N. (1996). *Mediating and negotiating marital conflicts*. Thousand Oaks, CA: Sage.

Erickson, J., & Henderson, A. (1998). Diverging realities: Abused women and their children. In J. Campbell (Ed.), *Empowering survivors of abuse: Health care for battered women and their children* (pp. 138–155). Thousand Oaks, CA: Sage.

Eriksson, M., & Hester, M. (2001). Violent men as good-enough fathers?—A look at England and Sweden. *Violence Against Women, 7*(7), 779–798.

Fagan, J., Stewart, D., & Hansen, K. (1983). Violent men or violent husbands: Background factors and situational correlates. In D. Finkelhor, R. Gelles, G. Hotaling, & M. Straus (Eds.), *The dark side of families: Current family violence research* (pp. 49–67). Beverly Hills, CA: Sage.

Faller, K. (1988). Criteria for judging the credibility of children's statements about their sexual abuse. *Child Welfare, 67*(5), 389–401.

Faller, K. (1991). Possible explanations for child sexual abuse allegations in divorce. *American Journal of Orthopsychiatry, 61*(1), 86–91.

Family Violence Project of the National Council of Juvenile and Family Court Judges. (1995). Family violence in child custody statutes: An analysis of state codes and legal practice. *Family Law Quarterly, 29*(2), 197–227.

Fantuzzo, J., & Mohr, W. (1999). Prevalence and effects of child exposure to domestic violence. *The Future of Children, 9*(2), 21–32.

Feld, S., & Straus, M. (1990). Escalating and desisting from wife assault in marriage. In M. Straus & R. Gelles (Eds.), *Physical violence in American families* (pp. 489–505). New Brunswick, NJ: Transition.

Finkelhor, D. (1994). Current information on the scope and nature of child sexual abuse. *The Future of Children, 4*(2), 31–53.

Finkelhor, D., Hotaling, G., & Sedlak, A. (1990). *Missing, abducted, runaway, and thrownaway children in America: First report: Numbers and characteristics, national incidence studies.* Washington, DC: U.S. Department of Justice.

Fleury, R., Sullivan, C., & Bybee, D. (2000). When ending the relationship does not end violence: Women's experiences of violence by former partners. *Violence Against Women, 6*(12), 1363–1383.

Follingstad, D., Rutledge, L., Berg, B., Hause, E., & Polek, D. (1990). The role of emotional abuse in physically abusive relationships. *Journal of Family Violence, 5*(2), 107–120.

Fray-Witzer, E. (1999). Twice abused: Same-sex domestic violence and the law. In B. Leventhal and S. Lundy (Eds.), *Same-sex domestic violence: Strategies for change* (pp. 19–41). Thousand Oaks, CA: Sage.

Furstenberg, F., & Cherlin, A. (1991). *Divided families: What happens to children when parents part.* Cambridge, MA: Harvard University Press.

Gardner, R. A. (1987). *The parental alienation syndrome and the differentiation between fabricated and genuine child sex abuse.* Cresskill, NJ: Creative Therapeutics.

Gardner, R. A. (1991). *Sex abuse hysteria: Salem witch trials revisited.* Cresskill, NJ: Creative Therapeutics.

Garrity, C., & Baris, M. (1994). *Caught in the middle: Protecting the children of high-conflict divorce.* New York: Lexington Books.

Gazmarian, J., Lazorick, S., Spitz, A., Ballard, T., Saltzman, L., & Marks, J. (1996, June 26). Prevalence of violence against pregnant women. *Journal of the American Medical Association (JAMA), 275*(24), 1915–1920.

Gazmarian, J., Petersen, R., Spitz, A., Goodwin, M., Saltzman, L., & Marks, J. (2000). Violence and reproductive health: Current knowledge and future research directions. *Maternal and Child Health Journal, 4*(2), 79–84.

Geddie, L., Beer, J., Bartosik, S., & Wuensch, K. (2001). The relationship between interview characteristics and accuracy of recall in young children: Do individual differences matter? *Child Maltreatment, 6*(1), 59–68.

Gelles, R. (1990). Violence and pregnancy: Are pregnant women at greater risk of abuse? In M. Straus & R. Gelles (Eds.), *Physical violence in American families* (pp. 279–286). New Brunswick, NJ: Transition.

Gelles, R. (1993). Alcohol and other drugs are associated with violence—they are not its cause. In R. Gelles & D. Loseke (Eds.), *Current controversies on family violence* (pp. 182–196). Newbury Park, CA: Sage.

Gelles, R., & Straus, M. (1988). *Intimate violence.* New York: Simon & Schuster.

Gender Bias Study Committee. (1989). Report of the Gender Bias Study of the Supreme Judicial Court. *Suffolk University Law Review, 23*(3), 575–683.

Gender Bias Study Committee. (1990). Gender Bias Study of the court system in Massachusetts. *New England Law Review, 24*(3), 745–856.

Giaretto, H. (1980). Humanistic treatment of father-daughter incest. In National Center on Child Abuse and Neglect (Ed.), *Sexual abuse of children: Selected readings* (Publication No. OHDS 78-30161, pp. 39–46). Washington, DC: U.S. Department of Health and Human Services.

Gleason, W. (1995). Children of battered women: Developmental delays and behavioral dysfunction. *Violence and Victims, 10*(2), 153–160.

Gondolf, E. (1988). *Research on men who batter: An overview, bibliography, and resource guide.* Bradenton, FL: Human Services Institute.

Gondolf, E. (1998a). Do batterer programs work? A 15 month follow-up of multi-site evaluation. *Domestic Violence Report, 3*(5), 65–66, 78–79.

Gondolf, E. (1998b). *Assessing woman battering in mental health services.* Thousand Oaks, CA: Sage.

Gondolf, E. (1999). MCMI-III results for batterer program participants in four cities: Less "pathological" than expected. *Journal of Family Violence, 14*(1), 1–17.

Gondolf, E. (2000). How batterer program participants avoid reassault. *Violence Against Women, 6*(11), 1204–1222.

Goodwin, M., Gazmarian, J., Johnson, C., Gilbert, B. C., Saltzman, L., & the PRAMS Working Group. (2000). Pregnancy intendedness and physical abuse around the time of pregnancy: Findings from the Pregnancy Risk Assessment Monitoring System, 1996–1997. *Maternal and Child Health Journal, 4*(2), 85–92.

Graham, D., Rawlings, E., Ihms, K., Latimer, D., Foliano, J., Thompson, A., Suttman, K., Farrington, M., & Hacker, R. (2001). A scale for identifying "Stockholm Syndrome" reactions in young dating women: Factor structure, reliability, and validity. In D. O'Leary & R. Maiuro (Eds.), *Psychological abuse in violent domestic relations* (pp. 77–100). New York: Springer.

Graham-Bermann, S. (1998). The impact of woman abuse on children's social development: Research and theoretical perspectives. In G. Holden, R. Geffner, & E. Jouriles (Eds.), *Children exposed to marital violence: Theory, research, and applied issues* (pp. 21–54). Washington, DC: American Psychological Association.

Green, A. (1991). Factors contributing to false allegations of child sexual abuse in custody disputes. In M. Robin (Ed.), *Assessing child maltreatment reports: The problem of false allegations* (pp. 177–189). New York: Haworth Press.

Greif, G., & Hegar, R. (1993). *When parents kidnap.* New York: Free Press.

Groth, N. (1982). The incest offender. In S. Sgroi (Ed.), *Handbook of clinical intervention in child sexual abuse* (pp. 215–239). Lexington, MA: Lexington Books.

Haj-Yahia, M. (1996). Wife abuse in the Arab society in Israel: Challenges for future change. In J. Edleson & Z. Eisikovits (Eds.), *Future interventions with battered women and their families* (pp. 87–101). Thousand Oaks, CA: Sage.

Hall, G. C. N. (1988). Criminal behavior as a function of clinical and actuarial variables in a sexual offender population. *Journal of Consulting and Clinical Psychology, 56*(5), 773–775.

Hall, G. C. N., & Crowther, J. (1991). Psychologists' involvement in cases of child maltreatment: Additional limits of assessment methods. *American Psychologist, 46*, 79–80.

Hamby, S. (1998). Partner violence: Prevention and intervention. In J. Jasinksi & L. Williams (Eds.), *Partner violence: A comprehensive review of 20 years of research* (pp. 210–258). Thousand Oaks, CA: Sage.

Hampton, R., Carrillo, R., & Kim, J. (1998). Violence in communities of color. In R. Carrillo & J. Tello (Eds.), *Family violence and men of color: Healing the wounded male spirit* (pp. 1–30). New York: Springer.

Hanks, S. (1992). Translating theory into practice: A conceptual framework for clinical assessment, differential diagnosis, and multi-modal treatment of maritally violent individuals, couples, and families. In E. Viano (Ed.), *Intimate violence: Interdisciplinary perspectives* (pp. 157–176). Washington, DC: Hemisphere.

Hanson, R. K., Gizzarelli, R., & Scott, H. (1994). The attitudes of incest offenders: Sexual entitlement and acceptance of sex with children. *Criminal Justice and Behavior, 21*(2), 187–202.

Hart, B. (1986). Lesbian battering: An examination. In K. Lobel (Ed.), *Naming the violence: Speaking out about lesbian battering* (pp. 173–189). Seattle, WA: Seal Press.

Hart, B. (1990a). *Safety planning for children: Strategizing for unsupervised visits with batterers.* Harrisburg: Pennsylvania Coalition Against Domestic Violence.

Hart, B. (1990b). Gentle jeopardy: The further endangerment of battered women and children in custody mediation. *Mediation Quarterly, 7*(4), 317–330.

Harway, M., & Hansen, M. (1993). Therapist perceptions of family violence. In M. Hansen & M. Harway (Eds.), *Battering and family therapy: A feminist perspective* (pp. 42–53). Newbury Park, CA: Sage.

Healey, K., Smith, C., & O'Sullivan, C. (1998). *Batterer intervention: Program approaches and criminal justice strategies* (Report No. NCJ-168638). Washington, DC: National Institute of Justice.

Heckert, A., & Gondolf, E. (2000). Assessing assault self-reports by batterer program participants and their partners. *Journal of Family Violence, 15*(2), 181–197.

Heise, L., Ellsberg, M., & Gottemoeller, M. (1999). Ending violence against women. *Population Reports, 50*(11), 1–43.

Heller, S., Larrieu, J., D'Imperio, R., & Boris, N. (1999). Research on resilience to child maltreatment: Empirical considerations. *Child Abuse and Neglect, 23*(4), 321–338.

Helton, A., McFarlane, J., & Anderson, E. (1987). Battered and pregnant: A prevalence study. *American Journal of Public Health, 77*(10), 1337–1339.

Herman, J. (1981). *Father-daughter incest.* Cambridge, MA: Harvard University Press.

Herman, J. (1992). *Trauma and recovery.* New York: Basic Books.

Hlady, L. J., & Gunter, E. J. (1990). Alleged child abuse in custody access disputes. *Child Abuse and Neglect, 14*(4), 591–593.

Holden, G., & Ritchie, K. (1991). Linking extreme marital discord, child rearing, and child behavior problems: Evidence from battered women. *Child Development, 62,* 311–327.

Holden, G., Stein, J., Ritchie, K., Harris, S., & Jouriles, E. (1998). Parenting behaviors and beliefs of battered women. In G. Holden, R. Geffner, & E. Jouriles (Eds.), *Children exposed to marital violence: Theory, research, and applied issues* (pp. 289–331). Washington, DC: American Psychological Association.

Holtzworth-Munroe, A., & Stuart, G. (1994). Typologies of male batterers: Three subtypes and the differences among them. *Psychological Bulletin, 116*(3), 476–497.

Hotaling, G., Straus, M., & Lincoln, A. (1990). Intrafamily violence and crime and violence outside the family. In M. Straus & R. Gelles (Eds.), *Physical violence in American families* (pp. 41–47). New Brunswick, NJ: Transition.

Hotaling, G., & Sugarman, D. (1986). An analysis of risk markers in husband to wife violence: The current state of knowledge. *Violence and Victims, 1*(2), 101–124.

Hughes, H., & Marshall, M. (1995). Advocacy for children of battered women. In E. Peled, P. Jaffe, & J. Edleson (Eds.), *Ending the cycle of violence: Community responses to children of battered women* (pp. 121–144). Thousand Oaks, CA: Sage.

Hughes, H. M., Parkinson, D., & Vargo, M. (1989). Witnessing spouse abuse and experiencing physical abuse: A "double whammy"? *Journal of Family Violence, 4,* 197–209.

Hurley, D. J., & Jaffe, P. (1990). Children's observations of violence: II. Clinical implications for children's mental health professionals. *Canadian Journal of Psychiatry, 35*(6), 471–476.

Jacobson, N., & Gottman, J. (1998). *When men batter women: New insights into ending abusive relationships.* New York: Simon & Schuster.

Jaffe, P., & Geffner, R. (1998). Child custody disputes and domestic violence: Critical issues for mental health, social service, and legal professionals. In G. Holden, R. Geffner, & E. Jouriles (Eds.), *Children exposed to marital violence: Theory, research, and applied issues* (pp. 371–408). Washington, DC: American Psychological Association.

Jaffe, P., Hurley, D. J., & Wolfe, D. (1990). Children's observations of violence: I. Critical issues in child development and intervention planning. *Canadian Journal of Psychiatry, 35*(6), 466–469.

Jaffe, P., Wolfe, D. A., & Wilson, S. (1990). *Children of battered women.* Newbury Park, CA: Sage.

James, B. (1994). *Handbook for treatment of attachment-trauma problems in children.* New York: Free Press.

Jasinski, J., & Williams, L. (1998). *Partner violence: A comprehensive review of 20 years of research.* Thousand Oaks, CA: Sage.

Johnston, J. (1992). *Proposed guidelines for custody and visitation for cases with domestic violence.* Corte Madera, CA: Center for the Family in Transition.

Johnston, J. (1994a, May). *Domestic violence and parent-child relationships in families disputing custody.* Paper presented at the National Family Court Seminar, Sydney, Australia.

Johnston, J. (1994b). High-conflict divorce. *The Future of Children, 4*(1), 165–182.

Johnston, J., & Campbell, L. (1988). *Impasses of divorce.* New York: Free Press.

Johnston, J., & Campbell, L. (1993a). A clinical typology of interparental violence in disputed-custody divorces. *American Journal of Orthopsychiatry, 63*(2), 190–199.

Johnston, J., & Campbell, L. (1993b). Parent-child relationships in domestic violence families disputing custody. *Family and Conciliation Courts Review, 31*(3), 282–298.

Johnston, J., Kline, M., & Tschann, J. (1989). Ongoing postdivorce conflict: Effects on children of joint custody and frequent access. *American Journal of Orthopsychiatry, 59*(4), 576–592.

Johnston, J., & Roseby, V. (1997). *In the name of the child.* New York: Free Press.

Jones, A. (1994). *Next time she'll be dead.* Boston: Beacon Press.

Jones, D. P. H., & McGraw, J. M. (1987). Reliable and fictitious accounts of sexual abuse of children. *Journal of Interpersonal Violence, 2*(1), 27–45.

Jones, D. P. H., & Seig, A. (1988). Child sexual abuse allegations in custody or visitation cases: A report of 20 cases. In B. Nicholson (Ed.), *Sexual abuse allegations in custody and visitation cases: A resource book for judges and court personnel* (pp. 22–36). Washington, DC: American Bar Association.

Jouriles, E., McDonald, R., Stephens, N., Norwood, W., Spiller, L. C., & Ware, H. S. (1998). Breaking the cycle of violence: Helping families departing from battered women's shelters. In G. Holden, R. Geffner, & E. Jouriles (Eds.), *Children exposed to marital violence: Theory, research, and applied issues* (pp. 337–369). Washington, DC: American Psychological Association.

Jouriles, E., & Norwood, W. (1995). Physical aggression toward boys and girls in families characterized by the battering of women. *Journal of Family Psychology, 9*(1), 69–78.

Kalmuss, D., & Seltzer, J. (1986). Continuity of marital behavior in remarriage: The case of spouse abuse. *Journal of Marriage and the Family, 48*, 113–120.

Kanuha, V. (1996). Domestic violence, racism, and the battered women's movement in the United States. In J. Edleson & Z. Eisikovits (Eds.), *Future interventions with battered women and their families* (pp. 34–50). Thousand Oaks, CA: Sage.

Karon, B., & Vandenbos, G. (1981). *Psychotherapy of schizophrenia: The treatment of choice.* New York: Jason Aronson.

Kashani, J., & Allan, W. (1998). *The impact of family violence on children and adolescents.* Thousand Oaks, CA: Sage.

Kaufman Kantor, G., & Straus, M. (1990). The "Drunken Bum" theory of wife beating. In M. Straus & R. Gelles (Eds.), *Physical violence in American families* (pp. 203–224). New Brunswick, NJ: Transition.

Kelly, J. (1993). Current research on children's postdivorce adjustment. *Family and Conciliation Courts Review, 31*(1), 29–49.

Kendall-Tackett, K. A., Williams, L. M., & Finkelhor, D. (1993). Impact of sexual abuse on children: A review and synthesis of recent empirical studies. *Psychological Bulletin, 113*(1), 164–180.

Kirkwood, C. (1993). *Leaving abusive partners*. Newbury Park, CA: Sage.

Kolbo, J., Blakely, E., & Engleman, D. (1996). Children who witness domestic violence: A review of empirical literature. *Journal of Interpersonal Violence, 11*(2), 281–293.

Koss, M., Goodman, L., Browne, A., Fitzgerald, L., Keita, G. P., & Russo, N. F. (1994). *No safe haven: Male violence against women at home, at work, and in the community*. Washington, DC: American Psychological Association.

Langford, L., Isaac, N. E., & Kabat, S. (1998). Homicides related to intimate partner violence in Massachusetts: Examining case ascertainment and validity of the SHR. *Homicide Studies, 2*(4), 353–377.

Langford, L., Isaac, N. E., & Kabat, S. (1999). *Homicides related to intimate partner violence in Massachusetts 1991–1995*. Boston: Peace at Home.

Langhinrichsen-Rohlins, J., Huss, M., & Ramsey, S. (2000). The clinical utility of batterer typologies. *Journal of Family Violence, 15*(1), 37–53.

Lawton, E., & McAlister Groves, B. (2000). Responding to domestic violence in custody cases. *Child Law Practice, 18*(12), 181–182, 186–187.

Leberg, E. (1997). *Understanding child molesters: Taking charge*. Thousand Oaks, CA: Sage.

Lemon, N. (1999). The legal system's response to children exposed to domestic violence. *The Future of Children, 9*(3), 67–83.

Lemon, N. (2000). Custody and visitation trends in the United States in domestic violence cases. In R. Geffner, P. Jaffe, & M. Sudermann (Eds.), *Children exposed to domestic violence: Current issues in research, intervention, prevention, and policy development* (pp. 329–343). New York: Haworth Maltreatment and Trauma Press.

Lerner, M. (1999). From safety to healing: Representing battered women with companion animals. *Domestic Violence Report, 4*(2), 1–2, 17–18, 28.

Levendosky, A., & Graham-Bermann, S. (2000). Trauma and parenting: An addition to an ecological model of parenting. In R. Geffner, P. Jaffe, & M. Sudermann (Eds.), *Children exposed to domestic violence* (pp. 25–36). New York: Haworth Maltreatment and Trauma Press.

Levendosky, A., Lynch, S., & Graham-Bermann, S. (2000). Mothers' perceptions of the impact of woman abuse on their parenting. *Violence Against Women, 6*(3), 247–271.

Leventhal, B., & Lundy, S. (Eds.). (1999). *Same-sex domestic violence: Strategies for change*. Thousand Oaks, CA: Sage.

Levinson, D. (1989). *Family violence in cross-cultural perspective*. Newbury Park, CA: Sage.

Liss, M., & Stahly, G. B. (1993). Domestic violence and child custody. In M. Hansen & M. Harway (Eds.), *Battering and family therapy: A feminist perspective* (pp. 175–187). Newbury Park, CA: Sage.

Lloyd, S., & Emery, B. (2000). *The dark side of courtship: Physical and sexual aggression*. Thousand Oaks, CA: Sage.

Lowen, A. (1985). *Narcissism: Denial of the true self*. New York: Jason Aronson.

MacFarlane, K., & Waterman, J. (1986). *Sexual abuse of young children*. New York: Guilford Press.

Magaña, H., & Taylor, N. (1993). Child custody mediation and spouse abuse. *Family and Conciliation Courts Review, 31*(1), 50–64.

Magen, R. (1999). In the best interests of battered women: Reconceptualizing allegations of failure to protect. *Child Maltreatment, 4*(2), 127–135.

Mahoney, P., & Williams, L. (1998). Sexual assault in marriage: Prevalence, consequences, and treatment of wife rape. In J. Jasinksi & L. Williams (Eds.), *Partner violence: A comprehensive review of 20 years of research* (pp. 113–157). Thousand Oaks, CA: Sage.

Malamuth, N., & Check, J. (1985). The effects of aggressive pornography on beliefs in rape myths: Individual differences. *Journal of Research in Personality, 19*, 299–320.

Maltz, A., & Holman, B. (1987). *Incest and sexuality: A guide to understanding and healing.* Lexington, MA: Lexington Books.

Margolin, G. (1998). Effects of domestic violence on children. In P. Trickett & C. Schellenbach (Eds.), *Violence against children in the family and community* (pp. 57–101). Washington, DC: American Psychological Association.

Margolin, G., John, R., & Foo, L. (1998). Interactive and unique risk factors for husbands' emotional and physical abuse of their wives. *Journal of Family Violence, 13*(4), 315–344.

Margolin, G., John, R., Ghosh, C., & Gordis, E. (1996). Family interaction process: An essential tool for exploring abusive relationships. In D. Cahn & S. Lloyd (Eds.), *Family violence from a communication perspective* (pp. 37–58). Thousand Oaks, CA: Sage.

Markowitz, F. (2001). Attitudes and family violence: Linking intergenerational and cultural theories. *Journal of Family Violence, 16*(2), 205–218.

Mart, E. (1999). Factitious disorder by proxy in forensic settings. *American Journal of Forensic Psychology, 17*(1), 69–82.

Massachusetts Department of Public Health. (n.d.). *What's the difference between anger management and certified batterer intervention programs?* Boston: Author.

Massachusetts Domestic Violence Visitation Task Force of the Probate and Family Court. (1994). *Domestic violence visitation risk assessment.* Madison, WI: Association of Family and Conciliation Courts.

Masson, J. (1984). *The assault on truth: Freud's suppression of the seduction theory.* New York: Farrar, Straus, & Giroux.

Mathews, D. (1995). Parenting groups for men who batter. In E. Peled, P. Jaffe, & J. Edleson (Eds.), *Ending the cycle of violence: Community responses to children of battered women* (pp. 106–120). Thousand Oaks, CA: Sage.

Maxwell, J. (1999). Mandatory mediation of custody in the face of domestic violence: Suggestions for courts and mediators. *Family and Conciliation Courts Review, 37*(3), 335–355.

McCloskey, L. A., Figueredo, A. J., & Koss, M. (1995). The effect of systemic family violence on children's mental health. *Child Development, 66*, 1239–1261.

McGraw, J. M., & Smith, H. A. (1992). Child sexual abuse allegations amidst divorce and custody proceedings: Refining the validation process. *Journal of Child Sexual Abuse, 1*(1), 49–61.

McIntosh, J. A., & Prinz, R. J. (1993). The incidence of alleged sexual abuse in 603 family court cases. *Law and Human Behavior, 17*(1), 95–101.

McKibben, L., De Vos, E., & Newberger, E. (1989). Victimization of mothers of abused children: A controlled study. *Pediatrics, 84*(3), 531–535.

McMahon, M., & Pence, E. (1995). Doing more harm than good? Some cautions on visitation centers. In E. Peled, P. Jaffe, & J. Edleson (Eds.), *Ending the cycle of violence: Community responses to children of battered women* (pp. 186–206). Thousand Oaks, CA: Sage.

Menard, A., & Turetsky, V. (1999). Child support enforcement and domestic violence. *Juvenile and Family Court Journal, 50*(2), 27–38.

Milner, J. (1998). Individual and family characteristics associated with intrafamilial child physical and sexual abuse. In P. Trickett & C. Schellenbach (Eds.), *Violence against children in the family and community* (pp. 141–170). Washington, DC: American Psychological Association.

Milner, J., & Chilamkurti, C. (1991). Physical child abuse perpetrator characteristics: A review of the literature. *Journal of Interpersonal Violence, 6*(3), 345–366.

Mitchell, W. (1992). Why Wape men don't beat their wives: Constraints toward domestic tranquility. In D. A. Counts, J. Brown, & J. Campbell (Eds.), *Sanctions and sanctuary: Cultural perspectives on the beating of women* (pp. 89–98). Boulder, CO: Westview Press.

Moore, A. (1997). Intimate violence: Does socioeconomic status matter? In A. Cardarelli (Ed.), *Violence between intimate partners: Patterns, causes, and effects* (pp. 90–100). Boston: Allyn & Bacon.

Morrison, R., Van Hasselt, V., & Bellack, A. (1987). Assessment of assertion and problem-solving skills in wife abusers and their spouses. *Journal of Family Violence, 2*(3), 227–238.

Myers, J. (1997a). *Evidence in child abuse and neglect cases* (3rd ed., 2 vols.). New York: Wiley.

Myers, J. (1997b). *A mother's nightmare—incest: A practical guide for parents and professionals.* Thousand Oaks, CA: Sage.

National Council of Juvenile and Family Court Judges. (1994). *Model code on domestic and family violence.* Reno, NV: Author.

Newberger, C., Gremy, I., Waternaux, C., & Newberger, E. (1993). Mothers of sexually abused children: Trauma and repair in longitudinal perspective. *American Journal of Orthopsychiatry, 63*(1), 92–102.

O'Keefe, M. (1998). Factors mediating the link between witnessing interparental violence and dating violence. *Journal of Family Violence, 13*(1), 39–57.

O'Leary, D. (1993). Through a psychological lens: Personality traits, personality disorders, and levels of violence. In R. Gelles & D. Loseke (Eds.), *Current controversies on family violence* (pp. 7–30). Newbury Park, CA: Sage.

Osofsky, J. (1998). Children as invisible victims of domestic and community violence. In G. Holden, R. Geffner, & E. Jouriles (Eds.), *Children exposed to marital violence: Theory, research, and applied issues* (pp. 95–117). Washington, DC: American Psychological Association.

Paradise, J., Rostain, A., & Nathanson, M. (1988). Substantiation of sexual abuse charges when parents dispute custody or visitation. *Pediatrics, 81*(6), 835–839.

Parker, B., McFarlane, J., Soeken, K., Torres, S., & Campbell, D. (1993). Physical and emotional abuse in pregnancy: A comparison of adult and teenage women. *Nursing Research, 42*(3), 173–177.

Paveza, G. (1988). Risk factors in father-daughter child sexual abuse. *Journal of Interpersonal Violence, 3*(3), 290–306.

Peled, E. (1998). The experience of living with violence for preadolescent children of battered women. *Youth and Society, 29*(4), 395–430.

Peled, E. (2000). The parenting of men who abuse women: Issues and dilemmas. *British Journal of Social Work, 30*, 25–36.

Peled, E., & Davis, D. (1995). *Groupwork with children of battered women.* Thousand Oaks, CA: Sage.

Peled, E., & Edleson, J. (1992). Multiple perspectives on groupwork with children of battered women. *Violence and Victims, 7*(4), 327–346.

Pence, E., & Paymar, M. (1993). *Education groups for men who batter: The Duluth model.* New York: Springer.

Penfold, P. S. (1982). Children of battered women. *International Journal of Mental Health, 11*(1–2), 108–114.

Pickering, R., Sykes, D., Narozniak, L., Pritchard, J., Meyer, M., Brown, R., Buck, B., Digiondomenico, E., & Tee, J. (1993). *Report of the Children Witnessing Wife*

Assault Working Group. Hamilton, Ontario: Association of Agencies for Treatment and Development.

Pithers, W. (1999). Empathy: Definition, enhancement, and relevance to the treatment of sexual abusers. *Journal of Interpersonal Violence, 14*(3), 257–284.

Pollack, W. (1998). *Real boys: Rescuing our sons from the myths of boyhood.* New York: Random House.

Pope, K. (1996). Scientific research, recovered memory, and context: Seven surprising findings. *Women and Therapy, 19*(1), 123–140.

Pope, K., Butcher, J., & Seelen, J. (2000). *The MMPI, MMPI-2, and MMPI-A in court.* Washington, DC: American Psychological Association.

Pope, K., & Feldman-Summers, S. (1992). National survey of psychologists' sexual and physical abuse history and their evaluation of training and competence in these areas. *Professional Psychology: Research and Practice, 23*(5), 353–361.

Prentky, R., Knight, R., & Lee, A. (1997). *Child sexual molestation: Research issues* (Report No. NCJ-163390). Washington, DC: U.S. Department of Justice.

Ptacek, J. (1997). The tactics and strategies of men who batter: Testimony from women seeking restraining orders. In A. Cardarelli (Ed.), *Violence between intimate partners: Patterns, causes, and effects* (pp. 104–123). Boston: Allyn & Bacon.

Raj, A., Silverman, J., Wingood, G., & DiClemente, R. (1999). Prevalence and correlates of relationship abuse among a community-based sample of low-income African American women. *Violence Against Women, 5*(3), 272–291.

Rapaport, K., & Burkhard, B. (1984). Personality and attitudinal characteristics of sexually coercive college males. *Journal of Abnormal Psychology, 93*(2), 216–221.

Reed, L. D. (1996). Findings from research on children's suggestibility and implications for conducting child interviews. *Child Maltreatment, 1*(2), 105–120.

Renzetti, C. (1997). Violence and abuse among same-sex couples. In A. Cardarelli (Ed.), *Violence between intimate partners: Patterns, causes, and effects* (pp. 70–89). Boston: Allyn & Bacon.

Reppucci, D., & Haugaard, J. (1993). Problems with child sexual abuse prevention programs. In R. Gelles & D. Loseke (Eds.), *Current controversies on family violence* (pp. 306–322). Newbury Park, CA: Sage.

Rosen, K. (1996). The ties that bind women to violent premarital relationships: Processes of seduction and entrapment. In D. Cahn & S. Lloyd (Eds.), *Family violence from a communication perspective* (pp. 151–176). Thousand Oaks, CA: Sage.

Rosen, L., & Etlin, M. (1996). *The hostage child: Sex abuse allegations in custody disputes.* Bloomington: Indiana University Press.

Rosewater, L. B. (1987). The clinical and courtroom application of battered women's personality assessments. In D. J. Sonkin (Ed.), *Domestic violence on trial: Psychological and legal dimensions of family violence* (pp. 89–94). New York: Springer.

Rossman, B. B. R., & Ho, J. (2000). Posttraumatic response and children exposed to domestic violence. In R. Geffner, P. Jaffe, & M. Sudermann (Eds.), *Children exposed to domestic violence* (pp. 85–106). New York: Haworth Maltreatment and Trauma Press.

Rotgers, F., & Barrett, D. (1996). *Daubert v. Merrell Dow* and expert testimony by clinical psychologists: Implications and recommendations for practice. *Professional Psychology: Research and Practice, 27*(5), 467–474.

Roy, M. (1988). *Children in the crossfire: Violence in the home—how does it affect our children?* Deerfield Beach, FL: Health Communications.

Rubenstein, S., & Lehmann, P. (2000). Mothers and children together: A family group treatment approach. In R. Geffner, P. Jaffe, & M. Sudermann (Eds.), *Children exposed to domestic violence* (pp. 185–206). New York: Haworth Maltreatment and Trauma Press.

Russell, M. N., & Frohberg, J. (1995). *Confronting abusive beliefs: Group treatment for abusive men.* Thousand Oaks, CA: Sage.

Saakvitne, K., Gamble, S., Pearlman, L. A., & Lev, B. T. (2000). *Risking connection: A training curriculum for working with survivors of childhood abuse.* Baltimore: Sidran Press.

Salter, A. (1988). *Treating child sex offenders and victims: A practical guide.* Newbury Park, CA: Sage.

Salter, A. (1995). *Transforming trauma: A guide to understanding and treating adult survivors of child sexual abuse.* Thousand Oaks, CA: Sage.

Satir, V. (1972). *Peoplemaking.* Palo Alto, CA: Science and Behavior Books.

Schafran, L. H. (1994). Gender bias in family courts. *Family Advocate, 17*(1), 22–28.

Schechter, S., & Edleson, J. (1998). *Effective intervention in domestic violence & child maltreatment cases: Guidelines for policy and practice.* Reno, NV: National Council of Juvenile and Family Court Judges.

Senate Committee on Post Audit and Oversight. (2001). *Guarding our children: A review of Massachusetts' Guardian ad Litem program within the Probate and Family Court.* Boston: Author.

Sheeran, M., & Hampton, S. (1999). Supervised visitation in cases of domestic violence. *Juvenile and Family Court Journal, 50*(2), 13–25.

Silverman, J., Andrews, G., Bancroft, L., Cuthbert, C., & Slote, K. (2001, June). *The Battered Mothers Testimony Project: Preliminary findings.* Paper presented at the Sixth International Conference on Children Exposed to Domestic Violence, London, Ontario.

Silverman, J., & Williamson, G. (1997). Social ecology and entitlements involved in battering by heterosexual college males: Contributions of family and peers. *Violence and Victims, 12*(2), 147–164.

Silvern, L., Karyl, J., & Landis, T. (1995). Individual psychotherapy for the traumatized children of abused women. In E. Peled, P. Jaffe, & J. Edleson (Eds.), *Ending the cycle of violence: Community responses to children of battered women* (pp. 43–76). Thousand Oaks, CA: Sage.

Sirles, E., & Franke, P. (1989). Factors influencing mothers' reactions to intrafamily sexual abuse. *Child Abuse and Neglect, 13*, 131–139.

Sonkin, D. J. (1987). The assessment of court-mandated male batterers. In D. J. Sonkin (Ed.), *Domestic violence on trial: Psychological and legal dimensions of family violence* (pp. 174–196). New York: Springer.

Sonkin, D. J., Martin, D., & Walker, L. (1985). *The male batterer: A treatment approach.* New York: Springer.

Sousa, C., & Cooper, J. (1997). *Understanding and responding to the adolescent perpetrator of dating violence: A manual for developing and facilitating prevention and intervention groups.* Cambridge, MA: Emerge.

Stahl, P. (1994). *Conducting child custody evaluations: A comprehensive guide.* Newbury Park, CA: Sage.

Stahl, P. (1999). *Complex issues in child custody evaluations.* Thousand Oaks, CA: Sage.

Stark, E., & Flitcraft, A. (1988). Violence among intimates: An epidemiological review. In V. Van Hasselt, R. Morrison, A. Bellack, & M. Hersen (Eds.), *Handbook of family violence* (pp. 293–317). New York: Plenum.

Stephens, R., Richardson, A., & Lewin, J. (1997). Bilateral subdural hematomas in a newborn infant. *Pediatrics, 99*(4), 619–620.

Stern, M., & Meyer, L. (1980). Family and couple interactional patterns in cases of father/daughter incest. In National Center on Child Abuse and Neglect (Ed.), *Sexual abuse of children: Selected readings* (Publication No. OHDS 78-30161, pp. 83–86). Washington, DC: U.S. Department of Health and Human Services.

Sternberg, K., Lamb, M., & Dawud-Noursi, S. (1998). Using multiple informants to understand domestic violence and its effects. In G. Holden, R. Geffner, & E. Jouriles (Eds.), *Children exposed to marital violence: Theory, research, and applied issues* (pp. 121–156). Washington, DC: American Psychological Association.

Straus, M. (1990). Ordinary violence, child abuse, and wife-beating: What do they have in common? In M. Straus & R. Gelles (Eds.), *Physical violence in American families* (pp. 403–424). New Brunswick, NJ: Transition.

Straus, M., & Gelles, R. (1990). How violent are American families? Estimates from the National Family Violence Resurvey and other studies. In M. Straus & R. Gelles (Eds.), *Physical violence in American families* (pp. 95–112). New Brunswick, NJ: Transition.

Straus, M., Gelles, R., & Steinmetz, S. (1980). *Behind closed doors: Violence in the American family.* New York: Anchor Books.

Straus, R. (1995). Supervised visitation and family violence. *Family Law Quarterly,* 29(2), 229–252.

Sudermann, M., Marshall, L., & Loosely, S. (2000). Evaluation of the London (Ontario) Community Group Treatment Programme for children who have witnessed woman abuse. In R. Geffner, P. Jaffe, & M. Sudermann (Eds.), *Children exposed to domestic violence* (pp. 127–139). New York: Haworth Maltreatment and Trauma Press.

Suh, E., & Abel, E. M. (1990). The impact of spousal violence on the children of the abused. *Journal of Independent Social Work,* 4(4), 27–34.

Summers, G., & Feldman, N. (1984). Blaming the victim versus blaming the perpetrator: An attributional analysis of spouse abuse. *Journal of Social and Clinical Psychology,* 2(4), 339–347.

Taylor, G., Barnsley, J., & Goldsmith, P. (1996). *Women and children last: Custody disputes and the family "justice" system.* Vancouver, British Columbia: Vancouver Custody and Access Support and Advocacy Association.

Thoennes, N., & Pearson, J. (1988a). Summary of findings from the Sexual Abuse Allegations Project. In B. Nicholson (Ed.), *Sexual abuse allegations in custody and visitation cases: A resource book for judges and court personnel* (pp. 1–19). Washington, DC: American Bar Association.

Thoennes, N., & Pearson, J. (1988b). Summary of recommendations from the Sexual Abuse Allegations Project. In B. Nicholson (Ed.), *Sexual abuse allegations in custody and visitation cases: A resource book for judges and court personnel* (pp. 279–286). Washington, DC: American Bar Association.

Thoennes, N., & Tjaden, P. (1990). The extent, nature, and validity of sexual abuse allegations in custody/visitation disputes. *Child Abuse and Neglect, 14,* 151–163.

Tjaden, P., & Thoennes, N. (2000). *Extent, nature, and consequences of intimate partner violence: Findings from the National Violence Against Women Survey* (Report No. NCJ-181867). Washington, DC: National Institute of Justice/Centers for Disease Control and Prevention.

Tolman, R., & Bennett, L. (1990). A review of quantitative research on men who batter. *Journal of Interpersonal Violence,* 5(1), 87–118.

Truesdell, D., McNeil, J., & Deschner, J. (1986, March/April). Incidence of wife abuse in incestuous families. *Social Work, 31,* 138–140.

Turrell, S. (2000). A descriptive analysis of same-sex relationship violence for a diverse sample. *Journal of Family Violence,* 15(3), 281–293.

Ulrich, Y. C. (1998). What helped most in leaving spouse abuse: Implications for interventions. In J. Campbell (Ed.), *Empowering survivors of abuse: Health care for battered women and their children* (pp. 70–78). Thousand Oaks, CA: Sage.

Utah Task Force on Gender and Justice. (1990). *Report to the Utah Judicial Council.* Salt Lake City, UT: Administrative Office of the Courts.

van der Kolk, B., & McFarlane, A. (1996). The black hole of trauma. In B. van der Kolk, A. McFarlane, & L. Weisaeth (Eds.), *Traumatic stress: The effects of overwhelming experience on mind, body, and society* (pp. 3–23). New York: Guilford.

Vestal, A. (1999). Mediation and parental alienation syndrome: Considerations for an intervention model. *Family and Conciliation Courts Review, 37*(4), 487–503.

Wagar, J., & Rodway, M. (1995). An evaluation of a group treatment approach for children who have witnessed wife abuse. *Journal of Family Violence, 10*(3), 295–306.

Waldner-Haugrud, L., Gratch, L. V., & Magruder, B. (1997). Victimization and perpetration rates of violence in gay and lesbian relationships: Gender issues explored. *Violence and Victims, 12*(2), 173–184.

Walker, L. (1979). *The battered woman.* New York: Harper & Row.

Walker, L. (1989). *Terrifying love.* New York: Harper & Row.

Walker, L., & Edwall, G. (1987). Domestic violence and determination of visitation and custody in divorce. In D. J. Sonkin (Ed.), *Domestic violence on trial: Psychological and legal dimensions of family violence* (pp. 127–152). New York: Springer.

Wallerstein, J. (1991). The long-term effects of divorce on children: A review. *Journal of the American Academy of Child and Adolescent Psychiatry, 30*(3), 349–360.

Wallerstein, J., & Blakeslee, S. (1989). *Second chances: Men, women, and children a decade after divorce.* New York: Ticknor & Fields.

Wallerstein, J., & Tanke, T. (1996). To move or not to move: Psychological and legal considerations in the relocation of children following divorce. *Family Law Quarterly, 30*(2), 305–332.

Websdale, N. (1999). *Understanding domestic homicide.* Boston: Northeastern University Press.

Websdale, N., Sheeran, M., & Johnson, B. (1998). *Reviewing domestic violence fatalities: Summarizing national developments.* Reno, NV: National Council of Juvenile and Family Court Judges.

Websdale, N., Town, M., & Johnson, B. (1999). Domestic violence fatality reviews: From a culture of blame to a culture of safety. *Juvenile and Family Court Journal, 50*(2), 61–74.

Weisz, A., Tolman, R., & Saunders, D. (2000). Assessing the risk of severe domestic violence: The importance of survivors' predictions. *Journal of Interpersonal Violence, 15*(1), 75–90.

Weitzman, L. (1985). *The divorce revolution: The unexpected social and economic consequences for women and children in America.* New York: Free Press.

West, C. (1998). Lifting the "political gag order": Breaking the silence around partner violence in ethnic minority families. In J. Jasinksi & L. Williams (Eds.), *Partner violence: A comprehensive review of 20 years of research* (pp. 184–209). Thousand Oaks, CA: Sage.

Whitney, P., & Davis, L. (1999). Child abuse and domestic violence in Massachusetts: Can practice be integrated in a public child welfare setting? *Child Maltreatment, 4*(2), 158–166.

Whitten, M. R. (1994). Assessment of attachment in traumatized children. In B. James (Ed.), *Handbook for treatment of attachment-trauma problems in children* (pp. 28–49). New York: Free Press.

Williams, L. M. (1994a). Recall of childhood trauma: A prospective study of women's memories of child sexual abuse. *Journal of Consulting and Clinical Psychology, 62*(6), 1167–1176.

Williams, L. M. (1994b). What does it mean to forget child sexual abuse? A reply to Loftus, Garry, and Feldman (1994). *Journal of Consulting and Clinical Psychology, 62*(6), 1182–1186.

Wilson, S. K., Cameron, S., Jaffe, P., & Wolfe, D. A. (1986). *Group program for children exposed to wife abuse.* London, Ontario: London Family Court Clinic.

Woffordt, S., Mihalic, D. E., & Menard, S. (1994). Continuities in family violence. *Journal of Family Violence, 9*(3), 195–225.

Wolak, J., & Finkelhor, D. (1998). Children exposed to partner violence. In J. Jasinksi & L. Williams (Eds.), *Partner violence: A comprehensive review of 20 years of research* (pp. 73–111). Thousand Oaks, CA: Sage.

Wolfe, D. (1985). Child-abusive parents: An empirical review and analysis. *Psychological Bulletin, 97*(3), 462–482.

YWCA of Western Massachusetts. (n.d.). *Visitation Center ground rules*. Springfield, MA: Author.

Zaragoza, M. (1991). Preschool children's susceptibility to memory impairment. In J. Doris (Ed.), *The suggestibility of children's recollections* (pp. 27–39). Washington, DC: American Psychological Association.

Zibbell, R. (1994). Psychological testing in family law cases. In C. Irskin (Chair), *A course in psychology for the family lawyer* (pp. 193–205). Boston: Massachusetts Continuing Legal Education.

Zorza, J. (1991). Woman battering: A major cause of homelessness. *Clearinghouse Review, 25*(4), 421–429.

Zorza, J. (1995). How abused women can use the law to protect their children. In E. Peled, P. Jaffe, & J. Edleson (Eds.), *Ending the cycle of violence: Community responses to children of battered women* (pp. 147–169). Thousand Oaks, CA: Sage.

Zorza, J. (1996). Protecting the children in custody disputes when one parent abuses the other. *Clearinghouse Review, 29*, 1113–1127.

Zubretsky, T., & Digirolamo, K. (1996). The false connection between adult domestic violence and alcohol. In A. R. Roberts (Ed.), *Helping battered women: New perspectives and remedies* (pp. 222–228). New York: Oxford University Press.

Index

About the Author

Lundy Bancroft has 14 years of experience working with batterers as a counselor and clinical supervisor, with involvement in over 2000 cases. He has also served extensively as a custody evaluator (Guardian ad Litem) and child abuse investigator, appears periodically as an expert witness in child custody and child welfare cases, and has led groups for teenage boys exposed to domestic violence. He has been training judges, probation officers, and other court personnel on men who batter and their effects on children for eight years, and has been a frequent presenter for child protective personnel, therapists, law enforcement, and medical providers. He has coauthored articles in the *New England Journal of Medicine* and the *Journal of Contemporary Psychology*, is coauthor of two nationally marketed curricula, one for working with batterers and one for teen dating violence education in schools, and is the author of *Why Does He Do That?: Inside the Minds of Angry and Controlling Men* (forthcoming in Fall 2002). In addition, a study he completed for the state of Massachusetts on approaches to meeting the service needs of children exposed to domestic violence is also forthcoming.

Jay G. Silverman, Ph.D., is Assistant Professor at the Harvard School of Public Health and Director of Violence Prevention Programs for the school's Division of Public Health Practice. He is a developmental psychologist with over 10 years of experience in domestic violence as a practitioner and researcher, including direct counseling experience with hundreds of men who batter. His work has been published in *Violence Against Women, Violence and Victims*, the *American Journal of Preventive Medicine*, the *Journal of Contemporary Psychology*, and the *Journal of the American Medical Association*. His research has included examinations of the social contextual influences on the etiology of battering, cross-cultural societal factors related to battering, experiences of battered immigrant women in the US, healthcare practitioners' responses to battered women in emergency departments, school-based primary prevention of domestic violence, help-seeking of battered women, health concerns and health-related behaviors of adolescent and adult women experiencing violence from male partners, and judicial behavior and the experiences of battered mothers in child custody cases.

Margaret Miller, Ed.D., is a psychologist and Clinical Director at the Family Advocacy Center at Baystate Medical Center in Springfield, Massachusetts. She specializes in treating children and adolescents who have been traumatized by sexual abuse and/or witnessing domestic violence, and in evaluating cases of suspected or alleged abuse.